D0902481

QUEER IDEAS

QUEER IDEAS

THE DAVID R. KESSLER LECTURES
IN LESBIAN AND GAY STUDIES

From the Center for Lesbian and Gay Studies, CUNY

THE FEMINIST PRESS AT THE CITY UNIVERSITY OF NEW YORK
NEW YORK

Published by the Feminist Press at the City University of New York
The Graduate Center
365 Fifth Avenue
New York, NY 10016
www.feministpress.org

First edition, 2003

Library of Congress Cataloging-in-Publication Data

Queer ideas : the David R. Kessler lectures in lesbian and gay studies / from the Center for Lesbian and Gay Studies, CUNY. — 1st ed., 2003.
    p. cm.
Includes bibliographical references.
    ISBN 1-55861-449-4 (pbk. : alk. paper) — ISBN 1-55861-448-6 (library cloth : alk. paper)
    1. Gay and lesbian studies—United States. I. City University of New York. Center for Lesbian and Gay Studies.
    HQ75.16.U6Q43 2003
    306.76'6'0973—dc22

                                                                2003021685

Text and cover design by Dayna Navaro
Printed in Canada on acid-free paper by Transcontinental Printing

09 08 07 06 05 04 03   5 4 3 2 1

CONTENTS

FOREWORD

Dave Kessler and I have known each other for some forty years. We met at Yale—I was a newly minted Ph.D. teaching in the Department of History and he was getting his credentials as a psychiatrist at the School of Medicine. We were part of a semi-clandestine group of budding gay academicians and professionals who—just by finding each other—helped to save our lives in those pre-Stonewall years. Dave stood out, and was ahead of the rest of us, in arguing insistently that we were *not*, as the official ideology of the day had it, sick creatures in need of cure.

When Dave moved to San Francisco, decades ago, he and I saw each other much less often but did manage to stay in touch. In May 1991, I was in California on a book tour and we arranged for one of our periodic get-togethers. Along with catching up on each other's lives, I had a specific agenda item I wanted to talk over with him. I wanted to tell him about the newest gleam in my eye—a research center to promote and disseminate reliable scholarship about gay and lesbian lives—and to enlist his active support.

The "gleam" had first been sparked five years earlier. I'd abruptly realized one day late in 1985 that, despite my resolute inattention to and cosmic ignorance of the world of finance, I'd accumulated a quite significant pension fund. I'd also arrived at a quite significant age. It was time to take steps, leave a responsible legacy.

Initially I had a general idea only: write a will that would leave the bulk of my estate to "the advancement of gay studies," probably in the form of an endowed professorship. But leave it to whom? Or where? My close friend Helen Whitney was at the time married to Benno Schmidt, recently named Yale's incoming president. Since I'd been an undergraduate at Yale and had taught there in the sixties, the confluence seemed noteworthy.

When I first approached Benno, his reaction was friendly though cautious. He told me right off that I simply didn't have enough money to endow a professorship, and that I needed to come up with a more manageable proposal. I immediately substituted "a gay research center," not at all sure whether that was more or less ambitious than a professorship. Benno said he wanted to think about it and to consult with Bart Giamatti, Yale's outgoing president, before proceeding further.

Benno soon got back to me to say that Bart (here I quote from my diary of January 19, 1986) had "immediately objected to establishing an endowment devoted to 'gay' anything." Gay, Giamatti had announced, was "an advocacy word." I tried arguing the parallel with black studies. Would Yale reject a center devoted to research about African Americans because some might argue that "black" was an advocacy word?

Benno then passed along Bart's suggestion that Yale might be interested if I left my estate to promoting, in some form, "the history of human sexuality." No, I said, that more generalized subject already had the university-affiliated Kinsey Institute, several established journals, and a significant cadre of researchers. In contrast, gay/lesbian studies had practically nothing.

As a fall-back, Benno next suggested that, to appease Bart, I substitute "homosexuality" for the incendiary "gay"; an endowment to study "the history of homosexuality" stood a better chance of finding favor with the powers that be. No, I said, "homosexuality" was a clinical term, loaded with negative moralistic judgments. Well then, Benno said, why don't we just put terminology aside for now while you see if you can gather together an organizing committee of bona fide scholars to work out a concrete proposal, complete with a set of by-laws. That seemed a reasonable, even necessary, next step in producing a workable "center." And so it was that a diverse and shifting group of scholars began a protracted set of meetings in my living room to talk through plans for the organization that would ultimately become the Center for Lesbian and Gay Studies—CLAGS.

But in the end it was not be situated at Yale. John Boswell, a distinguished and openly gay historian at Yale, ultimately withdrew his support several months into our discussions after we, as a group, rejected his demand that the center's daily operations be controlled by tenured Yale faculty members. Most of the women and some of the men on our committee pointed out to Boswell that acceptance of his proposal would necessarily result in a center controlled by a small group of white men—since Yale then had no tenured "out" lesbians or people of color, and few tenured women. From Boswell's stated point of view, this was perfectly acceptable. Boswell then, in a long letter to me—with a copy to Benno Schmidt—denounced the committee's deliberations as "unremittingly hostile" to Yale and severed all connection with us. Pleading his inability to get our proposal passed without the support of Yale's "gay star," Benno quickly bowed out.

The group was shocked and angry at what we took as Boswell's attempt to sabotage what he could not control. But there was considerable relief, too, at the breakdown in negotiations. Yale would have provided a prestigious legitimizing venue for gay studies, but the women on our committee especially had felt from the beginning that the price might be too high, that as a traditional bastion of white male privilege, Yale, at that time, was too hidebound an environment to harbor and nurture the gay world's vibrant diversity.

We turned to The City University of New York (CUNY), and what a difference it made! At our very first meeting, Harold Proshansky, president of the CUNY Graduate School, *thanked* us for bringing the idea of a gay/lesbian studies center to CUNY. "If anything," he said, "the time for creating such an institution is overdue." He not only offered to work actively with us to prepare strategies for winning approval from CUNY's Board of Trustees, but said he would personally ask a select group of progressive campus presidents (CUNY has some two dozen different undergraduate campuses) to kick in $5,000 each from their discretionary funds so that we would have at least a minimal budget to get us started.

Three days later I got a phone call from a decidedly down-in-the-mouth Proshansky. The CUNY chancellor, Joseph Murphy, had told him in no uncertain terms that although he would not openly oppose the establishment of such a center, he would not lift a finger to help it. And he told Proshansky that under no circumstances would he be permitted to approach campus presidents for contributions.

Murphy was at the time well known in leftwing circles, a champion of minority struggles. But as most of us had learned many times over in our lives, heterosexual lefties often just don't get it; our issues aren't real to them, our "cause" not quite reputable. Proshansky made it clear to me that we would ourselves have to raise all the start-up funds. To prove our "viability," he set the bar at $50,000—a substantial "nut" for academics lacking in fund-raising skills, foundation connections, or personal connections to the Rich and Famous.

"Good luck," Proshansky said. "You're going to need it." His tone was both sad and sardonic.

Well, we did do it, but it took nearly five years, nickel-and-diming it all the way. We literally passed the hat down the auditorium aisles at the scholarly events we began to organize early on, we harangued friends and pleaded with colleagues, we gradually discovered a few friendly program officers at foundations—and we were finally put over the top by a $20,000 bequest from a gay man none of us knew personally who had died of AIDS. In April 1991, the CUNY Board of Trustees made CLAGS an official Center of The Graduate School. A month later, I was in San Francisco having lunch with Dave Kessler.

Dave had kept posted over the years about our assorted tribulations and accomplishments, and was already one of CLAGS's most generous donors. Since he and I were old friends, I didn't have to waste any time, that day in May, before coming to the point: would he be interested in endowing a lecture series which each year would award and celebrate a scholar for his or her outstanding contribution to gay and lesbian studies? (As our consciousness expanded over the years, so did our terminology, with "bisexual," "transgender," and "queer" eventually being added in our literature to "gay and lesbian.")

Dave was immediately interested. And he made it clear that no further wooing or obeisance would be necessary. Dave, in contrast to many donors, is a modest, even self-effacing man who, when mention is made of his own significant role in changing stereotypes and treatment modalities within the psychiatric world, tends to blush and change the topic. What Dave said he did need was a little time to consult with his lawyer. In fact, it took very little time.

On November 19, 1992, in an auditorium packed to overflowing, Joan Nestle, cofounder of the Lesbian Herstory Archives, mounted the platform of the Graduate School auditorium to delirious applause and delivered the very first David R. Kessler Lecture. It was a night I'll never forget. Dave had flown in from San Francisco for the event, a festive dinner and cocktails had preceded, and Joan (as I wrote in my diary the next day) "did a marvelous job, recreating [the African American lesbian] Mabel Hampton's life out of bare fragments of evidence, showing how our lost voices *can* be reclaimed, and doing so with deep respect and feeling. Many were in tears at the end, including me. . . ."

I haven't missed a Kessler lecture since. Over time, "The Kessler" has become a widely anticipated annual event in academic gay circles, a festive gathering of the scholarly tribe, a celebration of our achievements, our unique perspectives, our trenchant challenges to traditional pieties.

Which is not to say that every lecture has been as triumphantly received as the first. Opinions—often reflecting whether one was pro- or anti-queer theory—differed widely year after year as to which celebrant did or did not reach those exacting initial heights.

Those devoted to speculative analysis listened to Monique Wittig's "Reading and Comments" with far more delight than they did to Barbara Smith's thoughtful presentation, traditionally grounded in factual specifics, about African American lesbian and gay history. Fans of queer theory were not nearly as smitten with John D'Emilio's talk on the life of Bayard Rustin as were those of us trained in the demands of evidentiary proof.

But so it inevitably goes with any ten-year-long sequence of events: the intensity varies, the format and focus shift, the reception wavers according to ideological tastes. Still, the Kessler lectures overall have retained a high standard for insight and eloquence, have celebrated a diverse group of scholars, writers, and activists, and have appealed to a wide range of consitituences. "The Kessler," year after year, has played to standing-room-only crowds. With this volume, happily, the lecture series can now be enjoyed by a wider audience.

Martin Duberman
New York City
October 2003

INTRODUCTION

As this book approached its last stages of preparation in the summer of 2003, the United States Supreme Court powerfully demonstrated a founding principle of lesbian/gay/bisexual/transgender/queer (LGBTQ) studies: that queer ideas can change the world. In the groundbreaking ruling in *Lawrence* v. *Texas*, the Court decreed at last that sodomy laws are unconstitutional. Thus it overturned the notorious 1986 decision in *Bowers* v. *Hardwick*, which had justified the arrest of adults having consensual sex by asserting that prohibitions against homosexual activity had "ancient roots" as well as a long legacy within U.S. law. Debunking the reasoning in *Bowers* in the majority opinion for *Lawrence*, Justice Anthony Kennedy wrote:

> At the outset it should be noted that there is no longstanding history in this country of laws directed at homosexual conduct as a distinct matter. Beginning in colonial times there were prohibitions of sodomy derived from the English criminal laws passed in the first instance by the Reformation Parliament of 1533. The English prohibition was understood to include relations between men and women as well as relations between men and men. . . . Nineteenth-century commentators similarly read American sodomy, buggery, and crime-against-nature statutes as criminalizing certain relations between men and women and between men and men. . . . The absence of legal prohibitions focusing on homosexual conduct may be explained in part by noting that according to some scholars the concept of the homosexual as a distinct category of person did not emerge until the late 19th century. See, e.g., J. Katz, *The Invention of Heterosexuality* (1995); J. D'Emilio & E. Freedman, *Intimate Matters: A History of Sexuality in America* (2d ed. 1997) ("The modern terms homosexuality and heterosexuality do not apply to an era that had not yet articulated these distinctions.") Thus early American sodomy laws were not directed at homosexuals as such but instead sought to prohibit nonprocreative sexual activity more generally. This does not suggest approval of homosexual conduct. It does tend to show that this particular form of conduct was not thought of as a separate category from like conduct between heterosexual persons. (2478–79)

Had Justice Kennedy been attending the annual David R. Kessler lectures at the Center for Lesbian and Gay Studies (CLAGS)? Had he been sitting among us in cognito (sans gown) all these years at the City University of New York (CUNY) Graduate Center? After all, at these gatherings, which honor scholars who have made substantial contributions to the expression and understanding of LGTBQ lives, he would have been exposed to exactly the sort of documentary evidence and theoretical analyses that enabled him both to recognize the capacious and unintended reach of colonial America's sodomy laws and to historicize "homosexual" as a category of identity. Each lecture offered, on the celebratory occasion of its delivery, new insights into and deep contemplations of LGTBQ studies, as well as personal and communal self-scrutiny. Together, in this volume, the lectures provide a rich map of the varied terrain of the field over a remarkably fecund period.

Dropping by for each lecture in the Kessler's first dynamic decade, Justice Kennedy might also have come to appreciate how Esther Newton's "butch career has been made possible by gay people who fought to create an alternative vision, a freer cultural space for gender and sexuality," or what makes Edmund White's lush novels political, or why, as Cherríe Moraga explains, "The fictions of our lives—how we conceive our histories by heart—can sometimes provide a truth far greater than any telling frozen to the facts." And, if he really listened, the Supreme Court Justice might even have agreed with Samuel R. Delany about the value of random and frequent cross-class encounters and the importance of public sex.

This last, in all seriousness, is an unlikely scenario. But, it *is* an imaginable one, thanks precisely to the paradigm-shifting, institution-rattling, and downright pulse-quickening work of the thinkers and writers who have brought LGTBQ studies into being. Initiated in 1992—before LGTBQ studies had found much of a foothold in American universities, much less been institutionalized in programs and departments, and through the rise in number of centers like CLAGS—the Kessler lecture series has featured pioneers in the field: Joan Nestle, Edmund White, Barbara Smith, Monique Wittig, Esther Newton, Samuel R. Delany, Eve Kosofsky Sedgwick, John D'Emilio, Cherríe Moraga, and Judith Butler.

As for what, exactly, that field has been and ought to be, these ten scholars would no doubt offer ten richly conflicting definitions. Indeed, anyone reading through *Queer Ideas* will discover what a wide range of approaches is not only accommodated, but in fact demanded, by LGTBQ inquiry. Interdisciplinary and unfixed, LGTBQ studies is a perpetual work in progress. So the essays gathered here, like shards in a kaleidoscope, work jointly to create a colorful and wondrous picture of a field of study that never sits still. Some of the lectures have themselves changed slightly in the transition to print and are published here with revisions made after the event. While some of the spontaneity of performance is gone, what stands maintains of the original intensity of each Kessler.

In their own distinct ways, all ten lecturers seized on the occasion of the Kessler to reflect on their personal and intellectual developments within queer thought, community, and/or politics. Some share the struggles of queer research—Smith contending with an archive that "exists in fragments, in scattered documents, in fiction, poetry, and blues lyrics, in hearsay and innuendo"; D'Emilio falling into near "mortal combat" with Bayard Rustin, the slippery subject of a biography. Others assess the intimacies that constitute queer life—Sedgwick in a therapist's office, Delany in Times Square movie houses. Some address issues of urgent moment—White considering the fate of gay fiction, and Butler, corporeal vulnerability and violence. And some—Moraga, Nestle, Newton, Wittig—trace a lesbian journey, real or imagined or both, that touches down in both hell and paradise. Their lectures speak in ten different registers, but you can hear in each voice a heady admixture of what Butler describes as a motive force for her own queer theory: rage and desire.

LGTBQ activism, too, has always been fueled by these feelings, and for all their divergence, the Kessler lecturers concur on one fundamental point: LGTBQ scholarship begins in, and remains tied to, a liberation movement. It's important to place these ten lectures in an intellectual and political context and describe the field they have helped to form, but not so easy to fill the story in neatly. Or, rather, it's *too* easy to offer an orderly account that doesn't capture the wonderfully messy, contentious, multifaceted activity of queer research. Nothing, least of all intellectual inquiry, follows a clean sequential narrative.

Unlike, say, the revolutionary physicist or literary critic whose new ideas can be shown to break with or develop out of previous traditions, early LGTBQ scholars were not entering into a field, but actually making it up as they went along. As D'Emilio notes in his Kessler lecture, the work had a distinct and self-conscious use-value. In the thrilling days of the early 1970s, he explains, "The excitement of reimagining and, in the process, reinventing our lives was balanced at times by a sense of being rudderless, of having not a clue as to what we were doing or where we were going, of having no history or tradition in which to anchor our activities." The new scholarship would provide such an anchor. But the course of the gay liberation movement and the inquiries it urged on—being powered, as it was, by love—never did run smooth. As we trace the broad trajectory of the birth and growth of LGTBQ studies, it's crucial to note from the outset that the development of the field is far tidier in the telling than in reality. What is certain is that it's impossible to relate any story about LGTBQ studies without repeatedly bumping into the names of the authors brought together in *Queer Ideas*.

THE FERVENT YEARS

LGTBQ studies has its origins in the gay activism that marks its symbolic birth with the Stonewall uprising of 1969. Though gay and lesbian publications and civil rights and social organizations had been functioning far earlier, and scholarship on sexuality had long been produced, Stonewall galvanized these wings of the emergent movement. Indeed, scholars who insisted that research on lesbian and gay lives, histories, and communities was both necessary and legitimate—and who produced that research—were very much working as *part* of the movement.

The writers in this volume place themselves and their work firmly within such activism (and recall disparate experiences of reception): D'Emilio consciously and eagerly produces "scholarship for the movement"; Newton credits her connection to community "via books and art, conferences and politics" with helping to make her own queerness possible; Moraga admits to feeling "betrayed" by "the white-entitlement of lesbianfeminism" and has to look elsewhere "for a radical revisioning of our lives." Edmund White participates in the "growth of the modern gay publishing movement" as books like his begin to win contracts from mainstream houses, while Smith creates publishing opportunities for those overlooked by the modern gay publishing movement with the grassroots establishment, Kitchen Table: Women of Color Press.

In other words, producing the research was not itself enough to forge a field. Pioneering scholars built institutions like Kitchen Table that made it possible for work to be disseminated, and even—as in the case of New York's Lesbian Herstory Archives, of which Joan Nestle was a founder—to be engaged at all. Other gay and lesbian archives were collected in other cities; gay papers and feminist journals proliferated. Those performing the typically voluntary labor to sustain these efforts were doing nothing short of creating the means of production of a revolutionary new scholarship.

Within academic institutions, LGTBQ scholarship emerged not only in relationship to the growing gay liberation movement, but also amid the explosion of women's studies and African American and other ethnic studies—precisely at the moment, that is, when universities were being radically reshaped by demands both that they open their doors to more diverse populations and that they admit new perspectives. But it would be some years before lesbian and gay studies would find any traction within the academy; those already in faculty positions often felt forced to stay in the closet to preserve their jobs. So while women's and ethnic studies fought for institutionalization, early gay and lesbian research was mostly being produced by such independent scholars as D'Emilio, Smith, and others—Allan Bérubé and Jonathan Ned Katz to name only two more—without the benefit of research grants or professorial salaries.

Soon, however, they joined with brave colleagues who did have academic positions in taking on, as Jeffrey Escoffier has put it, "the virulent homophobia of the academy" (13) In New York City, for example, D'Emilio and Nestle were active, along with Martin Duberman, Barbara Gittings, and Karla Jay, among others, in founding the Gay Academic Union (GAU). They produced a conference at CUNY's John Jay College in 1973 that drew three hundred people. D'Emilio chronicles the GAU's efforts in *Making Trouble: Essays on Gay History, Politics and the University.* Its statement of purpose, adopted in summer 1973 "after extensive debate," he writes, asserted:

> As gay men and women and as scholars, we believe we must work for liberation as a means for change in our lives and in the communities in which we find ourselves. We choose to do this collectively for we know that no individual, alone, can liberate herself or himself from society's oppression. The work of gay liberation in the scholarly and teaching community centers around five tasks which we now undertake: 1. to oppose all forms of discrimination against all women within academia; 2. to oppose all forms of discrimination against gay people within academia; 3. to support individual academics in the

process of coming out; 4. to promote new approaches to the study of gay experience; 5. to encourage the teaching of gay studies through-out the American educational system. (127)

Much of what these activist-scholars produced—like much of the early research in women's and ethnic studies—was work of recovery, in this instance, identifying and analyzing the experiences of gay and lesbian histori-cal subjects. Katz has described this "documentary impulse" as "defensive, a compensatory, reactive move against those who, directly or indirectly, denied the existence of our past." And precisely because of that denial and the invisi-bility it enforced, gay and lesbian research required what Katz calls "detective work," a "tracing of history's missing persons" ("Making Sexual History"). His own book, *Gay American History* (1976) is a foundational text in this tradition. Others, to mention only a few of dozens, include John Boswell's *Christianity, Social Tolerance and Homosexuality* (1980), a monumental revisioning of thir-teen centuries of western civilization; *Hidden from History: Reclaiming the Gay and Lesbian Past* (1989), an anthology edited by Martin Duberman, Martha Vicinus, and George Chauncey, Jr.; and Elizabeth Lapovsky Kennedy and Madeline D. Davis's *Boots of Leather, Slippers of Gold* (1993), a study of the les-bian community of Buffalo, New York, from the 1930s to the 1960s.

While many of these books chronicle the experiences of people from a wide range of class, ethnic, and racial backgrounds, the field as whole began to acquire what Smith calls, in her contribution to this volume, "a white dominant meta-narrative." Her own work, which sought to "understand Black lesbian and gay life in the context of both Black history and gay history," is one of countless contributions by scholars of color that have displaced that meta-narrative. Such works both place the context of communities of color at the center of their studies and insist on an analysis that disrupts the assumption of a universal gay or lesbian identity. Moreover, they build on Audre Lorde's influential argument (made powerfully in "The Master's Tools Will Never Dismantle the Master's House") that ignoring the differences among members of a group will not only inevitably shatter any joint effort or theory they undertake, but will also starve the project of its most generative resource. "Difference must not be merely tol-erated," Lorde declared, "but seen as a fund of necessary polarities between which our creativity can spark like a dialectic" (111).

QUEER THEORY

The search for and study of gay, lesbian, bisexual, and transgender subjects in a full range of contexts—which continues richly today—deepened as the field began to emphasize questions about what constitutes such a subject at all. Within the academy, at least, such issues were highlighted in response to two major influences that swept through universities in the 1980s, shaping the intellectual approach of a new generation of scholars in a wide variety of fields: French post-structuralist thought and the theories of Michel Foucault (whose work was first published in English in the 1970s).

But this "progress narrative" is too neat and unidirectional. Randolph Trumbach's research on same-sex activity in seventeenth and eighteenth-century England, for example, raised questions about identity categories before Foucault became fashionable (Trumbach, 1989). And Monique Wittig had long been exploring, as she puts it in her Kessler remarks, how "heterosexuality is not only an institution but a whole political regime." In her essays and experimental fiction, written over several decades, Wittig challenged the sex and gender binaries, even splitting or avoiding the use of pronouns in order to escape what she calls in her Kessler remarks "the gender trap."

What's more, such questions were not unique to LGTBQ scholarship: Debates about the contingencies of social construction and the power of discourses productively roiled women's and ethnic studies as well, producing important insights in gender and critical race theory. Still, researchers in LGTBQ studies began to call for a shift in focus from gay and lesbian people to the political/social/cultural/medical realm of human experience called sexuality. The impetus is summed up well in Joan Scott's influential essay, "The Evidence of Experience," where she argues:

> Histories that document the "hidden" world of homosexuality, for example, show the impact of silence and repression on the lives of those affected by it and bring to light the history of their suppression and exploitation. But the project of making experience visible precludes critical examination of the workings of the ideological system itself, its categories of representation (homosexual/heterosexual, man/woman, black/white as fixed immutable identities), its premises about what these categories mean and how they operate, and of its notions of subjects, origin and cause. Homosexual practices are seen as the result of desire, conceived as a natural force operating outside or in opposition to social regulation. (400)

Some scholars delved precisely into such critical examinations of the system itself, looking at the establishment and enforcement of sexual categories and practices, their social regulation, and the myriad ways these structures and their meanings shift over time and locale. Gayle Rubin, for one, traced the impact of moral panics about sex, showing, in "Thinking Sex," how they erupt and produce new systems of control (267–75). Judith Butler demonstrated the performativity of gender—the way it is produced "as an effect of the very subject it appears to express" ("Imitation" 24). In her much-cited book *Gender Trouble* (1990), she offers a model for examining the social reproduction and regulation of identity categories. Reflecting on that book at her Kessler lecture some eleven years after its publication, she suggested that its "perhaps naive example of drag" was intended to "make us question the means by which reality is made, and to consider the way in which being called real, being called unreal, can be not only a means of social control, but also dehumanizing violence."

Sedgwick was another pioneer in theorizing sexuality, demonstrating through meticulous and giddying literary analysis how to read through a queer lens. In her 1990 classic *Epistemology of the Closet* she mined the productive dissonances between two central ways of defining heterosexuality and homosexuality: a "minoritizing" view that holds that "there is a distinct population of persons who 'really are' gay," a "relatively fixed homosexual minority" (85), and a "universalizing" view that holds that "sexual desire is an unpredictably powerful solvent of stable identities," and that it is "of continuing, determinative importance in the lives of people across the spectrum of sexualities" (1).

Under the deliberately loose rubric of "queer theory"—a term whose coining is typically attributed to Teresa de Lauretis (iv) (who soon after distanced herself from it), and a practice that was at first most successfully pursued within literature and cultural studies—scholars from the post-structuralist generation elaborated a theoretical framework favoring Sedgwick's "universalizing" view. Little surprise that post-structuralism's skepticism toward sign systems and categories would be so appealing to queer theorists, as anybody coming to terms with a dissident sexuality has likely recognized that s/he couldn't so easily line up her/his experience on one end or the other of an absolute hetero/homo binary (while, in a heterosexist world, straight people can live securely in a false sense of sexual certainty). A theoretical framework that unsettles binaries, seeks to explode the formation of fixed categories or norms, and works to reexamine the direction of the arrows between cause and effect challenges the way knowledge production is domesticated and made subservient to hegemonic cultural norms. These projects have been fundamental to queer theory.

At the same time, arguably, the move to queer theory was a vigorous response to the ascendancy of identity politics in the Reagan era and the emerging dominance of a narrowly drawn civil rights agenda in the lesbian and gay movement, a distinct departure from the sexual liberation ethos of the Stonewall generation, which saw itself tied to movements for racial and economic justice. Indeed, the manifestos and analyses from the early movement collected in Karla Jay and Allen Young's *Out of the Closets* (1972), which call for breaking down social structures that sustain themselves by defining who's in and who's out, challenge gender norms, and propose desire as a lens for wider social scrutiny, sound more like queer theory than like the lobbying materials of today's mainstream gay rights organizations, for instance the large, Washington-based Human Rights Campaign. As books like Michael Warner's *The Trouble with Normal*, maintain, queer theory sets forth a radical liberationist agenda. The AIDS epidemic also had a huge impact on LGTBQ scholarship in the 1980s and 1990s, not only prodding scholars to produce important epidemiological studies but also pushing the field toward policy-oriented investigations, for instance, of the behavioral patterns of urban men having sex with men, and toward scrutiny of the very language and categories by which diseases are named, studied, and addressed within medical and cultural discourses. Work on HIV/AIDS by such scholars as Cathy Cohen, Douglas Crimp, and Cindy Patton are also foundational queer studies texts.

Paradoxically, though, as David Halperin notes "the more [queer studies] verges on becoming a normative academic discipline, the less queer 'queer theory' can plausibly claim to be" (113). Indeed, throughout the late 1980s and the 1990s, lesbian and gay studies was increasingly institutionalized (though not necessarily tamed, as Halperin would have it.) The first lesbian and gay studies conference, held at Yale University in 1989, drew hundreds of participants, and such conferences proliferated. Lesbian and gay caucuses within disciplinary associations soon followed, as did CLAGS and other research centers, as well as specialized journals, book series, and even programs of study.

If only because of the way academic institutions slice up the resources for which LGTBQ studies now competed with more established areas and disciplines, the field consolidated itself around sexuality per se. At least in the self-justifying language demanded of academic bureaucracies, proposals for new LGTBQ programs, courses, and even publications left the category of gender to women's studies and of race and ethnicity to African American studies, Latino/a studies, and other such programs, and staked out sexuality as the field's unique concern—even though much of the research being produced in lesbian and gay/queer studies interrogated the categories of gender, ethnicity, and race as vigorously as they did questions of sexual orientations and practices.

In the introduction to *The Lesbian and Gay Studies Reader* (1993), for instance, the editors set out the parameters of what they refer to as LG studies: For them, the proper object of analysis in women's studies is gender; in lesbian and gay studies, it is sexuality (Abelove, Barale, and Halperin xv). Yet in an influential 1994 article, "Sexualities Without Gender and Other Queer Utopias," Biddy Martin shows how much queer theory premises the instability and deconstructive potential of homosexual/heterosexual binarism on the presumed stability of gender distinctions (105). More recently, scholars in transgender studies have brought gender back into the mix, showing how, as Susan Stryker writes, the term transgender often "bears an intimate and in many ways polemically charged relationship" to the term queer, even as "*transgender* can in fact be read as a heterodox interpretation of *queer*" (149). With the interventions of such scholars as Aaron Devor, Jason Cromwell, Judith Halberstam, Joanne Meyerowitz, Shannon Minter, Viviane K. Namaste, Sandy Stone, and Stryker, to name only a few, transgender studies is pushing LGTBQ studies to recognize that hegemonic gender and sexuality norms are intersectionally related and mutually imbricated, and that there is much to be gained in unpacking the productive tensions between narratives of homosexuality and transsexuality. (But again, the caveat about a tidy genealogy: Esther Newton's seminal ethnographic study of drag queens in Kansas City, *Mother Camp*, was published in 1972.)

Similarly, the emergence of gay and lesbian studies as defined by the single identity category of sexuality tended effectively to constitute the analysis of racial oppression outside of the field. Works that focused on the experiences of lesbians of color, Cherríe Moraga and Gloria Anzaldúa's *This Bridge Called My Back* (1981) and Barbara Smith's *Home Girls: A Black Feminist Anthology* (1983), for example, were quicker to become central texts of women's studies programs than of gay scholarship. Nonetheless, the body of work generated by lesbian writers of color in the late 1970s and early 1980s called attention to the intersections of gender, race, class, and sexuality, pointing the way toward later theories of "hybridity" and postmodern notions of the fractured and socially constructed self.

Outside the academy, the rise of the "new social movements"—of the black civil rights movement, feminism, gay liberation, and more recently the transgender rights movement—worked to displace the "ontological priority" of the working class. The New Left notion that class was the central category of oppression, and that the elimination of class-based axes of oppression would also eliminate such "epiphenomenal" kinds of oppression as racism and sexism, gave way to "identity politics." In displacing class as the priority, often these new social movements asserted priorities of their own, often based on race- or gender-defined identity. In the feminist and gay liberation movements, at least, the question of how—and whose—identity was recognized and asserted was highlighted early on. In 1977, a Black feminist group in Boston, the Combahee River Collective, challenged the monolithic way in which feminist and gay and lesbian organizations understood and acted from their "own identity." In their "Black Feminist Statement" the collective declared their active commitment to "struggling against racial, sexual, heterosexual, and class oppression" and claimed as their task "the development of an integrated analysis and practice based upon the fact that the major systems of oppression are interlocking" (362). Their critique remained relevant two decades later, as Cathy Cohen notes in her assessment of queer activism. She writes:

> In contrast to the left intersectional analysis that has structured much of the politics of "queers" of color, the basis of politics of some white queer activists and organizations has come dangerously close to a single oppression model. Experiencing "deviant" sexuality as the prominent characteristic of their marginalization, these activists begin to envision the world in terms of a hetero/queer divide. (209)

Increasingly, LGTBQ scholars insisted that understanding power as operating through the construction of binary categories and systems of exploitation—race, gender, sexuality—requires that attention be paid to the way oppressions intersect and mutually reinforce each other. For example, Cohen and others have pointed to the process of welfare reform in the 1990s to demonstrate how heteronormativity is racially structured. Anjali Arondekar's work in critical race queer theory, Siobhan Sommerville's work in *Queering the Color Line*, and, more recently, investigations of the connections between LGTBQ studies and disabilities studies in works by such scholars as Lennard Davis, Kenny Fries, Robert McRuer, and Ruthann Robson are examples of investigations that not only cross paths with LGTBQ studies, but reconstitute it.

Intersectionality, then, is both a practical and a conceptual issue in LGTBQ studies. Judith Butler has put the question this way:

Within the academy, the effort to separate race studies from sexuality studies from gender studies marks various needs for autonomous articulation, but it also invariably produces a set of important, painful, and promising confrontations that expose the ultimate limits to any autonomy: the politics of sexuality within African American studies; the politics of race within queer studies, within the study of class, within feminism; the question of misogyny within any of the above; the question of homophobia within feminism—to name a few. ("Merely Cultural" 269)

The very slipperiness of "queer" has made debates over efforts to further institutionalize the field even more self-conscious—and, arguably, more generative—than they have been in other interdisciplinary areas. Among the urgent questions: Does LGTBQ studies have its own disciplinarity? Should it? Are there schisms in the field between, say, social scientists and humanists, or between those producing queer theory and those grounded in empirical work? How should relationships among the "constituencies" of LGTBQ studies—both inside and outside the university—and academic inquiry be mediated? How should an LGTBQ studies program be situated in relation to other interdisciplinary programs or departments, such as women's studies, diaspora studies, Chicano/a studies, disability studies, African American studies, cultural studies, and so on?

There is only one way to find answers: in the day-to-day grappling with the teaching and doing of LGTBQ studies. Praxis argues for an LGTBQ studies that creates productive spaces for the interrogation of sexualities and sexual minorities and the cultural and social processes by which they are named, shaped, and contested; such insights have percolated throughout LGTBQ scholarship in the United States, across traditional disciplines, with continued productive debate, over the last three decades. They are part of what sustains the radical impulse of the field and its promise to continue to produce new knowledges. As John D'Emilio put it in a talk he gave at the 1989 inauguration of the first gay and lesbian studies department in the United States, at City College of San Francisco, "We are involved in an effort to reshape a worldview and an intellectual tradition that has ignored, debased, and attacked same-sex relationships and that has, in the process, impoverished our understanding of the human experience and human possibilities" (158).

The Kessler Lectures and CLAGS: The First Ten Years

The Kessler lectures as annual event—and now, we trust, as a body of published texts—not only participate in the field's vast enrichment of our understanding of human experience and human possibilities, indeed, in reshaping worldviews—even the views of Supreme Court justices. They also look both forward and back at a field in formation, and always in struggle. To borrow a phrase from Moraga's lecture, every one of the essays here is "as much an autobiographical narrative as it is a dream waiting to happen based on some irrefutable facts."

Diverse as they are in outlook, angle, and emphasis, the ten lectures share an interest in both the means and methods of making LGBTQ knowledge, and in the meanings of lives lived—in community, in politics, sometimes in crisis, sometimes in ecstasy, always in bodies. The blending of theory and practice, the intellectual and the material, the abstract and the carnal, has been a feature of the Kessler from Nestle's inaugural lecture in 1992, which carefully examined "the fragile records of a tough woman" to demonstrate "another paradigm for doing history—not around coming out or bar culture, but around daily survival as a worker and an African-American woman who never apologized for her sexual life," to Butler's post-September 11 consideration, a decade later, of how political community is wrought as "passion and grief and rage, all of which tear us from ourselves, bind us to others, transport us, undo us, implicate us in lives that are not our own, fatally, irreversibly."

Even more than revealing common concerns, laying the lectures alongside each other allows them to talk back to one another—engaging in the sort of "discursive collision" that Delany finds, so crucially, in urban contact. D'Emilio's struggle with the "dual subjectivity" of a biographer suggests ways of thinking anew about Sedgwick's dialogue on love with a Platonic interlocutor. White's exulting in a "genuine feminist and queer literature" is answered, and then some, by Wittig's enthralling text. And so on. Compelling when delivered live on a special occasion, the lectures take on a new energy in provocative propinquity.

One significant aspect of the Kessler event could not be captured in this volume, but must be mentioned: the introductory tributes offered by colleagues of the lecturers, placing their works and lives in personal and political context. Vital thinkers and activists in their own rights, these introducers have provided analysis, warmth, and great sense of occasion. It's important to name them: For Nestle, Cheryl Clarke, Deb Edel, and Liz Kennedy; for White, David Bergman, J. D. McClatchy, and Felice Picano; for Smith, Naomi Jaffe, Mattie Richardson, and Evelyn C. White; for Wittig, Judith Butler (in absentia), Erika Ostrovsky, and Namascar Shaktini; for Newton, Judith Halberstam and William Leap; for Delany, Jeffrey Escoffier, Robert Reid-Pharr, and Eve Kosofsky Sedgwick; for Sedgwick, José Muñoz, Cindy Patton, and Michele Wallace; for D'Emilio, Allan Bérubé, Lisa Duggan, and Urvashi Vaid; for Moraga, Jacqui Alexander, Ricardo Bracho, and Irma Mayorga; for Butler, David Eng and Biddy Martin.

Along with the Kessler honorees, these speakers represent the vigor and variety of LGBTQ inquiry that course through CLAGS on a daily basis. Since its founding by Martin Duberman a dozen years ago, CLAGS has presented more than one hundred and twenty public programs where more than one thousand different people have offered their findings and posed new questions. We have awarded more than seventy fellowships and prizes for LGBTQ research. We have collaborated with dozens of academic, community, and activist organizations on programming. We have solidified LGBTQ studies at the CUNY Graduate Center—and beyond. The Kessler is the happy occasion when we celebrate not only the specific honorees, but also this explosion of activity that their work has been so instrumental in sparking.

ACKNOWLEDGMENTS

Many people have helped make the Kessler such a stimulating and festive event over the years: first and foremost, David Kessler, through his generosity and vision; also, Martin Duberman, whose inspiration and indefatigable labors brought CLAGS into being and sustained it through its early years; his first successor as CLAGS's executive director, Jill Dolan, who expanded CLAGS's roots and reach; the graduate students who have staffed CLAGS over this decade and pulled off one classy event after another; and, not least, the hundreds of community members who have come to share in the ideas and the merriment. The Graduate Center—and especially President Frances Degen Horowitz and Provost Bill Kelly—has been consistently supportive of CLAGS and the Kessler Lecture. On behalf of CLAGS we extend warm thanks.

Great thanks are due, too, to those who have done so much to bring this book to fruition. CLAGS's current staff—Preston Bautista, Hilla Dayan, Sara Ganter, Lavelle Porter, and Jordan Schildcrout—co-workers and comrades extraordinaire, gracefully did much of the nitty-gritty. It's been a pleasure to work with the Feminist Press, not just because it is a sister institution at CUNY, our beleaguered public university that keeps thriving despite constant budget cuts. What's more, our collaboration reasserts the foundational connection between feminism and LGTBQ investigation, recalling—as can't be done too often these days—how feminism has fueled theories of gay liberation. For all of us at CLAGS, we want to express our gratitude to everyone at the Feminist Press, and especially to Livia Tenzer, editorial manager, for bringing the idea to us in the first place, and for working so hard, and with such magnanimousness, to make it happen. For helping her compile the volume, special acknowledgement is owed to editorial interns Abby Collier, Loryn Lipari, and Jamie Stock, and to Karin Ballauf, senior editor at Milena Verlag (Austria) who did a residency at the press in spring 2003. Thanks, too, to Sande Zeig and Diane Griffin Crowder, who provided crucial support in preparing the lecture and biographical sketch of Monique Wittig.

On a personal note: This book goes to press just as the directorship of CLAGS is changing hands—as Alisa Solomon steps down after four years to return to research, teaching, and writing, and Paisley Currah takes up the reins. It feels fitting that in this moment when both of us are thinking about CLAGS's many accomplishments and future goals, we are called upon to offer these introductory remarks and acknowledgements to a book that invites just the sort of reflection we are in the mood to engage. Queer Ideas traces nothing short of a revolution in scholarship and social change. It's been a privilege to be a fellow traveler.

That's hardly to say that the transforming power of ideas has run its course. The Kessler's second decade is well underway. In 2002 Jonathan Ned Katz pondered "Making Sexual History" and as we go to press, we are preparing for a December 2003 Kessler lecture by Gayle Rubin. We eagerly anticipate the second volume of Queer Ideas in 2013—and those that will surely follow.

Alisa Solomon and Paisley Currah
New York City
September 2003

WORKS CITED

Abelove, Henry, Michèle Aina Barale, and David M. Halperin. Introduction. *The Lesbian and Gay Studies Reader*. Eds. Abelove, Barale and Halperin. New York: Routledge, 1993. xv–xvii.

Boswell. John. *Christianity, Social Tolerance and Homosexuality*. Chicago: U of Chicago P, 1980.

Butler, Judith. *Gender Trouble: Feminism and the Subversion of Identity*. New York: Routledge, 1990.

———. "Imitation and Gender Insubordination," *Inside/Out: Lesbian Theories, Gay Theories*, Ed. Diana Fuss. New York: Routledge, 1991. 13–31.

———. "Merely Cultural." *Social Text* 15 (Fall/Winter 1997): 265–277.

Cohen, Cathy J. "Punks, Bulldaggers and Welfare Queens: The Radical Potential of Queer Politics?" *Sexual Identities, Queer Politics*. Ed. Mark Blasius. Princeton: Princeton UP, 2001. 201–227.

Combahee River Collective. "A Black Feminist Statement." *Capitalist Patriarchy and the Case for Socialist Feminism*. Ed. Zillah R. Eisenstein. New York: Monthly Review, 1979. 362–372.

Cromwell, Jason. *Transman & FTMS*. Urbana: U of Illinois P, 1989.

De Lauretis, Teresa. "Queer Theory: Lesbian and Gay Sexualities, An Introduction." *Differences* 3.2 (1991): iii-xviii.

D'Emilio, John. "Inaugurating the First Lesbian and Gay Studies Department." *Making Trouble: Essays on Gay History, Politics and the University*. New York: Routledge, 1992. 155–159.

———. "The Universities and the Gay Experience." *Making Trouble: Essays on Gay History, Politics and the University*. New York: Routledge, 1992. 117–127.

Devor, Holly. *FTM: Female-to-Male Transsexuals in Society*. Bloomington: Indiana UP, 1997.

Duberman, Martin, Martha Vicinus and George Chauncey, eds. *Hidden from History: Reclaiming the Gay and Lesbian Past*. New York: Meridian, 1989.

Escoffier, Jeffrey. "Generations and Paradigms: Mainstreams in Lesbian and Gay Studies." *Gay and Lesbian Studies*. Ed. Henry L. Minton. New York: Hawarth, 1992. 7–26.

Halberstam, Judith. *Female Masculinity*. Durham: Duke UP, 1998.

Halperin, David. *Saint Foucault: Towards a Gay Hagiography*. New York: Oxford UP, 1995.

Jay, Karla and Allen Young. *Out of the Closets*. New York: Douglas, 1972.

Katz, Jonathan Ned. *Gay American History*. New York: Harper & Row. 1976.

———. "Making Sexual History: Obsessions of a Quarter Century." Eleventh Annual David R. Kessler Lecture at the Center for Lesbian and Gay Studies, City University of New York, December 6, 2002.

Kennedy, Elizabeth Lapovsky, and Madeline D. Davis. *Boots of Leather, Slippers of Gold*. New York: Routledge, 1993.

Lawrence v. Texas. No. 02–102. Supreme Ct. of the US. 26 June 2003. 2473 ff.

Lorde, Audre. "The Master's Tools Will Never Dismantle the Master's House." Comments at "The Personal and the Political Panel," Second Sex Conference, New York, 29 September 1979. *Zami, Sister Outsider, Undersong*. Quality Paperback Bookclub, 1993. 110–113

Martin, Biddy. "Sexualities Without Genders and Other Queer Utopias." *Diacritics* 24.2–3 (1994): 104–21. Rpt. in *Femininity Played Straight: The Significance of Being Lesbian*. New York: Routledge, 1996. 71–96.

McRuer, Robert and Abby L. Wilkerson, eds. *Desiring Disabilities: Queer Theory Meets Disability Studies*. GLQ 9.1–2 (2003)

Meyerowitz, Joanne. *How Sexed Changed: A History of Transsexuality in the United States*. Cambridge: Harvard UP, 2002.

Minter, Shannon. "Do Transsexuals Dream of Gay Rights?" *New York Law School Journal of Human Rights* XVII (2000): 589–621.

Moraga, Cherríe and Gloria Anzaldúa, eds. *This Bridge Called My Back: Writings by Radical Women of Color*. 1981. New York: Kitchen Table/Women of Color, 1983.

Namaste, Viviane K. *Invisible Lives: The Erasure of Transsexual and Transgendered People*. Chicago: U of Chicago P, 2000.

Newton, Esther. *Mother Camp*, Englewood Cliffs, N.J.: Prentice-Hall, 1972.

Rubin, Gayle. "Thinking Sex: Notes for a Radical Theory of the Politics of Sexuality." *Pleasure and Danger: Exploring Female Sexuality*. Ed. Carole S. Vance. New York: Routledge, 1984. 267–319.

Scott, Joan. "The Evidence of Experience." *The Lesbian and Gay Studies Reader*. Eds. Henry A. Abelove, Michèle Aina Barale, and David M. Halperin. New York: Routledge, 1993. 397–415.

Sedgwick, Eve Kosofsky. *Epistemology of the Closet*. Berkeley: U of California P, 1990.

Smith, Barbara, ed. *Home Girls: A Black Feminist Anthology*. New York: Kitchen Table/Women of Color, 1983.

Sommerville, Siobhan. *Queering the Color Line*. Durham, NC: Duke UP, 2000.

Stone, Sandy. "The *Empire* Strikes Back: A Posttranssexual Manifesto." *Bodyguards*. Eds. Julia Epstein and Kristina Straub. New York: Routledge, 1991. 280–304.

Stryker, Susan. "The Transgender Issue: An Introduction." *GLQ* 4.2 (1998): 145–158.

Trumbach, Randolph. "The Birth of the Queen: Sodomy and the Emergence of Gender Equality in Modern Culture, 1660–1750." *Making History: Reclaiming the Gay and Lesbian Past*. Eds. Martin Duberman, Martha Vicinus and George Chauncey. Meridan, 1989. 129–140.

Warner, Michael. *The Trouble with Normal*. New York: Free Press, 1989.

QUEER IDEAS

1992

JOAN NESTLE

EDMUND WHITE
BARBARA SMITH
MONIQUE WITTIG
ESTHER NEWTON
SAMUEL R. DELANY
EVE KOSOFSKY SEDGWICK
JOHN D'EMILIO
CHERRÍE MORAGA
JUDITH BUTLER

JOAN NESTLE

Joan Nestle is a sixty-three-year-old Jewish fem who came out in the working-class bars of New York City in the late 1950s. A teacher of writing in the SEEK Program at Queens College from 1966 to her retirement in 1995, she is also co-founder of the Lesbian Herstory Archives (established in 1974) and author of *A Restricted Country* (Firebrand Books, 1987; Cleis Books, 2002) and *A Fragile Union* (Cleis Books, 1998). Editor of *Persistent Desire: A Fem Butch Reader* (Alyson, 1992, out of print), Nestle is co-editor of seven other collections, the latest being *GenderQueer: Voices from Beyond the Binary* (Alyson, 2002). Her life's work is dedicated to those who have done so much with so little social or cultural respect.

"I LIFT MY EYES TO THE HILL"

The Life of Mabel Hampton
as Told by a White Woman

On Thursday nights, Mabel Hampton held court at the Lesbian Herstory Archives, opening the mail and gossiping with other archive workers. A devout collector of books on African American history and lesbian culture, in 1976 Ms. Hampton had donated her lesbian paperback collection to the archives. Surrounded by these books and many others, she shared in welcoming the visitors, some of whom had come just to meet her.

Another more public place we could count on finding Ms. Hampton in her later years was New York's Gay Pride march. From the early 1980s on, Ms. Hampton could be seen strutting down Fifth Avenue, *our* avenue for the day, marching under the Lesbian Herstory Archives banner, wearing her jauntily tilted black beret, her dark glasses, and a bright red T-shirt proclaiming her membership in SAGE (Senior Action in a Gay Environment). Later in the decades, when she could no longer walk the whole way, a crowd of younger lesbian women fought for the privilege to push her wheelchair down the avenue. Mabel Hampton, domestic worker, hospital matron, entertainer, had walked down many roads in her life—not always to cheering fans. Her persistent journey to full selfhood in a racist and capitalistic America is a story we are still learning to tell.

In recent years, I have been dazzled at our heady discussions of deconstruction, at our increasingly sophisticated academic conferences on gender representation, at the publication of sweeping communal and historical studies, and at our brave biographies of revered figures in American history in which the authors speak clearly about their subject's sexual identity. Mabel Hampton's is the story we are in danger of forgetting in our rush of language and queer theory.

Telling Mabel Hampton's history forces me to confront racism in my own relationship to her. Our two lives, Ms. Hampton's and mine, first intersected at a sadly traditional and suspect crossroads in the history of the relationships between black and white women in this country. These relationships are set in the mentality of a country that in the words of Professor Linda Meyers "could continue for over three hundred years to kidnap an estimated 50 million youths and young adults from Africa, transport them across the Atlantic with about half dying, unable to withstand the inhumanity of the passage."

In 1952, my small white Jewish mother took her breakfasts in a Bayside, Queens, luncheonette. Sitting next to her was a small black Christian woman.

For several weeks they breakfasted together before they each went off to work, my mother to the office where she worked as a bookkeeper, Ms. Hampton to the homes she cleaned and the children she cared for.

One morning, Ms. Hampton told me, she followed my mother out to her bus to say good-bye and my mother, Regina, threw the keys to our apartment out the bus window, asking whether Ms. Hampton would consider working for her. "I told her I would give her a week's trial," Ms. Hampton said.

This working relationship was not to last long because of my mother's own financial instability, but the friendship between my mother and Ms. Hampton did. I remember Ms. Hampton caring for me when I was ill. I remember her tan raincoat with a lesbian paperback in its pocket, its jacket bent back so no one could see the two women in the shadows on its cover. I remember, when I was twelve years old, asking my mother as we did laundry together one weekend whose men's underwear we were washing since no man lived in our apartment. "They are Mabel's," she said.

In future years, Regina, Mabel, and Mabel's wife, Lillian, became closer friends, bound together by a struggle to survive and by my mother's lesbian daughter. Ms. Hampton told me during one of our afternoons together that when Regina suspected I was a lesbian she called her late one night and threatened to kill herself if I turned out that way. "I told her, she might as well go ahead and do it because it wasn't her business what her daughter did and besides, I'm one and it suits me fine."

Because Ms. Hampton and I later formed an adult relationship, based on our commitment to a lesbian community, I had a chance much later in life, when Ms. Hampton herself needed care, to reverse the image this society thrives on, that of black women caring for white people. The incredulous responses we both received in my Upper West Side apartment building when I was Ms. Hampton's caretaker showed how deeply the traditional racial script still resonated. To honor her, to touch her again, to be honest in the face of race, to refuse the blankness of physical death, to share the story of her own narrative of liberation—for all these reason—it is she I must write about.

Ms. Hampton pointed the way her story should be told. Her legacy of documents so carefully assembled for Deborah Edel, who had met Ms. Hampton in the early seventies and who had all of Ms. Hampton's trust, tell in no uncertain terms that her life revolved around two major themes—her material struggle to survive and her cultural struggle for beauty. Bread and roses, the worker's old anthem—this is what I want to remember, the texture of the individual life of a working woman.

After her death on October 26, 1989, when Deborah and I were gathering her papers, we found a box carefully marked, "In case I pass away see that Joan and Deb get this at once, Mabel." On top of the pile of birth certificates and cemetery plot contracts was a piece of lined paper with the following typed entries:

1915–1919: 8B, Public School 32, Jersey City
1919–1923: Housework, Dr. Kraus, Jersey City

1923–1927: Housework, Mrs. Parker, Jersey City
1927–1931: Housework, Mrs. Katim, Brooklyn
1932–1933: Housework, Dr. Garland, New York City
1934–1940: Daily housework, different homes
1941–1944: Matron, Hammarlund Manufacturing Co., NYC
1945–1953: Housework, Mrs. Jean Nate
1948–1955: Attendant, New York Hospital
1954–1955: General, daily work
Lived 1935: 271 West 122nd Street, NYC
Lived 1939–1945: West 111th Street, NYC
Lived 1945–current (1955): 663 East 169th Street, Bronx, NYC

Compiled in the mid-fifties when Ms. Hampton was applying for a position at Jacobi Hospital, the list demanded attention—a list so bare and yet so eloquent of a life of work and home.

Since 1973, the start of the Lesbian Herstory Archives, I have felt Ms. Hampton's story must be told, but I am not a trained historian or sociologist. However, in the seventies, training workshops in doing oral histories with gay people were popping up around the city, and I attended every session I could. There, Jonathan Katz, Liz Kennedy, Madeline Davis, and I would talk for hours, trying to come up with the questions that we thought would elicit the kind of history we wanted: What did you call yourself in the twenties? How did you and your friends dress in the forties? What bars did you go to? In the late seventies, when I started doing oral history tapes with Ms. Hampton, I quickly learned how limited our methods were:

J.: Do you remember anything about sports? Did you know women who liked to play softball? Were there any teams?

M.: No, all the women, they didn't care too much about them—soft-balls—they liked the soft women. Didn't care about any old soft–ball. Cut it out!

I soon realized that Ms. Hampton had her own narrative style, which was tightly connected to how she had made sense of her life, but it wasn't until I had gone through every piece of paper she had bequeathed us that I had a deeper understanding of what her lesbian life had meant.

Lesbian and gay scholars argue over whether we can call a woman a lesbian who lived in a time when that word was not used. We have been very careful about analyzing how our social sexual representation was created by medical terminology and cultural terrors. But here was a different story. Ms. Hampton's lesbian history is embedded in the history of race and class in this country; she makes us extend our historical perspective until she is at its center. The focus then is not lesbian history but lesbians *in* history.

When asked "Ms. Hampton, when did you come out?" she loved to flaunt, "What do you mean? I was never *in*!" Her audiences always cheered this assertion of lesbian identity, but now I think Ms. Hampton was speaking of something more inclusive.

Driven to fend for herself as an orphan, as a black working woman, as a lesbian, Ms. Hampton always struggled to fully occupy her life, refusing to be cut off from the communal, national, and worldly events around her. She was never in, in any aspect of her life, if being "in" means withholding the fullest response possible from what life is demanding of you at the moment.

Along her way, Ms. Hampton found and created communities for comfort and support, communities that engendered her fierce loyalty. Her street in the Bronx, 169th Street, was *her* street, and she walked it as "Miss Mabel," known to all and knowing all, whether it was the woman representing her congressional district or the numbers runner down the block. How she occupied this street, this moment in urban twentieth-century American history, is very similar to how she occupied her life—self-contained but always visible, carrying her own sense of how life should be lived but generous to those who were struggling to make a decent life out of indecent conditions.

I cannot re-create the whole of Ms. Hampton's life, but I can follow her journey up to the 1950s by blending the documents she left, such as letters, newspaper clippings, and programs, with excerpts from her oral history and my interpretations and readings of other sources.

These personal daily documents represent the heart of the Lesbian Herstory Archives; they are the fragile records of a tough woman who never took her eyes off the hilltop, who never let racism destroy her love for her own culture, who never let the tyranny of class keep her from finding the beauty she needed to live, who never accepted her traditional woman's destiny, and who never let hatred and fear of lesbians keep her from her gay community.

None of it was easy. From the beginning, Ms. Hampton had to run for her life.

Desperate to be considered for employment by the City of New York, Ms. Hampton began to document her own beginnings in April of 1963:

To the county clerk in the Hall of Records, Winston-Salem, North Carolina:

> Gentlemen: I would appreciate very much your helping me to secure my birth papers or any record you may have on file, as to my birth and proof of age as this information is vital for the purpose of my securing a civil service position in New York. Listed below are the information I have to help you locate any records you may have.
>
> I was born approximately May 2, 1902 in Winston-Salem. My mother's name was Lulu Hampton or Simmons. I attended Teacher's College which is its name now at the age of six. My grandmother's name was Simmons. I lived there with her after the death of my mother when I was two months old. It is very important to me as it means a livelihood for me to secure any information.

On an affidavit of birth dated May 26, 1943, we find this additional information: Ms. Hampton was of the Negro race, her father's full name was Joseph Hampton (a fact she did not discover until she was almost twenty years old), and he had been born in Reidsville, North Carolina. Her mother's birthplace was listed as Lynchburg, Virginia.

This appeal for a record of her beginnings points us to where Ms. Hampton's history began; not in the streets of Greenwich Village, where she will sing for pennies thrown from windows in 1910 at the age of eight, not even in Winston-Salem, where she will live on her grandmother's small farm from her birth until 1909, but further back into a past of a people, further back into the shame of a country.

Ms. Hampton's deepest history lies in the middle passage of the Triangular Slave Trade, and before that in the complex and full world of sixteenth-century Africa. When Europe turned its ambitious face to the curving coastline of the ancient continent and created an economic system based on the servitude of Africans, Ms. Hampton's story began. The middle passage, the horrendous crossing of the waters from Africa to this side of the world, literally and figuratively became the time of generational loss. Millions died in those waters, carrying their histories with them. This tragic "riddle in the waters," as the Afro-Cuban poet Nicolás Guillén calls it, was continued on the land of the southern plantation system. Frederick Douglass writes, "I have no accurate knowledge of my age, never having seen any authentic record containing it." These words were written in 1845 and Ms. Hampton was born in 1902, but now as I reflect on Ms. Hampton's dedication to preserving her own documents, I read them as a moment in the history of an African American lesbian.

The two themes of work and communal survival that run so strongly throughout Ms. Hampton's life are prefigured by the history of black working women in the sharecropping system, a history told in great moving detail by Jacqueline Jones in her study, *Labor of Love, Labor of Sorrow: Black Women, Work, and Family from Slavery to the Present.* Though Ms. Jones never mentions lesbian women, Ms. Hampton and her wife of forty-five years, Lillian Foster, who was born in Norfolk, Virginia, carried on in their lesbian lives traditions that had their roots in the post-slavery support systems created by southern black women at the turn of the century. The comradeship of these all-women benevolent and mutual aid societies was rediscovered by Ms. Hampton and Ms. Foster in their New York chapters of the Eastern Star.

Even the work both the women did, domestic service for Ms. Hampton and pressing for Ms. Foster, had its roots in this earlier period. Jones tells us that "in the largest southern cities from 50 to 70 percent of all black women were gainfully employed at least part of the year around the turn of the century." In Durham, North Carolina, close to Ms. Hampton's birthplace, during the period of 1880 to 1910, "one hundred percent of all black female household heads, aged 20 to 24, were wage earners." Very likely, both Ms. Hampton's grandmother and her mother were part of this workforce.

"I'm Mabel Hampton. I was born on May the second 1902, in Winston-Salem, North Carolina, and I left there when I was eight years old. Grandma said I was so small that [my] head was as big as a silver dollar. She said that she did all she could to make me grow. One day she was making the bed and gettin' things together after she fed the chickens. She never let me lay in the bed; I lay in the rocking chair, and this day she put the clothes in the chair; when she carried 'em outside, she forgot I was in 'em and shook the clothes out and shook me out in the gardens out on the ground. And Grandma was so upset that she hurt me.

"My grandmother took care of me. My mother died two months after I was born. She was poisoned, which left me with just my grandma, mother's younger sister, and myself. We had a house and lived on a street—we had chickens, had hogs, garden vegetables, grapes and things. We had a backyard, I can see it right now, that backyard. It had red roses, white roses, roses that went upside the house. We never had to go to the store for anything. On Saturdays we go out hunting blackberries, strawberries, and peaches. My girlfriends lived on each side of the street: Anna Lou Thomas, Hattie Harris, Lucille Crump. Oh-OOh-O Anna Lou Thomas, she was good lookin', she was a good-lookin' girl.

"One day Grandma says, 'Mabel I'm goin' to take you away.' She left Sister there and we went to Lynchburg, Virginia, because Grandma's mother had died. I remember when I got there, the man picked me up off the floor and I looked down on this woman who had drifts of gray hair. She was kind of a brown-skinned woman and she was good lookin'. Beautiful gray hair she had. I looked at her and then he put me down on a stool and I set there. They sang and prayed and carried on. I went to sleep."

However pleasant Ms. Hampton's memories were of North Carolina, she had no intention of returning there later in her life. "Lillian tried her best to get me to go to Winston-Salem. I says, 'No, I don't want to.' She says, 'You wouldn't even go to my home?' I says, 'No, because with my nasty temper they'd lynch me in five minutes. Because they would see me walkin' down the street holdin' hands with some woman, they want to put me in jail. Now I can hold hands with some woman all over New York, all over the Bronx, and everywhere else and no one says nothing to me.'"

When she was seven years old, in 1909, Ms. Hampton was forced to migrate to New York. In her own telling there is a momentous sense that she was lost to whatever safety she had in that garden of roses.

"One morning I was in the bedroom getting ready for school [*a deep sigh*]. I heard Grandma go out in the yard and come back and then I heard a big bump on the floor. So I ran to the door and I looked and Grandma was laying stretched out on the floor. I hollered and hollered and they all came running and picked her up and put her on the bed. She had had a stroke. Grandma lived one week after she had that stroke. My mama's younger aunt, I'll never forget it, was combing my hair and I looked over at Grandma layin' in bed. She looked at me and I looked at her. And when my aunt got finished combing my hair, Grandma had gone away.

"They called my mother's sister in New York and she came so fast I think she was there the next day. I remember the day we left Winston-Salem. It was in the summertime. We went by train and I had a sandwich of liver between two pieces of bread. And I knew and felt then that things was going to be different.

After eating that sandwich I cried all the way to New York. My aunt tried to pacify me but it didn't do no good, seems as if my heart was broken."

Taken to a small apartment at 52 West Eighth Street, Ms. Hampton meets her uncle, a minister, who, within the year, will rape her.

In telling her story, Ms. Hampton has given two reasons for her running away at age eight from this home: one involves a fight with a white girl at school and the other, a terrible beating by her uncle after she had misspelled a word. Whatever the exact reason, it was clear that Ms. Hampton had already decided she needed another air to breathe.

"My aunt went out one day and he raped me. I said to myself, 'I've got to leave here.' He wouldn't let me sleep in the bed. They had a place where they put coal at, and he put a blanket down and made me lay there. So this day, I got tired of that. I went out with nothing on but a dress, a jumper dress, and I walked and walked."

Here begins an amazing tale of an eight-year-old girl's odyssey to find a place and a way to live. After walking the streets for hours, the young Ms. Hampton "comes to a thing in the ground, in the sidewalk, people was going down there." A woman comes by and thinks she recognizes the lost child. "Aren't you Miss Brown's little girl?" Before Ms. Hampton can answer, she places a nickel in her hand and tells her to go back home to Harlem. As Ms. Hampton says, "that nickel was a turning point in my life."

Instead of going uptown, Ms. Hampton boarded a Jersey-bound train and rode to the last stop. She came above ground and walked until she found a playground. "I seen all these children playin', white and black, all of them havin' a good time." She joins the children and plays until it begins to get dark. Two of the children take an interest in her and she makes up a story: "My aunt told me to stay here until she comes." The girl calls to her brother, "You go get the cops, I'll try to find her aunt." She brings a woman back with her—a Miss Bessie White—who begins to ask her questions. Ms. Hampton: "I looked down the street and from the distance I see the boy comin' with the cop so I decided to go with the woman. Bessie said, 'Come, I'll take you home.'"

Ms. Hampton will remain with the White family until she is seventeen years old. One member of the family, Ellen, particularly stays in her memory: "I seen a young woman sitting left of where I come in at. I say to myself, this is a good-looking woman; I was always admiring some woman. Oh, and she was. She had beautiful hair and she looked just like an angel. She got up out of the chair, she was kind of tall, and she says 'you come with me.' So she took me upstairs, bathed me, and said 'we'll find you some clothes.' She always talked very softly. And she says, 'you'll sleep with me.' I was glad of that.

"So I went and stayed with them. The other sister went on about lookin' for my aunt. I knew she never find her. See, I knew everything about me, but I kept quiet. I kept quiet for twenty years."

Mabel Hampton, from the very beginning of her narrative, speaks with the determination of a woman who must take care of herself. She will decide what silences to keep and what stories to tell, creating for herself a power over life's circumstances that her material resources seldom gave her.

For Mabel Hampton, the 1920s were both a decade of freedom and one of literal imprisonment. In 1919, when she is seventeen years old, she is doing housework for a Dr. Kraus of Jersey City. Her beloved Ellen, the first woman friend to hold Ms. Hampton in her arms, has died during childbirth. With Ellen gone, Ms. Hampton's ties to the White family are loosening; she will find work dancing in an all-women's company that performs in Coney Island and have her first requited lesbian love affair. She will discover the club life of New York. This is the first decade in which Ms. Hampton will pay a visit to the salon of A'Lelia Walker, the flapper daughter of Madam Walker, and be amazed at the multiple sexual couplings she observes. She will perform in the Lafayette Theater and dance at the Garden of Joy, both in Harlem. In this decade, she will make the acquaintance of Ethel Waters, Gladys Bentley, and Alberta Hunter. She will be one of the 150,000 mourners who sing "My Buddy" as the casket bearing Florence Mills, beloved singer, slowly moves through the Harlem streets in 1927. This is Ms. Hampton's experience of the period that lives in history books as the Harlem Renaissance.

But before all this exploration takes place, Ms. Hampton will be arrested for prostitution by two white policemen and be sentenced to three years in Bedford Hills Reformatory for Women by a Judge Norris. Ms. Hampton: "While we're standing there talking, the door opens. Now I know I had shut it. And two white men walk in—great big white men. 'We're raiding this house,' one of them says. 'For what?' 'Prostitution,' he says. I hadn't been with a man no time. I couldn't figure it out. I didn't have time to get clothes or nothing. The judge she sat up there and says 'Well only thing I can say is Bedford.' No lawyer, no nothing. She railroaded me."

When Ms. Hampton talks about her prison experience, she dwells on the kindnesses she found there: "It was summertime and we went back out there and sat down. She [another prisoner] says 'I like you.' 'I like you too.' She said no more until time to go to bed. We went to bed and she took me in her bed and held me in her arms and I went to sleep. She put her arms around me like Ellen used to do, you know, and I went to sleep."

But where Ms. Hampton found friendship, the board of managers of the prison area found scandal and disgrace. Opened in 1902 in a progressive era of prison reform, Bedford Hills under its first woman administrator, Katherine Davis, accepted the special friendships of its women inmates. But in 1920, word that interracial lesbian sex was occurring throughout the prison caused Ms. Davis to lose her job. The new administrators of the prison demanded segregated facilities, the only way, according to one of the men, to prevent interracial sex.

By the time I was doing the oral history with Ms. Hampton, she had left this experience far behind. She told me that she seldom told anyone about it; she would just say she had gone away for a while. But toward the end of her life, Ms. Hampton wanted her whole story to be told. She realized that her desire to be open about her life was not popular with her peers. "So many of my friends got religion now," she would say, "you can't get anything out of them."

While Mabel Hampton so generously shared her prison experience with me, I read about Bedford Hills in Estelle Freedman's book, *Their Sister's Keepers: Women's Prison Reform in America, 1830–1930.* When I read the following sentence in Freedman's book, "By 1919, we are told, about 75% of the prisoners were prostitutes, 70% had venereal disease, a majority were of low mental ability and ten percent were psychopaths," I was forced to see the lesbians encoded in this list. Mabel Hampton was among these counted women. As gays and lesbians, we have a special insight, a special charge in doing history work. We, too, have had our humanity hidden in such lists of undesirables. I started this work on Mabel Hampton because her life brought to the study of history the dignity of the human face behind the sweeping summaries. And because I loved her.

After thirteen months, Ms. Hampton is released from prison with the condition that she stay away from New York City and its bad influences. But Ms. Hampton cannot contain herself. A white woman with a gray car whom she met in Bedford comes to Jersey City to take her to parties in New York. When a neighbor informs on her, she is forced to return and complete her sentence at Bedford. Ms. Hampton later describes some of the life that the state had declared criminal.

"In 1923, I am about twenty years old. I had rooms at 120 West 122nd street. A girlfriend of mine was living next door and they got me three rooms there on the ground floor—a bedroom, living room, and big kitchen. I stayed there until I met Lillian in 1932. I went away with the people I worked for, but I always kept my rooms to come back to. Then I went into the show.

"Next door these girls were all lesbians, they had four rooms in the basement and they gave parties all the time. Sometimes we would have 'pay parties.' We'd buy all the food—chicken and potato salads. I'd chip in with them because I would bring my girlfriends. We also went to 'rent parties' where you go in and pay a couple dollars. You buy your drinks and meet other women and dance and have fun. But with our house we just had close friends. Sometimes there would be twelve or fourteen women there. We'd have pig feet, chittlins. In the wintertime, it was black-eyed peas and all that stuff. Most of the women wore suits. Very seldom did any of them have slacks or anything like that, because they had to come through the streets. Of course, if they were in a car, they wore the slacks. Most of them had short hair. And most of them was good-lookin' women too. And you wasn't supposed to jive with them, you know. They danced up a breeze. They did the Charleston, they did a little bit of everything. They were all colored women. Sometimes we ran into someone who had a white woman with them. But me, I'd venture out with any of them. I just had a ball.

"I had a couple of white girlfriends down in the village. We got along fine. At that time I was acting in the Cherry Lane Theater. I didn't have to go to the bars because I would go to women's houses. Like Jackie (Moms) Mabley would have a big party and all the girls from the show would go. She had all the women there."

In addition to private parties, Ms. Hampton and her friends were up on the latest public lesbian events. Sometime in February of 1927, Ms. Hampton attended the new play that was scandalizing Broadway, *The Captive*. Whatever her material struggle was in any given decade, Ms. Hampton sought out the cultural images she needed. Here, in a brief excerpt, is how she remembered that night at the theater.

Well, I heard about it and a girlfriend of mind had taken me to see this play, *The Captive*, and I fell in love—not only with *The Captive*, but the lady who was the head actress in it. Her name was Helen Mencken. So I decided I would go back—I had heard so much talk about it. I went back to see it by myself. I sat on the edge of my seat! I looked at the first part and I will always think that the woman was a lesbian. She played it too perfect! She had the thing down! She kissed too perfect, she had everything down pat. So that's why I kept going back to see it, because it looked to me it was part of my life. I was a young woman, but I said now this is what I would like to be, but of course, I would have to marry and I didn't want to marry [the play focuses on the seduction of a married woman by an offstage lesbian, who is also married], so I would just go on and do whatever I thought was right to do. I talked to a couple of my friends in Jersey City about the play. I carried them back, paid their way to see it, and they fell in love with it. There was plenty of women in that audience and plenty of men too! They applauded and applauded. This same girl with the green car, she knew her—Helen Mencken—and she carried me backstage and introduced me. Boy, I felt so proud! And she says, "Why do you like the show?" I said, "Because it seems a part of my life and what I am and what I hope to be." She says, "That's nice. Stick to it! You'll be alright."

The 1920s end with Mabel Hampton living fully "in the life" trying to piece together another kind of living from her day work and from her chorus line jobs. Later, when asked why she left show business, she will say, "Because I like to eat."

The Depression does not play a large role in Ms. Hampton's memories, perhaps because she was already earning such a marginal income. We know that from 1925 until 1937, she did day work for the family of Charles Baubrick. Ms. Hampton carefully saved all the letters from her employees testifying to her character:

Dec. 12, 1937:

To Whom It May Concern:
This is to certify that the bearer Mabel Hampton has worked for me for the last 12 years doing housework off and on and she does the same as yet. We have always found her honest and industrious.

Reading these letters, embedded as they were in all the other documents of Ms. Hampton's life, is always sobering. So much of her preserved papers testify to an autonomous home and social life, but these formal letters sprinkled through each decade remind us that in some sense Ms. Hampton's life was under surveillance by the white families who controlled her economic survival.

In 1935, Ms. Hampton is baptized into the Roman Catholic Church at St.

Thomas the Apostle on West 118th Street, another step in her quest for spiritual comfort. This journey would include a lifelong devotion to the mysteries of the Rosicrucians and a full collection of Marie Corelli, a Victorian novelist with a spiritualist bent. She will end the decade registering with the United States Department of Labor trying to find a job. She is told, "We will get in touch with you as soon as there is a suitable opening."

The event that changes Ms. Hampton's life forever happens early on in that decade, in 1932: while waiting for a bus, she meets a woman even smaller than herself, "dressed like a duchess," as Ms. Hampton would later say: Lillian Foster.

Ms. Foster remembers in 1976, two years before her death: "Forty-four years ago I met Mabel. We was a wonderful pair. I'll never regret it. But she's tough. I met her in 1932, September twenty-second. And we haven't been separated since in our whole life. Death will separate us. Other than that I don't want it to end."

Ms. Hampton, to the consternation of her more discreet friends, dressed in an obvious way much of her life. Her appearance, however, did not seem to bother her wife. Ms. Foster goes on to say: "A lady walked in once, Joe's wife, and she say, 'You is a pretty neat girl. You have a beautiful little home but where is your husband?' And just at that time, Mabel comes in the front door with her key and I said, 'There is my husband.'" The visitor added, "Now you know if that was your husband, you wouldn't have said it!" to which Ms. Foster firmly replied, "But I said it!"

Lillian Foster, born in 1906 in Norfolk, Virginia, shared much of the same southern background of Ms. Hampton, except that she came from a large family. She was keenly aware that Ms. Hampton was "all alone," as she often put it. Ms. Foster worked her whole life as a presser in white-owned dry-cleaning establishments, a job, like domestic service, that had its roots in the neo-slavery working conditions of the urban South at the turn of the century. These many years of labor in underventilated rooms accelerated Ms. Foster's rapid decline in her later years. But together with a group of friends, these two women would create a household lasting for forty-six years.

This household with friends took many shapes. When crisis struck and a fire destroyed their apartment in 1976, as part of the real estate wars that were gutting and leveling the Bronx, Ms. Foster and Ms. Hampton came to live with me and Deborah Edel until they could move back to their home. Later, Ms. Hampton would describe our shared time as an adventure in lesbian families. "Down here it was just like two couples, Joan and Deborah and Mabel and Lillian; we got along lovely, and we played, we sang, we ate; it was marvelous! I will never forget it. And Lillian, of course, Lillian was my wife. I had Joan laughing because I called Lillian 'Little Bear,' but when I first met her in 1932, she was to me, she was a duchess—the grand duchess. Later in life I got angry with her one day and I called her the 'little bear' and she called me 'the big bear' and of course that hung on to me all through life. And now we are known to all our friends as the 'big bear' and the 'little bear.'"

Ms. Hampton saved hundreds of little cards signed 'Little bear.' But when she appealed to government officials or agencies for help, as she often did as their housing conditions deteriorated, she said Ms. Foster was her sister.

Letter to Mayor Lindsay, 1969:

Dear Mr. Mayor,
I don't know if I am on the right road or not, but I am taking a chance;
now what I want to know is can you tell me how I can get an apartment,
I have been everywhere and no success. I am living at the above address
[639 E. 169th Street, Bronx] for 26 years but for about the past 10 years
the building has gone down terribly. For two years we have no heat all
winter, also no hot water. We called the housing authority but it seems
it don't help; everywhere I go the rent is so high that poor people can't
pay it and I would like to find a place before the winter comes in with
the rent that I can afford to pay. It is two of us (women) past 65. I still
work but my older sister is on retirement so we do need two bedrooms.
If you can do something to help us it will be greatly appreciated.

Thanking you in advance,
I remain, Miss Mabel Hampton.

Finding this letter marked a turning point in my work. Ms. Hampton's
request for a safe and warm house for herself and Ms. Foster now stands as the
starting point of all my historical inquiry: How did you survive?

In a document of a different sort, the program for a social event sponsored
by Jacobi Hospital, where she was employed for the last twenty years of her
working life, we discover that a Ms. Mabel Hampton and Ms. Lillian Hampton
are sitting at Table 25. These two women negotiated the public world as "sisters," which allowed expressions of affection and demanded a recognition of
their intimacy.

There is a seamless quality to Ms. Hampton's life that does not fit our usual
paradigm for doing lesbian history work. Her life does not seem to be organized around what we have come to see as the usual rites of gay passage, like
coming out or going to the bars. Instead, she gives us the vision of an integrated life in which the major shaping events are the daily acts of work,
friends, and social organizations, and the major definers of these territories are
class and race; in addition, she expects all aspects of her life to be respected.

Every letter preserved by Ms. Hampton written by a friend, co-worker, or
employer contains a greeting or a blessing for Ms. Foster. "I do hope to be
able to visit you and Lillian some evening for a real chat and a supper by a
superb cook! Do take care of yourself and my best to Lillian," Dolores, 1944;
"God bless and keep you and Lillian well always, I wish I could see you both
some times," Jennie, 1977.

The 1940s were turbulent years, marked by World War II and unrest at
home. While African American soldiers were fighting the armies of racial
supremacists in Europe, their families were fighting the racist dictates of a
Jim Crow society at home. Harlem, Detroit, and other American cities would
see streets become battlefields.

For African American working women like Ms. Hampton, the 1940s was the
decade of the slave markets, the daily gathering of Black women on the street

corners of Brooklyn and the Bronx to sell their domestic services to white women who drove by looking for cheap labor. In 1940, Ms. Hampton was part of this labor force as she had been for over twenty years, working year after year without worker's compensation, health benefits, or pension payments.

In September of 1940, she receives a postcard canceling her employment with one family: "Dear Mabel, please do not come on Thursday. I will see you again on Friday at Mrs. Garfinkels. I have engaged a part time worker as I need more frequent help as you know. Come over to see us."

Ms. Hampton did not let her working difficulties dampen her enthusiasm for her cultural heroes, however. On October 6, 1940, she and Ms. Foster are in the audience at Carnegie Hall, when at 8:30 P.M., Paul Robeson commands the stage. The announcement for this concert is the first document we have reflecting Ms. Hampton's lifelong love of the opera and her dedication to African American cultural figures and institutions.

In 1941, perhaps in recognition of her perilous situation as a day worker, Ms. Hampton secures the job of matron with the Hammarlund Manufacturing Company on West 34th Street, assuring her entrance into the new social security system begun just six years earlier by Franklin Roosevelt.

She still takes irregular night and day domestic employment so she and Ms. Foster can, among other things, on May 28, 1946, purchase from the American Mending Machine Company one Singer Electric Sewing Machine with console table for the price of $100. She leaves a $44 deposit and carefully preserves all records of the transaction.

On February 20, 1942, we have the first evidence of Ms. Hampton's involvement in the country's war efforts: a ditto sheet of instructions from the American Women's Voluntary Services addressed to all air raid wardens. "During the German attack on the countries of Europe, the telephone was often used for sabotage thereby causing panic and loss of life by erroneous orders. We in New York are particularly vulnerable in this respect since our great apartment houses have often hundreds even thousands under one roof. . . . The apartment house telephone warden must keep lines clear in time of emergency. Type of person required: this sort of work should be particularly suited for women whose common sense and reliability could be depended upon."

In August, Ms. Hampton is working hard for the Harlem branch of the New York Defense Recreation Committee, trying to collect cigarettes and other refreshments for the soldiers and sailors who frequent Harlem's USO. In December of 1942, she is appointed deputy sector commander in the air warden service by Mayor LaGuardia. The same year she will also receive her American Theater Wing War Service membership card. Throughout 1943, she serves as her community's air raid warden and attends monthly meetings of the 12th Division of the American Women's Voluntary Services Organizations on West 116th Street. During all this time, her country will maintain a segregated army abroad and a segregated society at home.

In January and February of 1944, she receives her fourth and fifth war loan citation. This support for causes she believed in, no matter how small her income, continues throughout Ms. Hampton's life. In addition to her religious causes, for example, she will send monthly donations to SCLC and the Martin Luther King Memorial Fund; by the end of the seventies, she is adding gay organizations to her list.

On March 29, 1944, Ms. Hampton attends the National Negro Opera Company's performance of *La Traviata*. This group believed in opera for the masses and included in its program a congratulatory message from the Upper West Side Communist Party. On its board sat Eleanor Roosevelt and Mary McCloud Bethune, both part of another moment in lesbian history. In 1952, this same company will present *Ouanga*, an opera based on the life of the first king of Haiti, Dessaline, who the program says "successfully conquered Napoleon's armies in 1802 and won the Black Republic's fight for freedom." Ms. Hampton will be in the audience.

Continuing her dedication to finding the roses amid the struggle, on November 12, 1944, Ms. Hampton will hear Marian Anderson sing at Carnegie Hall and add the program of this event to her collection of newspaper articles about the career of this valiant woman.

Ms. Hampton's never-ending pursuit of work often caused long absences from home, and Ms. Foster was often left waiting for her partner to return to their Bronx apartment on 169th Street, the apartment they had moved into in 1945, at the war's end, and which would remain their shared home until Ms. Foster's death in 1978.

> Dear Mabel:
> Received your letter and was very glad to hear from you and to know that you are well and happy. This leaves me feeling better than I have since you left. Everything is OK at home. Only I miss you so much I will be glad when the time is up. There is nobody like you to me. I am writing this on my lunch hour. It is 11 p.m. I am quitting tomorrow. I don't see anyone as I haven't been feeling too well. Well the 1/2 hour is up.
> > Nite nite be good and will see you soon.
> > Little Bear

In 1948, Ms. Hampton falls ill and cannot work. She applies for home relief and is awarded a grant of $54.95 a month, which the agency stipulates should be spent the following way: $27 for food; $21 for rent; 55¢ for cooking fuel; 80¢ for electricity; $6 for clothing, and for personal incidentals, she is allotted $1. But from these meager funds she manages to give comfort to friends.

> Postcard, August 9, 1948:

> Dear Miss Lillian and Mabel:
> The flowers you sent were beautiful and I liked them very much. I wear the heart you sent all the time. It was very nice to hear from you both. I am feeling fine now. I hope you are both in the best of health.
> > Love
> > Doris

In 1948, Ms. Hampton writes to the home relief agency telling the case-worker to stop all payments because she has the promise of a job.

The decade that began in war between nations and peoples ends in Ms. Hampton's version of history with a carefully preserved article about the international figure Josephine Baker. Cut out of the March 12, 1949, issue of the *Pittsburgh Courier* are the following words:

Well friends, fellow Negroes and countrymen, you can stop all that guess work and surmising about Josephine Baker. This writer knew Edith Spencer, Lottie Gee, Florence Mills, knew them well. He has also known most of the other colored women artists of the last thirty years. His word to you is that this Josephine Baker eminently belongs. She is not a common music hall entertainer. She has been over here for a long time, maybe 25 years. The little old colored gal from back home is a French lady now. That means something. It means for a colored person that you have been accepted into a new and glamorous and free world where color does not count. It means that in the joy of the new living you just might forget that "old oaken bucket" so full of bitter quaffs for you. It means that once you found solid footing in the new land of freedom, you might tax your mind to blot out all the sorry past, all the old associations, to become alien in spirit as well as in fact. It pleases me folks to be able to report to you that none of this has possessed Josephine. I tested her and she rang true. What she does is for you and me. She said so out of her own mouth. Her eyes glistened as she expostulated and described in vivid, charged phrases the aim and purpose of her work. She was proud when I told her of Lena and of Hilda [Simms]. "You girls are blazing trails for the race," I commented. "Indeed so," she quickly retorted. After she had talked at length of what it means to be a Negro and of her hope that whatever she did might reflect credit on Negroes, particularly the Negroes of her land of birth, I chanced a leading question. "So you're a race woman," I queried. I was not sure she would understand. But she did. "Of course I am," she replied. Yes, all the world's a stage and Josephine comes out upon it for you and for me.

In my own work, I have tried to focus on the complex interaction between oppression and resistance, aware of the dangers of romanticizing losses while at the same time aggrandizing little victories, but I am still awed by how a single human spirit refuses the messages of self-hatred and out of bits and pieces weaves a garment grand enough for the soul's and body's passion. Ms. Hampton prized her memories of Josephine Baker, Marian Anderson, and Paul Robeson, creating for herself a nurturing family of defiant African American women and men. When the *New York Times* closed its obituary on Ms. Hampton with the words "There are no known survivors," it showed its ignorance of how an oppressed people make legacies out of memory.

In our history of Ms. Hampton, we are now entering the so-called conforming 1950s, when white, middle-class heterosexual women, we have been told, are running in droves to be married and keep the perfect home. Reflecting on another vision, Ms. Hampton carefully cuts out and saves newspaper articles on the pioneer transsexual Christine Jorgensen. From 1948 until her retirement in 1972, Ms. Hampton will work in the housekeeping division of Jacobi Hospital, where she earns for herself the nickname "Captain" from some of the women she works with, who keep in touch with Ms. Hampton until their deaths many years later. Here she meets Ms. Jorgensen and pays her nightly visits in her hospital room.

From Ms. Hampton's documents: *Daily News* article, December 1, 1952, "Ex-GI Becomes Blond Beauty," contains a letter written by Jorgensen explaining to her parents why there is so much consternation about her case. She concludes, "It is more a problem of social taboos and the desire not to speak of the subject because it deals with the great hush hush, namely sex."

Ms. Hampton begins the decade earning $1,006 for a year's work and ends it earning $1,232. Because of lack of money, Ms. Hampton was never able to travel to all the places in the world that fascinated her; but in this decade she adds hundreds of pages of stamps to her overflowing albums, little squares of color from Morocco and Zanzibar, from the Philippines and Mexico.

Throughout her remaining years, Ms. Hampton will continue with her eyes on the hilltop and her feet on a very earthly pavement. She will always have very little money and will always be very generous. In the 1970s, Ms. Hampton discovers senior citizen centers and "has a ball," as she liked to say, on their subsidized trips to Atlantic City. She will lose her partner of forty-five years, Lillian Foster, in 1978.

After almost drifting away in mourning, she will find new energy and a loving family in New York's lesbian and gay community. She will have friendly visitors from SAGE and devoted friends like Ann Allen Shockley, who never fails to visit when she is in town. She will march in Washington in the first national lesbian and gay civil rights march. She will appear in films like *Silent Pioneers* and *Before Stonewall*. In 1987, she accompanies Deborah and her lover Teddy to California so she can be honored at the West Coast Old Lesbians Conference.

She will eventually have to give up her fourth-floor walk-up Bronx apartment and move in with Lee Hudson and myself, who along with many others will care for her as she loses physical strength. On October 26, 1989, after a second stroke, Ms. Hampton will finally let go of a life she loved so dearly.

Ms. Hampton never relented in her struggle to live a fully integrated life, a life marked by the integrity of her self-authorship. "If I give you my word," she always said, "I'll be there"—and she was.

On her death, her sisters in Electa Chapter 10 of the Eastern Star Organization honored her with the following words: "We wish to express our gratitude for having known Sister Hampton all these years. She became a member many years ago and went from the bottom to the top of the ladder. She has served us in many capacities. We loved her dearly. May she rest in peace with the angels."

Class and race are not synonymous with problems, with deprivation. They can be sources of great joy and communal strength. Class and race, in this society, however, are manipulated markers of privilege and power. Ms. Hampton had a vision of what life should be; it was a grand, simple vision, filled with good friends and good food, a warm home and her lover by her side. She gave all she could to doing the best she could. The sorrow is in the fact that she and so many others have had to work so hard for such basic human territory.

"I wish you knew what it's like to be me" is the challenge posed by a society divided by race and class. We have so much to learn about one another's victories, the sweetnesses as well as the losses. By expanding our models for what makes a life lesbian or what is a lesbian moment in history, we will become clearer about contemporary political and social coalitions that must be forged to ensure all our liberations.

We are just beginning to understand how social constructs shape lesbian and gay lives. We will have to change our questions and our language of inquiry to take our knowledge deeper. Class and race, always said together as if they meant the same thing, may each call forth their own story. The insights we gain will anchor our other discussions in the realities of individual lives, reminding us that the bread and roses, material survival and cultural identity, are the starting points of so many of our histories.

In that spirit, I will always remember our Friday-night dinners at the archives, with a life-size photography of Gertrude Stein propped up at one end of the table; Ms. Hampton sitting across from Lee Hudson; Denver, the family dog, right at Ms. Hampton's elbow; and myself, looking past the candlelight to my two dear friends, Lee and Mabel—each of us carrying different histories, joined by our love and need for one another.

Ms. Hampton's address at the 1984 New York City Gay Pride rally:

I, Mabel Hampton, have been a lesbian all my life, for eighty-two years, and I am proud of myself and my people. I would like all my people to be free in this country and all over the world, my gay people and my black people.

1993

JOAN NESTLE

EDMUND WHITE

BARBARA SMITH

MONIQUE WITTIG

ESTHER NEWTON

SAMUEL R. DELANY

EVE KOSOFSKY SEDGWICK

JOHN D'EMILIO

CHERRÍE MORAGA

JUDITH BUTLER

EDMUND WHITE

Edmund White has written sixteen books, including biographies of Marcel Proust and Jean Genet (for which he won the National Book Critics Circle Award). His autobiographical series of novels—*A Boy's Own Story, The Beautiful Room is Empty*, and *The Farewell Symphony*—is a landmark in contemporary gay fiction. He directs the Creative Writing Department at Princeton and lives in New York City with his partner, the writer Michael Carroll. For sixteen years White lived in Paris; he is an officer of Arts and Letters in France. His most recent publication is a historical novel, *Fanny: A Fiction*, which is narrated by Frances Trollope about the early feminist heroine Frances Wright.

THE PERSONAL IS POLITICAL
Queer Fiction and Criticism

In one sense, most of the fiction I like and all the fiction I write is political. If I sometimes sound like an apostle of art for art's sake, this esthetic bias should be judged against an endless fascination with politics. The power dynamics between populations, the jousting for position within a group, the struggle for dominance in a couple, even the empowering awareness of individual oppression—by all these definitions, politics has been a constant theme in my work, even or especially in my novels of pure fantasy, *Forgetting Elena* and *Caracole*.

I hope you'll forgive me for speaking so much about my own work. I am certainly aware of its limitations, and I by no means want to disguise my naïveté and shortcomings as a political commentator or activist. For instance, my nearly total silence in the face of AIDS, with the exception of my stories in *The Darker Proof*, I consider reprehensible, a lapsus I'm trying belatedly to fill with the novel I'm writing now, *The Farewell Symphony,* the sequel to my earlier autobiographical novels, *A Boy's Own Story* and *The Beautiful Room Is Empty.*

If I speak so much of my own books, I do so because I know the ins and outs of their publishing history. And since my career happened sometimes to parallel the birth and growth of the modern gay publishing movement, my story may be of some general interest.

In *Forgetting Elena*, my first published novel, which came out in 1973, I tried to put into practice an observation I'd made about the work of writers I'd admired. I'd realized that they were at their best when exploring themes about which they themselves were of two minds. A thesis novel that propounds an idea the author has completely mapped out in advance is not one I want to read or write. I prefer a book in which the writer sinks a probe into a question that is difficult to resolve but urgent to consider.

When I was a student Saul Bellow spoke to us along these lines about *The Brothers Karamazov*. He said that in a letter written to a friend during the composition of the novel, Dostoevsky complained that in "The Grand Inquisitor" he'd so convincingly repudiated God's world that in the next section he feared he couldn't conjure up some equally favorable arguments on behalf of his real credo—of universal harmony and the ascendancy of heart, feeling and faith over mind. Dostoevsky's dramatization of ideas struck me as the very way to stage my own political concerns. Proust had demonstrated the shortcomings of snobbism because he knew so intimately all about its allure, just as Elizabeth Bowen could write about the tragic conflict between unruly passion and crushing social convention in *The Death of the Heart* because she'd succumbed to passion and had been impressed by the luster convention gives to society.

Forgetting Elena is, among other things, a fantasy novel about the charm—and repulsiveness—of a closed society that has allowed the cult of beauty to replace genuine moral concerns. The denizens of my island kingdom, which sometimes resembles Fire Island, never stop to question if an act is good or bad so long as it is beautiful.

This estheticism produces sinister, even tragic consequences. And yet I lavished on those rituals and dances and costumes and nature worship all the affection I myself felt for the shimmering, ephemeral, erotically charged drama and décor of the Pines at the end of the 1960s, when gays were crowding out straights in the beach community and when, in the rest of the United States, the new gay movement was generating a fresh take on gender politics. Simultaneously, the new gay sensibility was concocting extravagant inventions in the ephemeral arts of fashion, lighting, flower arranging, party design, window dressing, disco dancing, drug sequencing and sexual performance. I was attracted to both gay politics *and* the gay sensibility, two very different entities; the tension humming under every page of *Forgetting Elena* was born out of this conflict.

Perhaps for all writers, but certainly for us lesbian and gay writers in the 1970s, every artistic decision we made had its political aspect. Should we write gay fiction at all? At that time there was no known market for our work, few bookstores that would carry it, precious few editors who would even read our manuscripts. Literary friends told us that we were betraying our high calling by ghettoizing ourselves. After all, the argument ran, many great writers had been lesbian or gay, but Willa Cather and Virginia Woolf and Elizabeth Bishop wrote for all humanity and would have found the label demeaning. It would be absurd to call them lesbian writers, just as it would be grotesque to call E. M. Forster or Henry James gay writers.

Since I'd had my first breakthrough with *Forgetting Elena*—a novel that no critic had identified as gay and that a notorious heterosexual, Vladimir Nabokov, had singled out for praise—my timorous friends were all the more insistent that I should not come out in print or, as they put it, "limit" myself.

Oddly enough Saul Bellow once again guided me. I read in his *Paris Review* interview that when he'd first started writing about the Jewish experience he'd been warned not to give up the writer's proudest birthright—his claim to universality (I say "his" advisedly). Fortunately Bellow had ignored the warnings.

Anyway, ever since I was a teenager I'd been writing unpublished and unpublishable gay fiction, not out of an enlightened or campaigning spirit but because I felt driven to exorcize my demons and establish my right to exist, on the page if not yet in society. At age fifteen I'd already written a coming-out novel, *The Tower Window*, never published, of course, and not even read in manuscript. Now, after *Forgetting Elena*, the very next book I wrote (in collaboration with Dr. Charles Silverstein) was *The Joy of Gay Sex*. In retrospect this book may look reckless (because of the subsequent AIDS crisis) or cynically commercial (because presumably we earned a lot of money) or blandly assimilationist (since the book appeared as a sequel to *The Joy of Sex*, a hugely successful guide for heterosexuals).

Queer history moves so quickly that even sixteen years later (*The Joy of Gay Sex* was published in 1977) that past moment is difficult to reconstruct. Needless to say, in 1977 no one could have foreseen the AIDS crisis of 1981 and at the time Dr. Silverstein and I were often criticized by people in the gay community for being conservative because we labeled certain sexual practices dangerous. We certainly didn't get rich, since we were paid a flat fee and a miserable percentage. The publishers told me I could write the book under a pen name; at that time my name was virtually unknown in any event. If this project now seems assimilationist, at the time assimilation itself seemed a provocative and progressive idea. There were so few openings in the united front against homosexuality that only the sexual revolution seemed a possible point of entry.

Our book, moreover, was much more a guide to gay practical problems (for instance, how to write a will in favor of a lover) or psychological hurdles (how to come out at work, for example) than a sex manual, which we knew from Masters and Johnson's findings was far less a problem for gays than for straights. We felt courageous signing our real names to a book that would be sold across the country over the counter in major bookstores—a book that attempted to assuage fears, diminish guilt, combat puritanism, sanction sex. After 1981 we were naturally distressed that the book was still in print, but our efforts to revise it were ignored by the publishers, who had now been absorbed by American Express. Recently Dr. Silverstein and Felice Picano were at last able to bring out a safe-sex version, for which I wrote an introduction.

In my next novel, *Nocturnes for the King of Naples*, my narrator writes a long letter to an absent beloved who might, depending on one's interpretation, either be an older man or God. Mary Gordon, the then newly discovered Catholic novelist, gave me a blurb saying my novel had re-invented "devotional literature." Although I wrote the book out of my private poetic obsessions, I was certainly aware that in a country like the United States where homosexuals have suffered so much at the hands of organized religion, it was a useful literary act, if only for my 5,000 readers, to place an overtly gay love story in a mystical tradition that blends the carnal with the spiritual, a tradition that includes Saint John of the Cross, the Sufi poet Rumi and Baroque poets such as John Donne.

But perhaps the most dramatic choice was the decision not to explain gay lives but simply to present them. In the novel I'm writing now, which starts in the late 1960s, before Stonewall, I have a passage that reads:

> Back then I was anything but an objective observer. I was a moralist, if that meant I wanted to suggest new ways of acting through examples and adjectives that were subtly praising or censorious. I knew as well as anyone else that homosexuality was an aberration, a disease, but in my fiction I pretended otherwise. I gave my characters problems, minor problems that struck me as human, decorous, rather than

the one irrevocable tragedy of being blasted from the start. I showed my homosexual characters living their lives openly and parallel to those of their heterosexual friends: pure fiction. I pretended the homosexual characters had homes, loves, careers if not exactly the same at least of a similar weight and dignity. But my greatest invention was that I let my queers think about everything except the one subject that obsessed them: how they came to be this way, how they could evince the world's compassion rather than hate, and how they could be cured of their malady. I knew I didn't have the equilibrium or self-acceptance of my characters, but I thought of pretending as if (hadn't a whole German philosophy been based on the words "as if?") this utopia already existed I could authenticate my gay readers if not myself.

Curiously even *The Joy of Gay Sex* had advocated a warmer, more sensual view of sex than I myself could muster. This hortatory and utopian aspect of gay writing sometimes vexed straight readers. I remember that John Gardiner, the author of *On Moral Fiction*, told me that he considered *Nocturnes* immoral because in it the father breezes right past his son's confession of homosexuality. The father, if anything, seems relieved that his son won't be competing with him for women. Gardiner thought such broad-mindedness (or egotism) was unrealistic, hence immoral. He didn't understand that I was trailblazing.

States of Desire: Travels in Gay America, published in 1980, took a half-admiring, half-castigating look at the triumphant clone culture that was about to be transformed beyond recognition by AIDS. As a socialist I was worried by the materialism, selfishness and racism I detected among successful white clones, but at the same time I had to admire the in-your-face confidence of this group in confronting Christian fundamentalist Anita Bryant, for instance. The most obvious political agenda of the book was to show the wide variety of gay lives. I also turned the travel-book format into a platform for writing mini-essays about man-boy love, racism, sado-masochism, agism, and so on.

Perhaps the least obvious but most telling political decision was to address a sophisticated gay reader. If previously I'd written for an older European heterosexual woman, an ideal reader who helped me to screen out in-jokes and preaching to the converted, I now pictured my reader as another gay man. Up until now many gay nonfiction books had been pleas for compassion or primary guides to gay folklore addressed to an open-minded if uninformed straight audience. I decided to work on the principle behind the *New Yorker* that pretends all readers are Manhattanites, a policy that flatters even Iowans. I thought by writing for other gays I could get beyond the See-Dick-Run level and apologetic tone of most gay commentators, a tone that had begun to bore me.

If *A Boy's Own Story*, published in 1982, was my best-received book, it succeeded partly because it seemed to fill an empty niche in the contemporary publishing ecology, the slot of the coming-out novel. What I wanted to show was the harm psychotherapy had done to homosexuals and the self-hatred that was forced on a young gay man by a society that could conceive of homosexuality only as a sickness, sin or crime. What allowed me to write it and its sequel, *The Beautiful Room is Empty*, was the conviction I'd picked up in consciousness-raising groups in the early 1970s that the personal is political. This simple phrase, more than any other, opened the way to a genuine feminist and queer literature. We learned that what we'd endured and survived was not too subjective or peculiar to be of interest to readers. We also learned that what we'd lived through was not a neurosis in need of treatment but a shared experience that called for political action. My strategy in *The Beautiful Room is Empty* was to present a gay hero so self-hating that even the most retrograde reader would become impatient with his inner torment and welcome with relief the Stonewall uprising, which is the concluding scene of that novel. I felt my strategy had worked when Christopher Lehmann-Haupt, an avowed heterosexual, wrote in his *New York Times* review that he found himself longing for the hero to settle down and get on with his life, even if it was gay.

The consciousness-raising group seemed not a bad model for the queer artistic and critical community. During a typical session we took a single theme—gays and religion, say—and each person was asked to give a personal testimony bearing on the subject. No one was permitted to advise another person or interpret her or his testimony—practices more appropriate to group therapy, which assumed the individual was out of step, than to the CR group, which was convinced society needed to be reformed. Only after everyone had spoken did we seek to find certain common themes, if there were any, and to envisage a remedial political action. For instance, if everyone, in speaking about coming out, testified to the blackout of information about homosexuality in the schools while growing up, we might plan actions that would provide it now.

The part of the formula that seems important to recall today is that no one had the right to challenge the political correctness of another person's story. Politics entered the process only after all the stories were told. Political correctness is a matter for criticism, not creativity.

Neither Marxist nor Freudian nor deconstructionist arguments have persuaded me to abandon the romantic creed that art is an expression of human freedom at its highest, virtually the only arena not subject to compromise, fear, contingency, and accommodation. Fiction is based on human feelings, including those of hate, lust, greed, and self-pity, and no one has the right to deny another person's emotions or to correct her or his account of them. To say, "I know what you're feeling or what you should be feeling better than you yourself know," is redolent of the psychotherapeutic Fascism we queers have done so much to combat.

In recent years I've had the occasion to reread the novels of Jean Genet. They are genuinely perverse, often infantile, always shocking. They glorify passion and crime and exalt treachery. In my analysis of Genet's defiant Satanism I never let myself lose sight of the fact that he, like me, like every homosexual before gay liberation, could choose only among the same three metaphors for homosexuality—as sickness, crime or sin. Almost all other homosexual writers chose sickness as their model since it called for compassion from the heterosexual reader.

Genet chose the other two, sin and crime, which turned out to define the fiercer, prouder position. Genet wants to intimidate and alternately to seduce his heterosexual reader, not beg him for forgiveness. Instead of tea and sympathy, Genet offers vitriol and impudence.

A political analysis of Genet's fiction must recognize that regardless of his explicit message or his stated provocations, he invented the drag queen for literature with Divine in *Our Lady of the Flowers*, a novel that also gives the most detailed picture we have of the slang and customs of the gay community in Montmartre just before the war. In a similar fashion *The Miracle of the Rose*, although anything but a work of realism, gives the most detailed picture we have of sex and love at Mettray, the reform school Foucault also discusses in *Discipline and Punish*, just as *The Thief's Journal* is the most complete record that exists of the Barrio China in Barcelona, the stronghold of marginal Spain during the years of anarchy and civil war. The point is that we may feel uncomfortable when Genet relentlessly endorses male-female role-playing or equates homosexuality with treachery, but if we, first, acknowledge that his sexuality was formed by prison, and second, look beyond his attitudinizing to the actual content of his books, he is as useful a writer today as he was fifty years ago.

In interpreting Genet I'd learned a lesson from the struggles over Larry Kramer's *Faggots* in the 1970s. American gay commentators had mostly denounced the book for daring to criticize gay promiscuity, then considered a cornerstone of gay freedom. However, an important socialist review in Britain, *Gay Left*, took a very different stand and praised *Faggots* because it was set in the heart of the gay community and showed how gay people interact, not just as lovers but also as friends. This interaction was to be contrasted with the supposedly affirmative books and films of the period that invariably placed a loving lesbian or gay couple in an idyllic bucolic setting far from a gay social or cultural context, thereby covertly suggesting once again that only the alibi of love redeems a queer and that love can flourish only outside the supposedly neurotic and hostile ghetto.

Today many of the attacks staged by the Left on books are launched in the name of the politics of identity, the principle that each minority can and should speak only for itself and that outsiders should be banned from doing so. Much can be said in favor of this position and each of us can attest that we've learned more about African Americans from Toni Morrison than William Faulkner, that we feel Andrew Holleran understands gays better than Norman Mailer does, and that Maxine Hong Kingston knows more about China than does Pearl Buck. These preferences, however, are esthetic and need no defense. Readers are naturally attracted to versions of an experience that are more detailed, more convincing, veristic, shaded. Yet we resist having this preference codified into a policy. Can only Salman Rushdie write about India? Most Indians agree that *Kim* is the best book about nineteenth-century India, despite Kipling's imperialist politics. I once asked one of my writing students, an African American lesbian, what she thought about the politics of identity. With a little smile and a verbal shrug she said that after she heard Ishmael Reed say that black women didn't have the right to write about black men, she had decided to throw in the towel.

Many of the current battles over literature are being fought in the universities and are an effort to insert gay books or feminist books or African American books or the books representing other minorities into the canon.

When I published three years ago an article in the *New York Times Magazine* about the current state of gay fiction, I received dozens of letters from teachers asking me for a reading list, including the list I was using in a lesbian and gay literature course I was teaching at Brown that I'd mentioned. Some people seemed uncertain about which lesbian and gay books should be considered classics. Others had made their pick and wanted to introduce their favorite titles into the canon, the reading list of introductory literature courses.

I myself am in favor of desacralizing literature, of dismantling the idea of a few essential books, of retiring the whole concept of a canon. A canon is for people who don't like to read, people who want to know the bare minimum of titles they must consume in order to be considered polished, well rounded, civilized. Any real reader seeks the names of more and more books, not fewer and fewer.

The notion of a canon implies that we belong to something called Western Civilization that is built on a small sacred library and that that library is eternal and universal and important in the way no individual reader can ever be. I would say that every part of such an assumption is misguided. The United States is no more Western than Eastern, no more English than Spanish, no more Christian than Jewish or Buddhist. We must accept the full implications of pluri-culturalism. We must no longer attempt to introduce a few gay titles or a Chinese-American title into a canon that begins with Aristotle and Plato or the Bible. Even the hierarchy inherent in the concept of a canon must be jettisoned. In Latin a canon is a ruler, a rule or a model and the relevant primary meaning of the word is "an authoritative list of books accepted as Holy Scripture." No matter that the canon, even among the most conservative readers, shifts from one generation to the next. Look at the Harvard Five-Foot Shelf of Classics, once considered definitive. Few people today read Charles Dana's *Two Years Before the Mast* or Whittier's poetry, but for my grandparents such books were unquestionably canonical, as was *The Pilgrim's Progress* or William Dean Howells's *The Rise of Silas Lapham*.

Literature courses should teach students how to read, not what to read. Students can acquire from teachers the rigorous pleasure of close reading, of comparison and analysis, of broadened sympathies and finer moral discrimination. Students can be taught to be skeptical, to label rhetorical strategies, to uncover political subtexts, to spot allusions, to recognize the anxiety of influence and to detect the function of such fictional structures as mystery, suspense and characterization. They can't be taught to like or even finish the *Nicomachean Ethics*. Our reading lists should be long, heterodox, seductive and they should include many contemporary works; as John Ashbery once said, "We should begin at the beginning, that is, the present." The mind of a particular student, far from being just one more vessel into which the divine liquor of canonical wisdom is poured, is, at the moment of reading, the *unique* theater on which Shakespeare's plays are staged or the *only* altar where Bacon's Idols are overturned. A book exists only when a living mind re-creates it and that re-creation comes into being only through the full imaginative participation of a particular sensibility.

I've tried to show, in taking the example of my own work, the political assumptions I had to make in order to write some of my books. From there I've grazed past such explosive current questions such as political correctness, artistic freedom and canon formation. I've suggested that whereas criticism can be correct, fiction itself is immune from such a judgment. Whereas criticism can discuss the political dimensions of fiction, in a novel whose dimensions are always richer and more subtle than at first one might suspect, it is less a question of explicit authorial message and more a matter of the milieu represented, the ideal reader addressed, the utopia adumbrated.

That our feelings run high when we discuss queer fiction only attests to the central role it plays in the formation of our new culture. It sometimes seems more people discuss fiction than read it, but this intense scrutiny, even anxiety, reveals that for us, perhaps more than for any other group, fiction is a way of preserving the past, recording the present, creating the future. Until recently there were few openly queer political leaders, social philosophers, literary critics, outspoken celebrities willing to take stands on important questions. When such stands do get taken, all too often they sound narrowly polemical and divisive. Philosophy is too abstract, history too circumstantial, politics too peremptory to show in precise, glowing detail the way an individual lives through a particular moment. To use the philosopher Richard Rorty's terms, only fiction does equal justice to private irony and public liberalism. Or to come back to our own vocabulary, only our fiction fully demonstrates how the personal is political.

1994

JOAN NESTLE
EDMUND WHITE
BARBARA SMITH
MONIQUE WITTIG
ESTHER NEWTON
SAMUEL R. DELANY
EVE KOSOFSKY SEDGWICK
JOHN D'EMILIO
CHERRÍE MORAGA
JUDITH BUTLER

BARBARA SMITH

Barbara Smith is an author and independent scholar who has played a groundbreaking role in opening up a national cultural and political dialogue about the intersections of race, class, sexuality, and gender. In her work as a critic, teacher, activist, lecturer, and publisher—she founded Kitchen Table: Women of Color Press—Smith was among the first to define an African American women's literary tradition and to build Black women's studies and Black feminism in the United States.

Her articles, essays, literary criticism, and short stories have appeared in a variety of publications including the *New York Times Book Review, Ms.,* the *Black Scholar, Gay Community News,* the *Guardian,* the *Village Voice,* and the *Nation.* She has edited three major collections about Black women: *Conditions Five, The Black Women's Issue* (with Lorraine Bethel); *All the Women Are White, All the Blacks Are Men, But Some of Us Are Brave: Black Women's Studies* (with Gloria T. Hull and Patricia Bell Scott); and *Home Girls: A Black Feminist Anthology.* She is also the co-author with Elly Bulkin and Minnie Bruce Pratt of *Yours in Struggle: Three Feminist Perspectives on Anti-Semitism and Racism.* Smith is a general editor of *The Reader's Companion to U. S. Women's History* with Wilma Mankiller, Gwendolyn Mink, Marysa Navarro, and Gloria Steinem. A collection of her essays, *The Truth That Never Hurts: Writings on Race, Gender, and Freedom* was published by Rutgers University Press in 1998. She resides in Albany, New York.

AFRICAN AMERICAN LESBIAN
AND GAY HISTORY

An Exploration

In 1979 Judith Schwarz of the Lesbian Herstory Archives sent out a question-naire on issues in lesbian history to women working in this just-developing field. Among the twenty-four women who responded were Blanche Wiesen Cook, Lisa Duggan, Estelle Freedman, Joan Nestle, Adrienne Rich, Carol Smith-Rosenberg, and myself. Our responses were published in the women's studies journal *Frontiers*, in an issue devoted entirely to lesbian history.

In response to the question "How can our work be inclusive of the total les-bian experience in history, particularly given the barriers that race, class, age, and homophobia raise in many societies?" I answered as follows:

> I wanted to say something about the ways that racial and economic oppression will affect trying to do research on Black lesbian history. . . . I feel there is a gold mine of facts to find out, but the problem is that there are so few Black lesbians to do this. . . . The women who have the training and the credentials to do this kind of research don't even have feminist politics, let alone lesbian politics. . . . Many women who have the politics don't have the academic credentials, training, or material resources that would permit them to do the kind of research needed. Right now I can only think of one other Black woman besides myself who has all the resources at her disposal, and who is actively reporting on Black lesbian material she is discovering in her work: Gloria T. Hull. It's depressing, but I'm living for the day when it will change.[1]

Fifteen years later, as I research a book on the history of African American lesbians and gays, my earlier comments make my involvement in this project seem inevitable. My writing, teaching, activism, and work as a publisher have always embodied the commitment to challenge invisibility, to make a place for those of us who are unseen and unheard. Despite the building of a Black lesbian and gay political movement since the 1970s and the simultaneous flowering of Black lesbian and gay art, Black lesbians and gays are still largely missing from the historical record.

The history of African American lesbians and gays currently exists in frag-ments, in scattered documents, in fiction, poetry, and blues lyrics, in hearsay, and in innuendo. Ideally, what I would like to create is a chronological narrative that traces evidence of same-gender sexual and emotional connections between people of African descent in this country for as many centuries back as possible. Realistically, because of how relatively little work has been done in this field, the finished work will undoubtedly be thematically focused rather than a comprehensive chronicle of the last four hundred years of homosexual, homoemotional, and homosocial experiences in African American life. My more achievable goal is to arrive at an accurate and useful analytical and theoretical framework for understanding the meaning of Black lesbian and gay life in the United States.

Such a framework has not been developed and applied to Black lesbian and gay experience by previous researchers, the majority of whom have been European Americans, whose primary focus has not been African American subject matter. The complex scope of Black lesbian and gay history has yet to be defined by Black lesbian and gay scholars, and it has also not been written by persons who are expert in African American studies. Until now Black lesbian and gay history has largely been written in juxtaposition to the history of white lesbians and gays and has been presented in works in which the history of white gays or lesbians constitutes the dominant narrative. The fascinating examples of Black lesbian and gay life that other historians have discovered are quite useful and suggestive, but the interpretative context in which this information exists as a part of a white dominant meta-narrative leaves many questions unanswered. The most alarming omissions result from insufficient or nonexistent attention to the pervasive impact of racism and white supremacy upon the lives of all African Americans regardless of sexual orientation, and upon the attitudes and actions of whites as well.

Most of what has been written about Black lesbians and gays has attempted to understand them in relationship to other gays who are of course white. Even when a serious attempt is made to understand Black gay experience within the Black experience as a whole, analytical errors still surface. My project is to understand Black lesbian and gay life in the context of both Black history and gay history. The major questions I want to answer which have not been previously addressed are 1. How did Black lesbians and gays view their own existences within Black communities during various historical eras? And 2. How did other members of Black communities view them? In short, what has the existence of African American homosexuality meant to Black people of various sexual orientations over time?

Before looking at some examples of how Black lesbian and gay experience has been approached and avoided, I would like to explain my decision to research the history of both men and women. Because I see this as a definitional project, it seemed impossible to understand fully the history of one gender without understanding the history of the other. The kinds of questions I want to explore cannot be accurately addressed by looking at Black lesbian or Black gay experience in isolation. In the future I hope that other researchers will focus with much more clarity on the specific histories of Black lesbians, gays, bisexuals, or transgendered people because of my attempt to create a more general framework. For example, we might see separate studies concerning Black lesbian participation in Black women's clubs and sororities; Black gay men's impact upon gospel and other sacred music; Black women who passed as men; or drag performance in African and African American culture.

My own experience as a Black lesbian during the past two decades indicates that Black lesbians and gay men are linked by our shared racial identity and political status in ways that white lesbians and gays are not. These links between us are sociological, cultural, historical, and emotional and I think it is crucial to explore this new terrain together.

The amount of published historical research which focuses specifically upon African American lesbians and gays is minimal, particularly when compared to the growing body of lesbian and gay research as a whole. In the Center for Lesbian and Gay Studies of the City University of New York's first *Directory of Lesbian and Gay Studies*, for 1994–1995, which lists six hundred scholars, five individuals list an interest in Black lesbian and gay historical topics and seven more mention interest in researching African American subject matter in other disciplines.[2] It has always been obvious to me that the difficult, often hostile working conditions that Black academics face as a result of racism in white institutions would make their involvement in explicitly lesbian and gay research an even higher risk activity than it is for European American scholars. There are several courageous younger Black academics, however, some still in graduate school, who are beginning to work in this area.

I value the efforts of the handful of white historians who have made the attempt to include material concerning people of color in their work. Jonathan Ned Katz's groundbreaking documentary collections, *Gay American History*, first published in 1976, and the *Gay/Lesbian Almanac*, published in 1983, are models to this day of racial, ethnic, gender, and class inclusivity. Elizabeth Kennedy's and Madeline Davis's *Boots of Leather, Slippers of Gold*, which is based upon oral histories, also demonstrates a conscious commitment to racial and class diversity. The New York Public Library's 1994 exhibition "Becoming Visible: The Legacy of Stonewall," curated by Mimi Bowling, Molly McGarry, and Fred Wasserman, displayed a level of racial and gender diversity that is rare in cultural productions organized by European American gays and lesbians.

Other scholars have uncovered valuable evidence of Black lesbian and gay existence before Stonewall, especially during the 1920s in Harlem. The analyses of this information, however, sometimes overlook important meanings, advance inaccurate interpretations, or fail to place Black lesbian and gay experience into the context of Black American life. The most distorting error is either to ignore or give inadequate weight to the realities of racism, segregation, and white supremacy as they shape African American lesbian and gay people's existences.

Jazz Age Harlem, for example, is now recognized as the site of a vibrant Black gay cultural and social life which rivaled that of Greenwich Village. Yet there is insufficient discussion of exactly how racial segregation shaped the growth of this so-called Black lesbian and gay community. Since a large proportion of New

York's Black population lived in Harlem during the 1920s, as a result of citywide housing discrimination, the gay community that arose there was obviously shaped by quite different forces than more intentional white enclaves in other parts of Manhattan. This geographic apartheid raises questions about whether the Harlem Black community's seemingly greater tolerance for visible homosexuals was evidence of more accepting attitudes about sexuality and difference or was merely a structural accommodation to the reality of segregation which forced all types of Black people to live together in one location. Perhaps it was a subtle combination of both.

We also know very little about Black lesbian and gay existence in other cities during this period. Was the manifestation of Black lesbian and gay life in Harlem and the way in which it was viewed by heterosexual African Americans an exceptional case or might parallels be drawn to what was going on in other urban centers?

Another set of assertions that needs to be investigated concerns Harlem's class composition. The issue of class identity in the Black community is exceedingly complex, often confusing, and cannot be evaluated by using measures identical to those used for whites. Racial oppression has a profoundly negative impact upon African Americans' economic opportunities, their class and social status. To this day the average income levels of African Americans remain at or near the bottom of the U.S. scale and a tiny percentage of Blacks are in fact wealthy or upper class. When various attitudes about homosexuality are attributed to members of Harlem's upper or middle classes, there needs to be much more specific explanation of who comprised these strata and also what their numbers were relative to the population of Harlem as a whole.

An avenue of inquiry that I have wanted to pursue for some time is a revisionist history of the Harlem Renaissance itself. As I began to discover that more and more of the Harlem Renaissance's leading writers were gay, bisexual or lesbian, I knew that the meaning of this pivotal epoch in Black culture needed to be seriously reevaluated. What does it mean that the major outpouring of Black literature, art, and cultural consciousness in this century prior to the Black Arts Movement of the sixties and seventies was significantly shaped by Blacks who were not heterosexuals? How would those who celebrate this period for its major intellectual and artistic achievements view it if they fully realized how much it was a queer production? The crucial impact of lesbian, bisexual, and gay artists and intellectuals upon the formation of the Renaissance has meaning and needs to be systematically explored.

Harlem has become a symbolic catchall for the discussion of pre-Stonewall Black lesbian and gay existence. Other regions of the country need to be studied and the Harlem experience itself needs to be revisited with a much stronger consciousness of the myriad economic, political, and social factors that shaped African American life during that era.

An example of a problem of interpretation occurs in George Chauncey's *Gay New York: Gender, Urban Culture, and the Making of the Gay Male World.* This work makes a major contribution to increasing understanding of gay life in the early part of this century and Chauncey's discussion of Harlem during the 1920s and 1930s provides significant information and insights. In one instance, however, in an effort to equalize Black and white experience, the specificity of Black experience is not taken sufficiently into account. The author describes in detail the history of Harlem's Hamilton Lodge Balls, the largest drag events to occur in New York during this era. He notes that this annual event was unique because it attracted an interracial crowd of both participants and observers at a time when racial segregation in social settings was virtually universal. Chauncey writes:

> The balls became a site for the projection and inversion of racial as well as gender identities. Significantly, though, white drag queens were not prepared to reverse their racial identity. Many accounts refer to African-American queens appearing as white celebrities, but none refer to whites appearing as well-known black women. As one black observer noted, "The vogue was to develop a 'personality' like some outstanding woman," but the only women he listed, Jean Harlow, Gloria Swanson, Mae West, and Greta Garbo, were white.[3]

Chauncey is correct to imply that white drag queens' racism prevented them from adopting Black female personas, but my initial response to this passage was that there was in fact no comparable group of Black women to be imitated. Despite the popularity of some Black women entertainers during this period, there were no Black women who functioned as internationally recognized glamour icons. There were no Black women movie stars; no Black women worked as fashion models in white contexts. White Americans simply did not see Black women as beautiful; indeed, the racist stereotypes of our physical appearances define us as quite the opposite. The white world certainly did not confer fame upon Black women for either their physical attributes or outstanding accomplishments. Josephine Baker had to leave the United States for Paris in order to achieve stardom during this very period. Chauncey also does not explore the racial implications of Black men wanting not merely to be female for a night, but white as well.

When I discussed this passage with my colleague Mattie Richardson at Kitchen Table: Women of Color Press, she pointed out that if white males had chosen to portray Black women, they very likely would have donned blackface to complete the effect. Such a racial masquerade undoubtedly would have upset Blacks in an atmosphere that Chauncey describes as already racially charged.

An example of an analytical error that affects the entire thesis of a work occurs in Tracy Morgan's article "Pages of Whiteness: Race, Physique Magazines, and the Emergence of Gay Public Culture, 1955–1960." Although Morgan acknowledges the negative racial climate in the United States during this period, she describes the exclusion of Black men from white physique publications as a conscious strategy that white gay men pursued in order to appear more acceptable and to help neutralize their queerness. She writes:

In thinking about race and gay community formation, it might be important to ask how patterns of white, gay racism may have been "useful," in terms of the "wages of whiteness" thesis, in assisting white gay people to attain greater social and cultural privilege as, at least, "not black" outcasts in American culture. . . .

Summoning forth white-skin privilege as a salve and smoke screen in a quest for respectability, physique magazines were part of a larger phenomenon within mid-twentieth-century gay community formation that often sought individual, privatized solutions to group problems. . . .

Gay maleness became synonymous with whiteness. Black, gay men became invisible—the representation of 1950s homosexuality demanded their repression.[4]

Although excluding Black men might have had the result of minimally enhancing white gay men's social position, their original motivation for such exclusion was no doubt based upon unquestioning conformity to the racial status quo. Morgan does not take into account that racism, white supremacy, and segregation were universally institutionalized, accepted, and practiced by whites of all classes, genders, sexual orientations, and geographic regions. The average white person did not have to decide to exclude Black people from every aspect of their social, economic, and personal lives. U.S. society was organized to ensure that this would always be the case. The "decision" to enforce white supremacy and to reap its benefits had been made long before white gay men in urban settings began publishing physique magazines in the mid-twentieth century. By the time these men reached maturity, unless their families were highly exceptional, complete racial segregation would have been a norm, a cherished and familiar way of life. Just as their fathers did hire Blacks, their schools and churches did not admit them, and their neighborhoods refused to house them, their magazines did not publish physique photographs of Black men.

Morgan confuses the causes for racism with the resulting benefits. She writes, "Most lesbian and gay publications, to this very day, continue to draw on white-skin privilege as one of their main vestiges of respectability" (124). If racial exclusion is primarily a strategy used by a disenfranchised group, why are straight magazines equally white in their content? Her thesis inaccurately assumes that white gays have a significantly different value system about race than other whites, and that if it were not for their attempt to enhance their credibility with white heterosexuals, they would be much more racially inclusive.

I do not want to dissuade scholars from investigating and including material about people of color. Indeed, current queer studies needs to be much more racially and ethnically inclusive, but at the same time it also needs to demonstrate a thorough consciousness of the racial and class contexts in which lesbians and gays of color actually function.

African American historical research would seem to offer more avenues into Black lesbian and gay experience. The field of Black history, which has roots in the Negro History movement of the early twentieth century, offers extensive and complex documentation of African American life. The overwhelming problem, however, is that there is virtually no acknowledgment within the confines of African American history that Black lesbians and gays ever existed.

The reasons for this silence are numerous. Homophobia and heterosexism are of course the most obvious. But there is also the reality that Black history has often served extrahistorical purposes that would militate against bringing up "deviant" sexualities. In its formative years, especially, but even today, Black history's underlying agenda frequently has been to demonstrate that African Americans are full human beings who deserve to be treated like Americans, like citizens, like men. I use "men" advisedly because until approximately twenty years ago there was little specific focus upon the history of Black women. Those who subscribe to certain strains of Afrocentric thought can be even more overtly hostile to Black lesbian and gay historical projects. The conservative agendas of some Afrocentric or Black nationalist scholarship encourage condemnation of what they define as European-inspired perversion, a conspiracy to destroy the Black family and the race. The themes of uplift, of social validation, and of prioritizing subject matter that is a "credit to the race" have burdened and sometimes biased Black historical projects. Chauncey points out that in the early part of this century "many middle-class and churchgoing African Americans grouped . . . [bulldaggers and faggots] with prostitutes, salacious entertainers, and 'uncultured' rural migrants as part of an undesirable and all-too-visible Black 'lowlife' that brought disrepute to the neighborhood and the race."[5] "Lowlife" is exactly the image I had of the lesbian lifestyle when I was growing up in the pre-Stonewall 1950s and 1960s. I am not even sure where I got this from since sexuality in general and lesbianism in particular were seldom explicitly discussed, yet this subliminal message greatly contributed to my fear of coming out.

It is difficult to imagine traditional African American historians going out of their way to explore lesbian and gay life, or to reveal evidence of it when they happen across it while researching other topics. Arnold Rampersad's biography of Langston Hughes illustrates the opposite tendency of going out of one's way to ignore or suppress such information. It is hard to imagine Black historians combing through court and police records (as some white lesbian and gay scholars have done) to find evidence of Black homosexuality. I have weighed the implications of utilizing these kinds of sources myself, especially in today's political climate in which the right wing seeks to criminalize all people of color as part of their racist agenda.

An example of how an otherwise highly informative work can obscure Black lesbian history occurs in *Black Women in America: An Historical Encyclopedia*, whose principal editor is Darlene Clark Hine. This groundbreaking two-volume, 1,500-page reference work presents an exhaustively researched picture of Black American women. It contains interpretative articles that cover historical issues and organizations as well as hundreds of biographical entries describing individual Black women. The index alone is 150 pages long; however, there are only six entries listed under "Lesbianism." Certainly the encyclopedia includes many more women who were in fact lesbian or bisexual, but because discussion of a Black woman's sexuality is not usually considered relevant, unless her orientation is heterosexual, contributors either omitted or suppressed this material. I found myself reading between the lines and trying to evaluate the work's beautiful photographic images in an effort to guess which of the many women documented might be ones I should investigate further for my study. These omissions will necessitate that others do a great deal of this primary research all over again.

Another type of omission in *Black Women in America* occurs in entries which describe women who are known to be lesbian or bisexual, especially musicians and entertainers such as Alberta Hunter and Jackie "Moms" Mabley, but who are not identified as such. The comments in the encyclopedia on the heiress A'Lelia Walker, whose legendary salons were attended by queer luminaries of the Harlem Renaissance as well as by other lesbians and gays, illustrate how reticence about sexuality can result in an incomplete portrait of an historical figure. The author, Tiya Miles, writes:

> A'Lelia Walker was not accepted by everyone in the Harlem community, however. Some begrudged the fact that she was the daughter of a washerwoman. Some also objected to her fast-paced social life and unusual style of dress, which included turbans and jewelry. Some of her contemporaries called her the "De-kink Heiress." James Weldon Johnson's wife, Grace Nail Johnson, who was known as the social dictator of Harlem, refused to attend Walker's parties.[6]

A photograph of A'Lelia shows her not only in a turban, but in shiny, high, black leather boots with harem pants tucked inside of them, leaning back casually with one of her legs bent and her foot propped up on the bench on which she is sitting. This is neither ladylike dress nor a ladylike pose. Walker was obviously willing to challenge the gender expectations of her time.

Mabel Hampton's description of some of A'Lelia's "less formal" parties quoted in Lillian Faderman's *Odd Girls and Twilight Lovers* offers other reasons for Walker's negative reputation:

> [They were] funny parties—there were men and women, straight and gay. They were kinds of orgies. Some people had clothes on, some didn't. People would hug and kiss on pillows and do anything they wanted to do. You could watch if you wanted to. Some came to watch, some came to play. You had to be cute and well-dressed to get in.[7]

Probably Grace Nail Johnson and other members of the Black bourgeoisie knew about such goings-on and ostracized Walker as a result, as well as for the reasons that Miles cites.

The most painful paradoxes among the encyclopedia's entries are those that describe my contemporaries, women who I personally know to be lesbians, but who are unwilling to publicly acknowledge the fact. This is the group that will pose one of the most significant challenges for my research. The myriad closeted contemporary figures who are artists, activists, athletes, and entertainers, both male and female, constitute what I already think of as the chapter I cannot write. But I plan to write it anyway. I have no intention of outing anyone, but want to analyze instead what it means on a variety of levels that there are so many prominent African Americans whose stories are well known in lesbian and gay circles, but whom I cannot include because they are unwilling to relinquish their heterosexual privilege and name themselves.

The fear of being rejected by and losing credibility in the Black community is undoubtedly one of the most significant disincentives to coming out, and this is particularly true of our closeted cultural and political leaders. Since I have personally experienced some of the difficult consequences of being honest about my sexual orientation, I will not say fears are groundless. However, the increase in the numbers of Black people who can now be counted as allies in movements for sexual and gender freedom is the direct result of our actively challenging oppression instead of accommodating to it. It is my hope that this historical project will play a part in enlarging the space in which people of all sexualities can live and struggle.

NOTES

1. Judith Schwarz, "Questionnaire on Issues in Lesbian History," *Frontiers: A Journal of Women Studies* 4, no. 3 (Fall 1979): 5, 6.

2. Center for Lesbian and Gay Studies, *The CLAGS Directory of Lesbian and Gay Studies* (New York: Center for Lesbian and Gay Studies, The City University of New York, 1994), *passim*.

3. George Chauncey, *Gay New York: Gender, Urban Culture, and the Making of the Gay Male World, 1890–1940* (New York: Basic Books, 1994), 263.

4. Tracy Morgan, "Pages of Whiteness: Race, Physique Magazines, and the Emergence of Gay Public Culture, 1955–1960," *Found Object*, no. 4 (Fall 1994): 112, 123, 124. All subsequent references to this work will be designated in the text.

5. Chauncey, *Gay New York*, 253.

6. Tiya Miles, "A'Lelia Walker (1885–1931)," in *Black Women in America: An Historical Encyclopedia*, ed. Darlene Clark Hine et al. (Brooklyn, N.Y.: Carlson Publishing, 1993), 1205.

7. Lillian Faderman, *Odd Girls and Twilight Lovers: A History of Lesbian Life in Twentieth-Century America* (New York: Penguin, 1991), 76.

1995

MONIQUE WITTIG

The French novelist, poet, and social theorist **Monique Wittig** was a founding member in the feminist movement that emerged in late-1960s France. Her literary and theoretical works are today recognized for their essential contributions to feminist theory and lesbian and gay theory worldwide, as well as to the movement for lesbian and gay rights.

Wittig won major critical acclaim and the coveted Prix Médicis with her first novel, *The Opoponax* (1964). A sensitivity to the nuances of language, and in particular its encoding of gender, marked all of her fiction: *Les Guérillères* (1969), *The Lesbian Body* (1973), *Lesbian Peoples: Materials for a Dictionary* (co-authored with Sande Zeig, 1975), and *Virgile, non* (1984; translated as *Across the Acheron*, 1987). These works offered a powerful illustration of her philosophy of lesbian materialism, a theoretical position she set forth in a series of essays collected in *The Straight Mind* (1992), a term she coined.

Wittig's work has been translated into a dozen languages, including German, Dutch, Finnish, Japanese, and Spanish. Her collaboration with Zeig resulted most recently in a feature film based on her short story, "The Girl" (2001), directed by Zeig. Monique Wittig was a professor at the University of Arizona, Tucson.

READING AND COMMENTS
Virgile, non/Across the Acheron[1]

I'm very honored to be here tonight, invited by the Center for Lesbian and Gay Studies to present the David Kessler Lecture. I would like to thank the people who have talked on my behalf: Namascar Shaktini, Erika Ostrovsky, and Judith Butler, via the voice of Ann Pellegrini. Again, thank you very much. You really did a wonderful job.

I have decided tonight to read to you, to read from my work. But first I want to say something. I could not have written what I wrote in the United States in this last year while I was living in France. I'm alluding particularly to the essays published in *The Straight Mind*. There I reached a point difficult for me to go beyond, when I considered that heterosexuality is not only an institution but a whole political regime. I suggest you read *Politics* by Aristotle to be convinced of my point.

I have several works still unpublished in the United States which I would like you to know. This is why tonight I'm going to read with Barbara Page of Vassar College from the book which is called in French *Virgile, non*. Published in France, in England, and Holland, it's not published here. So I would like to share it with you, if possible. I will read the text in French, and Barbara will read the English.

Virgile, non is written around a real and imaginary San Francisco, with its hell, its limbo, and its utopian paradise. As in the *Divine Comedy* by Dante, it's a paradigm of a three-fold reality in three-dimensional description, but unlike in Dante, hell is domination, limbo is provisory exit, and paradise, utopia.

I would like to say, between us, I never used the words "women" or "men" in any of my books. But particularly in this one, because I knew what happened in English when "they" was translated into "the women," completely ruining my effort with the pronouns, this time I said, I'm not going to use the pronoun ["they"], or any pronoun. Instead I used my own name for a character. I used the lost souls. And I thought with the lost souls, we are not going to talk about men or women, biological realities, we are going to talk about creatures, abstraction, fiction. And that's why I chose this way of doing it. Now, I know this is not quite what happened in the translation. But the translator is not faulty. I must say that mostly I love my translator, David Le Vay, because he has a sense of the words, of the vocabulary. He knows exactly where I want to put the accent, the rhythm, and everything like that. But, because we cannot work together, he cannot exactly know what I have in my mind. That's all.

For me the text of *Virgile, non,* or as it's called in English, *Across the Acheron,* functions both as a film and a kind of *Beggar's Opera* à la John Gay or à la Brecht, composed of a series of songs. I mentioned Dante, whose *Divine Comedy* was my matrix. *Virgile, non* does not mean "no to Virgil," the poet I love, but it says "no" to Virgil as a guide, since in this book the guide is Manastabal. Manastabal is far, far from being as sweet as the sweet Virgil.

The device which consists of using one's own name for the name of a character I borrowed from Genet. I mean, I know other writers have done it, but this time I thought about Genet—as a reference to him. And this book leans upon parody to express the distance and amazement a homosexual perspective has on the straight world. It is no wonder, then, that I chose San Francisco for the site of the novel.

In addition, it's a Latin city for me, where I could connect with my own language. French is a heavy language when compared to English, but somehow one needs its weight for certain writings. And I wanted to link my actual writing with *The Opoponax,* my first book, and use once again "one"—that is "on" [Fr.]—to escape the gender trap.

So we are going to read a few passages of *Virgile, non.* . . . I chose to read the first pages in succession. Like that, you will have an idea of the structure of the book.

Chapter 1: Ouverture/Overture

Les aires sont dépourvues de toute ornementation. Le sable passe en lames fines et dures sur les surfaces battues. Celle qui se dit mon guide, Manastabal, marche en avant de moi. Encore heureux qu'on n'ait pas à porter des tuniques pour entreprendre ce voyage tout ensemble classique et profane car elles seraient en un instant arrachées par le vent. Au lieu de ça, la tenue et la démarche de Manastabal, mon guide, ont quelque chose de familier. Sa chemise gonflée lui claque autour du torse et des bras. Le vent plaque ses cheveux contre son crâne dont la forme est visible. Elle a les mains dans les poches de son jean et marche comme dans un film muet. J'ai beau voir quand elle se tourne vers moi qu'elle émet un sifflement avec ses lèvres, je ne peux pas l'entendre. La bandoulière du fusil presse sur la base de mon cou et dans le creux de mes omoplates. Il ne m'est pas permis de savoir par le cours de la marche si on suit une direction définie. L'espace est si plat qu'il donne à voir la circularité de la planète à l'horizon. On semble donc marcher exactement au milieu de la terre. On suit en effet le chemin qu'il faut prendre pour aller en enfer puisque c'est là que, selon elle, Manastabal, mon guide, me conduit. Comme le vent persiste et s'accélère, on marche au ralenti en s'appuyant de tous les muscles contre le volume de l'air, trop heureux de n'avoir pas les members arrachés. J'ouvre la bouche pour demander si c'est encore loin là où on va, la rafale s'y engloutit, empêchant tout son de passer. Enfin je parviens en forçant l'allure à rattraper Manastabal, mon guide et à poser un bras sur ses épaules. On s'arrête alors et se regarde face à face. On a des traits distordus par la pression de l'air et ce n'est pas un sourire que forment les lèvres écartées des gencives. Qu'attend-elle? Va-t-elle me prendre sur ses épaules pour me faire faire le passage? Mais le passage de quoi? Il n'y a pas de fleuve ici. Il n'y a pas de mer.

○

The space is devoid of ornamentation. The sand passes in fine, hard waves over the beaten surfaces. Manastabal, she who calls herself my guide, walks ahead of me. Fortunately, we don't have to wear tunics for this journey, which is both sacred and profane, for they would be instantly torn off by the wind. Instead, the dress and gait of Manastabal, my guide, are somehow familiar. Her billowing shirt flaps round her chest and arms. The wind flattens her hair against her skull, revealing its shape. She has her hands in the pockets of her jeans and walks as in a silent film. When she turns towards me I can see from her lips that she is making a whistling sound, but I can't hear it. The sling of my rifle presses on the base of my neck and in the hollow of my shoulder-blades. The course we are following does not allow me to determine whether we are taking a definite direction. The space is flat, flat enough to reveal the circularity of the planet on the horizon. So we seem to be walking at the exact center of the earth. In fact we are following the route which must be taken to arrive in Hell, since it is there that Manastabal, my guide, says she is taking me. As the wind persists and quickens we walk more slowly, leaning with every muscle against the expanse of air, only too glad not to have our limbs torn off. I open my mouth to ask if we still have a long way to go; the blast rushes into it, preventing any sound. At last, forcing the pace, I manage to catch up with Manastabal, my guide, and place an arm round her shoulders. Then we stop and look at each other, face to face. Our features are distorted by the pressure of the air, and as our lips curl back over our gums they form no smile. What is she waiting for? Is she going to take me on her shoulders to get me to make the crossing? But what crossing? There's no river here. There's no sea.

This first passage, "Ouverture," I imagined as a film. In fact, the precise film I thought of was *Orphée* by Cocteau, where Heurtebise helps Orphée to go back in time, moving in slow motion, fighting against the wind. I was thinking about what Erika [Ostrovsky] said about transformation and about what Racine used to say about the treatment of a fable: when you take a fable already existing, if you want to transform it, you cannot upset the text—the fable or the text or the matrix—immediately. You have to follow it point by point, and that's what I did in that text. Before the transformation can take place, you have to move along with the original fable. And in Dante as well, the wind blows incessantly, like it does in that first passage and other passages of the book.

(Il n'y a rien où on va, Wittig, du moins rien que tu ne connaisses déjà. On va bien dans un autre monde comme tu crois, mais le soleil l'éclaire tout comme celui d'où on vient. Et il te faudrait des trésors d'ingéniosité pour faire passer pour héroïques les soupirs, les cris de douleur, d'angoisse, de terreur et d'incertitude qui s'y poussent. Les âmes damnées que tu vas rencontrer sont vivantes même si elles font des voeux ardents pour ne plus l'être. Elles sont anonymes et je te défie bien de leur trouver des particularités propres à leur fabriquer un manteau de gloire. Pour elles, l'horreur et l'irrémissibilité de la souffrance ne sont pas causées par l'ignominie des actions. Je t'emmène voir ce que partout on peut voir en plein jour.)

A son discours, tous les cercles de l'enfer réunis s'ouvrent et du gouffre ne parviennent qu'une lumière glauque et des gémissements si horribles qu'on n'ose pas en deviner la nature. Mes genoux flanchent aussitôt et je dis:

(S'il en est ainsi, inutile d'aller plus loin.)

Le sable du desert s'aplatit en lames de faux régulières et incessamment balayées. Je lutte contre le vent pour garder l'équilibre comme Manastabal, mon guide, parle en ces mots:

(Si je te comprends bien, Wittig, la peur te donne comme un coup sur la tête et t'emplit de lâcheté. Crois-tu que tu puisses te détourner de ce voyage nécessaire. Sache donc que je suis ici avec toi sur la recommandation de celle qui t'attend au paradis et s'est mise en peine de te voir si mal embarquée pour l'enfer. Voici l'objet qu'elle m'a donné en gage.)

Je reconnais le flacon d'éther que celle qui est ma providence m'a donné autrefois comme un remède en de certaines extrémités. C'est ce même objet qu'elle m'envoie en m'engageant à aller de l'avant afin de la retrouver au bout du chemin. Ses paroles, telles que Manastabal, mon guide, me les transmet, claquent comme des coups de fusil contre le volume de l'air, vrombissant autour de mes oreilles, galvanisant mes muscles. S'il le faut donc j'irai jusqu'au bout de l'enfer pour retrouver de l'autre côté au milieu des anges celle qui m'a donné le goût du paradis par ses bienfaits. Je dis donc à Manastabal, mon guide:

(Guide-moi, je ferai de mon mieux pour te suivre. Qu'il pleuve ou qu'il vente, qu'il neige ou qu'il grêle, qu'il tonne ou qu'il fasse une chaleur à crever, j'irai. Je n'aurai pas besoin que tu me portes sur ton dos, comme il est de tradition pour ce genre de passage. Même au contraire je pourrai te porter un peu si besoin est.)

A ces mots, Manastabal, mon guide, émet un rire qui claque mes nerfs désagréablement. Se pourrait-il qu'on soit déjà en enfer? Mais non, je ne vois autour que poussière et tourbillons de vent qui s'y ruent.

°

(There's nothing where we are going, Wittig, at least nothing you don't know already. We're certainly entering another world, as you imagine, but the sun shines on it just as it shines on the world we are leaving. Sighs, cries of pain, anguish, terror and uncertainty are uttered there, and you'd need vast ingenuity to describe them as heroic. The condemned souls you are about to meet are alive, despite their fervent wish to be dead. They are anonymous, and I challenge you to find any quality about them that clothes them in glory. In their case the horror and irremissibility of suffering are not caused by the ignominy of their deeds. I'm taking you to see what can be seen anywhere in broad daylight.)

At these words all the conjoined circles of Hell open and from the abyss rise only a glaucous light and groans so horrible that I daren't think about their nature. My knees give way at once and I say:

(If it's like this, there's no point in going any farther.)

The desert sand flattens out into scythe-blades, forming and fading into continuous, regular waves. I struggle against the wind to keep my balance as Manastabal, my guide, utters these words:

(If I understand you correctly, Wittig, fear affects you like a blow on the head and fills you with cowardice. Do you think you can draw back from this vital journey? Understand that I am with you here at the command of her who awaits you in Paradise and grieves to see you so poorly prepared for Hell. Here is the object she gave me as a pledge.)

I recognize the flask of ether that she who is my Providence gave me in the past as a remedy in certain extreme situations. She is sending me the same object now as she commits me to go forward and meet her at the end of the road. Her words, as Manastabal, my guide, transmits them to me, crack like rifle-shots against the expanse of air, humming round my ears, galvanizing my muscles. So if I have to, then, I shall go to the farthest end of Hell, and on the other side, among the angels, I shall meet again the woman whose loving deeds have given me the taste of Paradise. So I say to Manastabal, my guide:

(Guide me, I'll do my best to follow you. Come rain or wind, snow or hail, thunder or stifling heat, I shall go. You won't have to carry me on your back, as is traditional with this type of crossing. On the contrary, I could even carry you a little if necessary.)

At these words Manastabal, my guide, utters a laugh that grates unpleasantly on my nerves. Could we be in Hell already? But no, I see only dust and whirling eddies of wind around me.

In this last passage we just read the reference is still to Dante. There is for Dante the same fear that Wittig feels. Of course, it's a parody and the goal is to reach the Wittig character's Beatrix. I am now going to read "The Eagle." In Dante there are also various kinds of monsters and animals.

Chapter 3: L'aigle/The Eagle

J'épaule mon fusil pour m'entraîner. Je ne vois pas de cible possible, sauf à prendre pour telle l'énorme rouleau de sable qui à l'horizon s'approche, poussant devant lui des entassements de branches sèches, roulées elles aussi dans la forme d'énormes balles de laine. Outre que la cible est trop éloignée, elle se déplace également trop vite pour qu'il soit possible de prévoir une ligne de tir. C'est pourquoi je m'exerce au maniement rapide de l'arme, la saisissant d'une main, de l'autre relâchant le magasin à balles, le rechargeant, épaulant, pressant sur la gâchette, tirant au hasard dans la direction du nuage ocre, arrêtant brusquement de tirer de peur que le vent ne rabatte la balle sur ma figure. Un aigle des sables descend en tournant au-dessus de ma tête. Il ne semble pas empêché de voler par les tourbillons contradictoires du vent qui se heurte soi-même. Son vol est régulier et puissant comme il se doit pour un aigle. L'apparition de l'aigle est bienvenue tant il me semble qu'il y a des siècles que je n'ai pas vu âme qui vive. Manastabal, mon guide, ne revient pas. Pour regarder dans la direction d'où elle est partie, je détourne mes yeux de l'aigle qui en profite pour fondre à la hauteur de ma figure et s'apprête à m'attaquer. Comme il est tout près de moi maintenant, il est trop tard pour épauler mon fusil et viser. Je me contente donc de tirer en l'air pour faire fuir l'aigle. Au lieu de ça il devient enragé et se précipite sur moi, ailes déployées, serres tendues, bec ouvert, disant:

(Vas-tu arrêter ce jeu imbécile avec ton fusil et tes balles ou faut-il que je te laboure la figure de telle sorte qu'aucune de tes amantes ne puisse plus te reconnaître?)

Je voudrais lui poser des questions mais à la place je lui tape sur le corps de toutes mes forces avec la crosse de mon fusil. Le choc rend un son creux et métallique. L'aigle tombe à terre dans un bruit de fer-raille, ses ailes sont agitées de soubresauts mécaniques tandis que la voix enrayée d'un automate répète au ralenti les mêmes phrases:

(Que tu le veuilles ou non, Wittig, l'esclavage a la voix enrouée—ici, rire. N'essaie pas de péter plus haut que ton cul, misérable créature. Tu es née poussière et tu redeviendras poussière.)

La voix se bloque sur un couinement comme je donne à l'aigle des coups de pied répétés et que je crie:

(Ferme ta gueule vieux radoteur. Pierre que roule n'amasse pas mousse et le silence est d'or.)

Le robot gît à mes pieds, disloqué, enfoncé dans le sol par sa chute et mes coups, et déjà à moitié recouvert par les soulevées de sable en forme de lames de faux qui n'arrêtent pas de balayer la surface plate du desert.

I raise my rifle for practice. I see no possible target, unless I take as such the enormous roll of sand approaching from the horizon, pushing in front of it piles of dry branches, which are also rolled into the shape of enormous balls of wool. Not only is the target too distant, it moves too quickly for me to plan any line of fire. That is why I practise the rapid handling of the weapon, grasping it with one hand, releasing the magazine with the other, reloading, aiming, pressing the trigger, firing at random in the direction of the ochre cloud, suddenly ceasing to fire lest the wind beats the bullet back into my face. A desert eagle descends, circling above my head. It does not seem to be prevented from flying by the whirling gusts of wind that blow from opposite directions and buffet each other. Its flight is even and powerful, as is proper for an eagle. The appearance of the eagle is all the more welcome, since I feel I have not seen a living creature for centuries. Manastabal, my guide, does not return. To look in the direction where she departed I glance away from the eagle, which seizes the opportunity to sweep down to the level of my face and prepare to attack me. As it is now so close to me, it is too late to level my rifle and take aim. So I content myself with firing into the air to scare the eagle away. Instead it becomes enraged and hurls itself at me, wings outspread, talons outstretched, beak open, saying:

(Cut out this stupid nonsense with your gun and your bullets, or I'll claw your face so deeply that not one of your lovers will recognize you again.)

I should like to ask it some questions, but instead I strike it on the body with my rifle-butt as hard as I can. The blow renders a hollow, metallic sound. The eagle falls to the ground with a clanking noise, its wings agitated by mechanical jerks, while the jammed automaton voice slowly repeats the same phrases:

(Whether you like it or not, Wittig, slavery has a hoarse voice. Here, you can laugh. Don't aim too bloody high, you wretched creature. Dust you were born and to dust you will return.)

The voice sticks in a screech as I kick the eagle over and over again and cry:

(Shut up, you driveling old fool. A rolling stone gathers no moss and silence is golden.)

The robot lies at my feet, broken up, buried in the ground by its fall and my kicks, and already half covered under the scythe-blades of the rising sands that constantly sweep over the flat surface of the desert.

In the passage "The Eagle" we just read, the sandstorm is comparable to those one can see in New Mexico. And I must say that I was very impressed by those sandstorms. Also, "slavery has a hoarse voice" is borrowed from Shakespeare, but I cannot say from what play now, because this borrowing is such an old one. It appears already in my first paper (political papers), so I can't remember, and I don't agree, of course.

Chapter 4: La laverie automatique/The Laundromat

(Est-ce pour m'insulter et te moquer de moi que tu viens dan ce cercle, transfuge, renégate? Tu gonfles tes biceps, tes triceps, tes dorsaux. Tu sautes sur tes cuisses et tu plies tes genous, dans une position de combat. Tu pousses des cris d'orfraie at tu vas disant, voyez je n'en suis pas une car je ne me fais ni baiser, ni ramoner, ni troncher, ni enfiler. Tu vas t'affublant d'un nom qui n'a plus cours depuis deux mille quatre cents ans. Tu me le balances à la gueule comme un miroir à alouettes. Crois-tu donc que je ne vois pas le piège? De deux maux cependant je choisis le moindre. Car mieux vaut se faire baiser, ramoner, troncher, enfiler par un ennemi qui a de quoi, que par toi qui n'en as pas. Va-t'en d'ici et laisse-moi mener ma barque comme je l'entends. Va baiser où tu appartiens et ne quitte surtout pas la rue Valencia. Va-t'en retrouver les gouines répugnantes comme même l'une d'entre elles les désigne, quoique pour moi *puantes* conviendrait mieux. Car c'est bien là tout ce qui tu sais, faire lécher des culs qui ne se montrent pas au grand jour. Vole donc vers tes plaisirs, cours vers le coin de la vingt-quatrième rue pour retrouver tes pareilles. Pour la plupart d'ailleurs vous n'avez ni feu ni lieu. Ne parlons pas de la foi réciproque, elle n'existe pas chez vous. Vous n'en prétendez pas moins vouloir sortir tout notre sexe de sa servitude. Il y a de quoi mourir de rire, si ce n'est que ma bile m'étouffera avant, quand je songe que la seule chose qui vous intéresse, c'est de la corrompre tout entier, notre sexe. Croi-tu que je n'aie pas des oreilles pour entendre? Je sais tout de la peste lesbienne qui doit selon vos dires gagner de proche en proche toute la planète. Il n'y a pas longtemps une prophétesse inspirée a vitupéré contre vous et supplié, avec des larmes sur les joues, incessamment prostrée dans des prières ardentes, rampant sur les genoux, qu'on vous empêche de corrompre les enfants dans les écoles. Avec la voix du juste, cette sainte personne a rappelé la parole sacrée selon laquelle il vaudrait mieux vous mettre à toutes la pierre au cou, infâmes créatures, et vous noyer jusqu'à la dernière, plutôt que de laisser par vous le scandale arriver.)

A ce point de leur discours, je me tiens à quatre pour ne pas les traiter de mégères, et je me souviens à temps que j'ai adopté le genre noble pour donner un peu d'éclat à notre sexe asservi, car il vaut mieux laisser à l'ennemi le soin de le traîner dans la boue, ce qu'il ne se gêne jamais pour faire. D'autant que je viens de goûter une certaine douceur dans leur hargne, leur ressentiment, pour ne pas dire leur haine. En effet ne s'agit-il pas des mêmes créatures qui, tant qu'il n'a pas encore été question du péril mauve, n'ont pas eu d'yeux quand on les a croisées dans la rue. Ce sont celles pour qui j'ai autrefois écrit: "Chiennes rampantes, pas une de vous ne me regarde. Elles me marchent à travers. Elles me prennent à l'arrêt, saisie, réduite à une impuissance que je qualifierai d'ignoble. Un long bras nu me traverse le thorax. C'est du temps que je suis par elles un eunuque." Leur haine actuelle donc si elle n'est rien d'autre témoigne au moins qu'on fait peur. Et si elles ont délibérément et avec la plus grande mauvaise foi caricaturé le gai avertissement qu'on appelle le péril mauve en en parlant comme de la peste lesbienne, c'est aussi, cela, l'expression d'une effroi presque sacré, soit:

(Père, père, ne me rejette pas, moi qui suis à tes genoux, jette un regard sur moi et vois que je suis exactement comme tu m'as faite. Ne permets pas que je tombe aux mains de ces maudites créatures et me perde dans les ténèbres du mal. Ne dit-on pas qu'elles procèdent à des rapts et comme si cela ne suffisait pas qu'elles droguent leurs malheureuses victimes pour pouvoir leur faire plus commodément subir les derniers (dernières) sévices (délices)—ah père, père, pourquoi m'as-tu abandonnée?)

Aussi bien, dès qu'elles ont eu commencé, je me suis mise à marcher de long en large dans la laverie automatique, essayant mon style noble pour attirer leur attention et disant:

(Malheureuses! Ecoutez-moi!)

Mais elles ne m'ont pas écoutée. J'ai lancé mes bras vers le ciel (que j'ai pris à témoin) en criant:

(Sapho m'est témoin que je ne vous veux aucun mal puisque au contraire je suis venue ici comme votre défenseur et redresseur de torts car je soupçonne que, comme les maux, ils pullulent parmi vous.)

Elles restent sourdes à mes exhortations sauf une qui pousse un grand hullulement en écorchant le nom de notre grand prédécesseur dans un glapissement tenu sur le *o*. Elle est la seule du reste dont le nom chéri a touché les oreilles. Je me maudis d'avoir jeté dans cette bataille un des rares noms don't on n'ait pas à rougir. A bout, je leur crie:

(Misérables créatures, écoutez-moi!)

Mais elles, dans leur bouleversement et leur agitation, se tiennent dans un cercle qui tange de droite à gauche, tandis que de leur bouche sort un sifflement. Comme aucun mot ne semble pouvoir atteindre leur compréhension, je me mets à poil entre deux rangées de machines à laver et je m'avance parmi elles, non pas telle Vénus sortie des eaux, ni même telle que ma mère m'a faite, mais enfin avec deux épaules, un torse, un ventre, des jambes et le reste. Je n'ai donc rien de spécial à exhiber si ce n'est la parfaite conformité humaine avec les personnes de mon sexe, une similitude des plus évidentes et banales, et je dis:

(Vous voyez bien que je suis faite du même bois que vous, nous appartenons à la même armée si ce n'est pas le même corps. Il n'y a pas à se méprendre sur mes intentions, elles sont pacifiques. C'est ce qu'ainsi je vous témoigne.)

Mais je n'ai pas eu fait un pas dans ce simple appareil qu'aussitôt elles se mettent à tourner sur elles-mêmes en s'arrachant les cheveux dans la plus pure tradition classique, telles des toupies ou des derviches tourneurs, en poussant des gémissements forcenés, certaines, je peux dire, éructant, tandis que l'une d'elles se met à crier (au viol, au viol) et à se précipiter dans toutes les directions, et, comme elle ne peut pas aller bien loin, arrêtée au'elle est dans son élan par les machines à laver et les séchoirs électriques qui obstruent tout l'espace, après s'être cognée aveuglément contre chacun des appareils l'un après l'autre, poussée par sa seule terreur, atteint la rue par hasard en répétant le même phrase insane (au viol, au viol). Une autre dans son effroi se jette dans un séchoir qui tourne encore et fait là le plus beau charivari. Enfin il y a des chances que ces furies me réserveraient le même sort que les bacchantes à Orphée si un événement extérieur sous la forme d'une cape miraculeusement volée à un séchoir par Manastabal, mon guide, et jetée sur moi pour dérober aux regards ma nudité, cause d'après elle de tout ce chahut, ne les en empêchait. Mais elle ne va pas assez vite que je n'entende leur cris:

(Regardez, elle est couverte de poils des pieds à la tête, son dos même est poilu.)

Je me regarde avec étonnement: d'est vrai, j'ai des poils longs, noir et luisants qui me couvrent tout le corps, remplaçant ce qui n'était jusqu'alors qu'un duvet. Je dis donc:

(Ah, voilà qui va me tenir chaud en hiver!)

Mais déjà je les entends dire dans un nouveau hurlement:

(Regardez, elle a des écailles sur la poitrine, sur les épaules et sur le ventre.)

Je baisse les yeux vers ma personne physique une fois de plus et voilà que les poils sont derechef remplacés par des écailles dures et brillantes que je trouve du plus bel effet et qui ne vont pas manquer de resplendir au soleil. Déjà je redresse la tête, quand une d'entre elles rugit en pointant le milieu de mon corps:

(Regardez, il est long comme un long doigt. Coupez-le, coupez-le.)

Et à ce point-là, je n'ai pas le temps de vérifier la véracité de leurs dires en jetant un coup d'oeil à l'objet incriminé car déjà elles se ruent sur moi. Je n'ai pas le mauvais esprit de leur dire que, pour ce qui est de le couper, elles se trompent de continent (car se moquer de son propre malheur avilit), quoique je ne doute pas une minute que ce soient leurs pareilles qui se livrent à de telles pratiques dans les pays dont ont dit que c'est la coutume et qu'une fille ne peut pas s'en passer. Manastabal, mon guide, m'entraîne dans la rue en disant:

(Eh bien, Wittig, es-tu convaincue maintenant que c'est bien en enfer que je te mène? Vas-tu encore nier à outrance? Et livrer bataille pour me persuader du contraire?)

A moitié défaillante sous l'effet de la peur, soigneusement enveloppée de la cape qui dissimule ce qu'on ne saurait voir, secouée dan ma fierté, tremblante, je crie:

(Dans notre propre ville, qui l'eût cru, qui l'eût dit? Ah je t'en prie, Manastabal, mon guide, emmène-moi boire un coup, je n'en peux plus.)

°

(You deserter, you renegade, have you come into this circle to insult me and laugh at me? You flex your biceps, your triceps, your dorsal muscles. You crouch down on your thighs and bend your knees, ready for combat. You shriek at the top of your voice and go around saying, look, I'm not one of those, for I won't let myself be fucked or screwed, balled or poked. You go about using a name that's been out of date for two thousand four hundred years. You dangle it in front of me like a decoy. Do you think I don't see the trap? Yet I'm choosing the lesser of two evils. For it's better to be fucked or screwed, balled or poked by an enemy who's got what it takes than by you who haven't. Get out and let me do my own thing. Go and fuck where you belong and, whatever happens, don't leave Valencia Street. Go and find the repulsive dykes, as even one of their number calls them, although I find *stinking creatures* more appropriate. For that's really all you know about, how to lick the backsides that don't dare show themselves in daylight. So fly off to your pleasures, hurry to the corner of Twenty-Fourth Street to meet up with your kind. And most of you haven't a place to call your own. Don't let's talk about being faithful to each other. That sort of thing doesn't exist among you. But it doesn't stop you from claiming that you want to lead our entire sex out of servitude. It's enough to make me die laughing, if bile didn't choke me first, when I think that the only thing which interests you is the corruption of our entire sex. Do you think I haven't ears to hear? I know all about the lesbian plague which, according to you, will gradually take over the whole planet. It's not long since an inspired prophetess railed at you and, with tears running down her cheeks, constantly prostrated in ardent prayer, crawling on her knees, implored that you should be stopped from corrupting children in the schools. With the voice of the righteous this holy individual recalled the sacred word, according to which it would be better to hang mill-stones round your necks, vile creatures, and drown the lot of you, rather than have an outcry because of you.)

At this point in their discourse it is all I can do not to treat them as shrews, and I remember in time that I have adopted the noble style to lend a little glamour to our enslaved sex, for it's better to leave our enemies the job of dragging it through the mud, something they never hesitate to do. The more so since I have come to detect a certain gentleness in the belligerence, their resentment, not to mention their hatred. After all, aren't these the same creatures, who, while there was still no question of the mauve peril, wouldn't look up when you passed them in the street. They are the women of whom I once wrote: "Grovelling bitches, not one of you looks at me. They walk across my path. They catch me when I stop, when I'm brought up short, reduced to an impotence which I'll describe as revolting. A long, bare arm lies across my chest. From that time, because of them, I've been a eunuch." Their present hatred, then, if nothing else, at least proves that I frighten them. They have probably, deliberately, and with the worst of bad faith, caricatured the lesbian warning known as the mauve peril by speaking of it as the lesbian plague; and that too is the expression of an almost holy dread, such as:

(Father, Father, don't reject me, I who am at your knees. Look down at me and see that I am exactly as you created me. Don't allow me to fall into the hands of these accursed creatures and be lost in the darkness of evil. Don't people say that they carry out abductions and, as if that were not enough, they drug their wretched victims so that it is easier to inflict on them the ultimate cruelties (delights). Father, Father, why hast thou forsaken me?)

In any case, once they'd begun, I started to walk up and down in the laundromat, trying out my grand style in order to attract their attention, saying:

(You wretches! Listen to me!)

But they didn't listen to me. I raised my arms to Heaven (which I took as witness), calling out:

(Sappho is my witness that I wish you no harm. On the contrary, I've come here to defend you and redress your wrongs, for I suspect that they multiply among you, like evil deeds.)

They remain deaf to my exhortations, save for one woman who utters a loud wailing, mispronouncing the name of our great predecessor by sustaining a long squeal on the *o*. She is the only one in fact whose ears were touched by the beloved name. I curse myself for having thrown into this battle one of the rare names for which one need not blush. I've had enough. I shout at them:

(Wretched creatures, listen to me!)

But in their confusion and agitation they stand in a circle, swaying from right to left, while they emit a king of whistling sound. Since no word seems to penetrate their understanding, I strip naked between two rows of washing-machines and advance among them, not like Venus emerging from the waves, nor even as my mother bore me, but at any rate with two shoulders, a torso, a belly, legs and the rest. So I have nothing special to exhibit, only perfect human conformity with persons of my own sex, a most obvious and commonplace similarity, and I say:

(You can see clearly that I'm made of the same stuff as you. We belong to the same army, if not the same unit. There's no need to mistake my intentions. They're peaceful. This is how I'll prove it to you.)

But before I can take one step in this state of nudity they immediately begin to spin round, tearing their hair in the purest classical tradition, like tops or whirling dervishes, uttering frenzied cries, some of them, I'm sure, belching; one of them starts to cry (rape, rape), rushing about in all directions; she can't get very far, for she's brought up short in her dash by the washing-machines and the spin-driers which block all the space, so, after blindly colliding with each of the machines in turn, driven by pure terror, she accidentally reaches the street, repeating the same mad phrase (rape, rape). Another in her terror throws herself into a drier that is still spinning and makes a terrible racket. These furies might reserve for me the same fate as the Bacchantes inflicted on Orpheus, but an external event stopped them: Manastabal, my guide, miraculously stole a cloak from a drier and threw it over me to conceal my nudity—the cause, she said, of all this uproar. But she doesn't move fast enough to stop me hearing their cries:

(Look, she's covered with hair from head to foot, even her back's hairy.)

I look at myself in astonishment: it's true, long, black, glossy hair covers my entire body, replacing what had previously been only down. Then I say:

(Ah, here's something to keep me warm in winter!)

But already I can hear them say, yelling again:

(Look, she has scales on her chest, on her shoulders and on her belly.)

I look down at my body once again and see that the hair has now been replaced by hard, shiny scales that I find most attractive. They won't fail to glitter in the sun. I look up again and one of the women, pointing at the center of my body, bellows:

(Look, it's as long as a middle finger. Cut it off, cut if off.)

And at this point I haven't time to verify the truth of their remarks by looking at the incriminated object, for they're already flinging themselves at me. I'm not vicious enough to tell them that when it comes to cutting it off, they've got the wrong continent (for it's degrading to mock one's own misfortune); all the same I don't doubt for a minute that it's women like them who indulge in such practices in those countries where this is said to be the custom, and no girl can avoid it. Manastabal, my guide, drags me out into the street, saying:

(Well, Wittig, are you convinced now that it's really Hell where I'm taking you? Will you still deny it to the bitter end? And start fighting to persuade me to the contrary?)

Half fainting in my fear, carefully wrapped in the cloak that conceals what should not be seen, shaken in my self-respect, trembling, I cry:

(In our own city, who would have believed it, who would have said it? Oh, I beg you, Manastabal, my guide, take me for a drink. I've had enough.)

In this passage the references were to a poet whom you know certainly: Judy Grahn. Maybe you don't know "It Was a Dyke," because it was published a long time ago. The other reference is to Djuna Barnes's *The Book of Repulsive Women*. Also, all the insults you have heard in that passage I have heard myself, said by a neighbor of mine who was shouting at me so loud that the whole building could hear these insults from top to bottom, every night.

NOTES

1. Monique Wittig's comments have been transcribed from the videotape of her Kessler Lecture and are presented here with only minimal editing.

1996

JOAN NESTLE
EDMUND WHITE
BARBARA SMITH
MONIQUE WITTIG
ESTHER NEWTON
SAMUEL R. DELANY
EVE KOSOFSKY SEDGWICK
JOHN D'EMILIO
CHERRÍE MORAGA
JUDITH BUTLER

ESTHER NEWTON

Esther Newton is Professor of Anthropology and Kempner Distinguished Professor at Purchase College, State University of New York. She is a founder and co-chair of the Lesbian and Gay Studies Program at the College, and the author of numerous articles and of *Mother Camp: Female Impersonators in America* (University of Chicago Press). *Cherry Grove, Fire Island: 60 Years in America's First Gay and Lesbian Town* (Beacon Press 1993) and *Margaret Mead Made Me Gay: Personal Essays, Public Ideas* (Duke University Press 2000) both won the Ruth Benedict Award of the Society of Lesbian and Gay Anthropologists of the American Anthropological Association. Her next project is a memoir based on "My Butch Career." She lives in New York City in a traditional lesbian family: two Standard Poodles, one Norfolk Terrier, three cats, and her partner, performance artist Holly Hughes.

MY BUTCH CAREER

A Memoir

Gay, Laura thought to herself. *Is that what they call it? Gay? She was acutely uncomfortable now. It was as if she were a child of civilization, reared among the savages, who suddenly found herself among the civilized. She recognized them as her own. And yet she had adopted the habits of another race and she was embarrassed and lost with her own kind.*

(Bannon 1983)

PROLOGUE: ALICE-HUNTING

I met Gertrude Stein in 1961, on the cover of a book. Inside were lots of facts and dates and witty sayings of hers but not the one thing I wanted most to know: Was Gertrude Stein a dyke?

So I ran out and found *The Autobiography of Alice B. Toklas*, thinking what a nervy idea to write someone else's autobiography, they must have been lovers, but it didn't say so any more than the first book had. It was all impersonal and too much about famous men, but there were many, many hints. And the more books and photographs I found the more I thought yes. But it's one thing to think yes and something else to know it.

Little by little this idea of being Gertrude began to grow inside my head. It wasn't yet about living in Paris or about writing, but about being accepted as an equal by men within a very small select circle, and of living in a happy domesticated couple with heaps of good food. So naturally, the big thing was to find an Alice.

But finding an Alice wasn't easy. At first it wasn't easy because some therapist said I should go out with men, and none of the men were at all like Alice. After several years I'd used up all the men and the therapist too, and was still as gay as ever. Just then I became one of a few women in a fancy graduate school, with lots of small select men who accepted me as an equal, so the time for Alice seemed right. But none of the women I met really deep down wanted to be an Alice. No matter how Alice they seemed, it always turned out that secretly they too wanted to be Gertrude, even if they'd never read anything about her. Unbelievable as it sounds, all those Alices wanted to use me as a model for becoming Gertrude themselves. And as they became more Gertrude, I fought with them more and desired them less.

This is because, speaking frankly, Gertrudes have a couple of faults—being bossy and being babies—and they like to be the only bossy baby in the house. And the aspiring Gertrudes—this is how I saw the situation—probably wanted Alices of their own or at least a more neutral sort of person than I was. And as for desire, I wanted to be the one who was doing something to an Alice who wanted something, not the other way around.

However, there was no giving up on this idea of Gertrude and Alice. Certainly I couldn't be Alice myself, and without an Alice I couldn't be Gertrude, which was for me the only way to be gay. And I was gay. So little by little I began to think that the reason why I couldn't find an Alice must be that I wasn't a genius. If only I could be a genius then absolutely Alice must appear. It was 1968.

Just then they showed the feminist protest of the Miss America contest on TV. Nothing had made me so excited since the day I'd first seen Gertrude's photograph, and I joined a consciousness-raising group. The other women had all been in the radical left and they were politically aware. And just as I was desperately longing to be Gertrude, these young women said that class privilege was wrong. I had been earning money on my first teaching job, and even though I still hadn't found an Alice, I'd been collecting good furniture and other things I thought a Gertrude sort of person should have in her home. And furthermore, my "sisters" most definitely didn't believe in "roles," meaning they were sick of having their boyfriends boss them around. They didn't approve of Gertrude and Alice's way of living either, which seemed to them just like a husband and wife.

Then I met Louise. At first she wore miniskirts and eye makeup. On our first date we went to see *King Kong* and afterwards Louise did a very funny imitation of Kong smelling Fay Wray's underpants. Because of her long blonde curls and sequined blouses, I never asked what it meant that Louise played King Kong. She could cook very well and made things like avocado and mushroom sandwiches, so I was thrilled and we moved in together.

But as time went on it got more and more mixed up who was really King Kong and who Fay Wray. Louise's hair got shorter and shorter. All the time we were going separately and together to feminist meetings, where it was always said that there were no more "roles," so there was no way to talk about our predicament. It was bad to be a "heavy" (meaning other people felt small because you were too big), and I was, and if Louise wanted to be King Kong in bed why couldn't I be Alice?

I began to doubt everything except being gay and wrote about all the doubts in a journal. Soon writing got to be more and more on my mind. And the more I liked doing it and having it on my mind, the more I began to feel Gertrude-like as a writer, just as I was rejecting her because what feminist wants to be accepted as an equal by men or be waited on by an Alice in a cozy couple surrounded by select fews? No, I was too Gertrude, that was the trouble. If only I were less Gertrude I'd meet someone who was less Alice and this would solve the problem.

> *The butch is either the magical sign of lesbianism, or a failed, emasculated and abjected man.*
>
> (Munt 1998)

Because of my chromosomes—xx as far as I know—and a reproductive biology, which is, or rather was, capable of giving birth, my sex is female. During my lonely childhood among the savages, I was stuck in the girl gender, which is linked, worldwide, to hard work, low pay, and disrespect, though this is not the only reason why for me, neither being female nor being a woman has ever been easy or unequivocal. Later, when I found gay life and started to become civilized, I was given a second gender.[1] This gay gender, butch, makes my body recognizable and it alone makes sexual love possible. But being butch has been problematic, too. How could it not be?

Butch is my handle and my collective name; a tribe, the late lamented writer Paul Monette called us gay people. My life's work has been inspired by and primarily written for these gay communities, entities that are no less powerful for being symbolic.

Remember that scene in *The Well of Loneliness*, where Stephen Gordon grieves over the reflection of her masculine body? Well, mirrors have always made me queasy, too. Maybe for the same reasons why I get anxious sometimes, even today, going around with other butches. Our forbidden looks are reflected back even bigger when butches hang out. In them I see what I look like, and how I look still has the power to shock me: sometimes because my masculine self-awareness, my ego body image is startled, for example, by the breasts or hips I see in the naked mirror; other times because I look so different from how, as a woman, I know I am supposed to look. In a documentary I once saw about dwarfs, a woman not much taller than a fire hydrant tells the impartial camera how at first she had recoiled from joining an association of little people because "I was horrified when I saw them. I had told myself, 'You don't look like that.'"

The other night I dreamed I came upon a brown bear surrounded by a boisterous crowd of street people. I approached the bear obliquely from the back; it was sitting upright and motionless in a hole, only the back of its torso and head were visible. The people were shouting at it and throwing garbage. I realized that they meant in the end to kill it and were only tormenting it for the fun of destroying a robust, beautiful animal who was hopelessly outnumbered. I woke in terror and threw myself into my girlfriend's arms. "It's you, the bear," she said. "But it's only a dream."

Is my butch body worth any more than the bear's, or is the hatred it inspires its only value? Certainly, butches have been the target of medical intervention to correct our grievous mistakes, our unshakeable belief in how we should look and move. My body commits every one of these movement "mistakes"—for example, hands on hips, *fingers forward*—that are used to diagnose Gender

Identity Disorder, a category of mental illness listed in the *DSM-IV*.[2] Luckily, when my friction of teenage misery burst into flames, I escaped the Thorazine and shock treatments others endured through the middle-class option of therapy to cure what still proved to be an intractable "case" of gender dysphoria and homosexual desire. But there is still a terror of calling attention to myself, of naming myself what is plain to see.

Child Monster

My child body was a strong and capable instrument somehow stuffed into the word "girl." I was the first kid up the jungle gym, as good as any of the boys at stoop ball. All my friends were boys; girls were dumb. I had nothing in common with them.

When I was about seven, a ten-year-old boy I idolized, a guy I was playing sex games with, thinking we were buddies and I could be him, showed me I was no boy by trying to use me as a sexual favor for his real buddies. My rage and shame over his betrayal threw me into a shock whose traumatic effects have proven to be lifelong. The guys had made me understand that they were the boys, and I was something other, a body to be used by them. Thus ended my life as a boy. But it didn't make me a girl. It made me an antigirl, a girl refuser, caught between genders.

Like "gay community," the female body is also an imaginary construct. Any body is shaped by being lived in. My own intrepid body and dominating (though needy) personality seemed to others—and to my child self—to be masculine, and these perceptions (should they be called fears? convictions?) bore out Oscar Wilde's dictum that life imitates art. My body ate masculinity and thrived on it. Endless hours playing stickball, later tennis, basketball, competitive physical games I loved. The horse books and baseball books that appealed to me. All those dark Saturday mornings at the kids matinee in the Superior Theater, the local movie house, dreaming myself into Tyrone Power, Errol Flynn the buccaneer running his sword through villainous Basil Rathbone. This masculinity, my masculinity, is not external; it permeates and animates me. Nor is it a masquerade. In my own home, when no one is present, I still sit with my legs carelessly flung apart.

I saw other female bodies: my mother's, the others girls' at summer camp where my parents had sent me, hoping without saying so that somehow their femininity would rub off on me, which it did not. But spending every summer with girls made me feel more at ease with them, and showed me there were ways of being a girl that might just work. There were counselors who were physically confident and well coordinated like me, who could handle nervous horses and slam tennis balls. For the first time I had tomboy friends and even wound up liking regular, feminine girls more, despite their teasing because even in my bunk I always wore that blue Brooklyn Dodgers baseball cap.

Eleven is supposed to be the age when girls lose confidence. That's how old I was when my divorced mother dragged me to California. On the drive cross-country, I spun around and around inside one desperate thought: that if I'd been a boy this exile from everything familiar in New York City could not have happened.

My Favorite Photo

In my favorite photo, the setting is urban, a kids' playground. In the background was a 1940s baby carriage and a grim brick building, public toilets. My WASP mother and her little guy sit on a bench thigh to thigh. Her chestnut hair is braided around her head like a laurel wreath or a halo. She wears a plain cotton dress. She holds her legs together and smiles into the camera, but one knee is exposed. The edge of her skirt partly covers my thigh.

I must have been four or five. My mother thought bathing suit tops for little girls premature, a commercially motivated imposition of femininity, so I wear a boy's bathing suit. Little boots stuffed with socks beside me. My legs spread comfortably apart, feet swinging free. You can tell I'm a girl because my brown hair covers my ears. I am leaning into the crook of my mother's arm. Protectively, she circles my shoulders from behind. The outside hand pulls me into her; the closer one seems to ward off some danger to my chest. I stare out—unsmiling—as if to say, This is my spot.

Like my dark father, I am attracted to my mother's fair skin and light eyes. Is this a form of self-hate, a delicious eroticism, or both?

Desire among the Savages (Sue Wilson)

Palo Alto, California. By accident, Sue Wilson sat next to me in high school honors English. She was busty and inactive, the kind of girl that boys liked. Not that she showed what she had, like those so-called "cheap" Mexican girls. She was a "nice" white girl, neatly dressed in straight skirts and blouses with round collars, only the top button undone. Assured, easy in her body, Sue was definitely feminine.

What was it, to be feminine? I tried to learn. Inside the girls' clothing I loathed, inside the traitorous body that had grown into an alien shape, inside the suburban teenager who had to beg for an allowance and the use of the car, the me that was as free and big as Tyrone Power setting sail contracted to the vanishing point. I had understood, all over again, that there was no choice. I *had* to be a girl.

How did the girls do it? Practicing in front of the mirror, tugging the stiff crinolines this way and that, the rolled-down bobby sox, charm bracelets, flared skirts, straight skirts, Peter Pan blouses, Pendleton outfits . . . What was it? No clothing, no borrowed gesture ever performed the magic, made me right.

The other girls just *were* it. Sue Wilson, for instance. The teacher read the best compositions aloud in class. Sue wrote that her father was in the Army. She'd been born in Turkey. I thought her writing was beautiful. Was there still something of Constantinople inside that WASPy blandness?

She asked me over to study for a test. Sue's room was right out of *Seventeen* magazine; her bed even had a canopy and stuffed animals on the pillow. We sat under the canopy. As she ran through a plot synopsis of *Cry, The Beloved Country*, I began to sweat. My eyes kept going to her blonde hair, and to her breasts, thick and fragrant as a rose bush I couldn't help but stick my nose into—because of the way just the top of her cleavage showed when she bent over the book. My body felt grotesque, bulky. Was I getting my period? There were no cramps. My ears were hot. My arms and hands seemed so huge and separate, almost out of control. I saw myself as a plague of locusts swarming all over her smooth creamy skin. Did Sue notice she was sitting next to a monster? I almost ran out of her house.

This fierce impulse to shake her up, to kiss her mouth, even to squeeze her breasts, it was sexual, it was how I imagined that men got turned on to women. Someone had passed me *The Well of Loneliness* in a brown paper bag, so I knew there had been a masculine girl like me in England. The kids called it "lesbian." It might as well have been "leper." No one in my high school wore green on Thursday for fear of being called one. That other lepers might be in Africa or even England was as good as saying there were none, here in the Bay Area.

I expected Sue would avoid me after that. I avoided everyone. Several weeks later, coming home from the dentist full of Novocain, I stared dispassionately in the bathroom mirror at my sullen, strong-jawed face. This face looked very ugly, very wrong. The big dark eyes scared me. What was inside there? Reaching into the medicine cabinet, I unwrapped a razor blade and cut a slash by the side of my mouth. "I can't feel anything," I said aloud as the blood dripped down my neck.

A WASP in Jew's Clothing

We are never simply women or men. Our American genders are always embodied as "races." These so-called races have a haphazard relation to biology, yet, like being queer, they are all too real, culturally speaking, in their consequences for individuals. My body was always definitely white when considered in relation to black people or Asian people. "White" was the given as I grew up, so I was not aware of how I became a white girl, or how the signs and smells of whiteness permeated me. Nor of all the perks and pleasures provided me within that dispensation.

My mother's coloring is fair. She came from old Yankee stock. All her ancestors but one had come over before the Revolution, one of them on the *Mayflower*. As I write this I am in Provincetown with my girlfriend, who is also, not coincidentally, a WASP; there is a plaque here dedicated to those same Mayflower Pilgrims who, in 1620, first landed in America. What possible leap of imagination connects me to my ancestor—his name was Peregrine White—without whom I would not exist? And why would I want to, except that our pasts must be owned? My WASP ancestors and people like them conquered the country, cheated the Indians and then disowned them, kept African slaves. They also bravely crossed the Great Plains in covered wagons, founded towns like Peoria, Illinois, freed the slaves out of conviction, and gave birth in hard circumstances.

While my mother always talked proudly about her ancestors and relatives I knew I was different from these people we hardly ever saw. Within whiteness there are subtleties and equivocations. Not all so-called white people are the same, or equal.

I was a red diaper baby. My mother had a thing for Jewish men. She met lots of them in the Communist Party she had joined out of a Depression-era liberal social conscience and to enrage her conservative father, a general in the U.S. Army. One of those left-wing Jews my WASP mother liked was my father, a man just as tyrannical as the general, and a womanizer who eventually had six wives. For a few years, until he tired of her, my father cast his erotic net over my mother and she didn't struggle. She had the hots for him. How intensely I resented that! He joined our circle late: while he had been away fighting Nazis I had been her little husband.

My father's parents were struggling immigrants from the Ukraine. He rejected Judaism right after his bar mitzvah—some mistreatment of his family by the local synagogue, he said, but really, the model of Jewish scholarly manhood repelled and shamed him. My father took up boxing in college—when I was six or seven, he tried to teach me never to telegraph my punches—and as a soldier he volunteered to be an artillery spotter, one of the most dangerous assignments. He was my masculine ideal.

When we lived in New York my parents sent me to one of those commie pinko progressive schools—anthropologist Margaret Mead was said to have been a founder—that believed in letting children "be themselves." As a nine-year-old, let's say, my everyday school outfit was sneakers, jeans, and a polo shirt, and for dress-up I was the Lone Ranger, whom I called the Long Ranger so my father called me the Short Ranger.

Once when I was in my late thirties and had freed myself from his domination, my father and I had dinner near where he lived. As we stood on the corner of Broadway and 91st Street waiting for the light to change, I realized with a creepy shock that we were dressed nearly the same—running shoes, jeans, and plaid shirt—and were both standing with hands on our hips, *fingers forward*, a couple of tough Jewish guys.

My father was dark and, as luck would have it, I am too, though not as dark as he was. A mutt is what my students call us American mixed breeds. Recently I've begun to think of my butch self as bicultural and to appreciate my hybrid vigor. Because of growing up in New York among my father's Jewish relatives I'm at home among Jews, though ignorant of the religion. Because of being raised by my WASP mother, though, my sensibility is more akin to the WASPS I don't resemble. I came to understand that I wasn't as white as they were. My mother once corrected a hospital nurse who remarked on our resemblance as mother and daughter, "But her father was of a completely different race!"

Privilege Is Part of Me

> *Once [Ann Lister] inherits her uncle's estate, indeed, her social position actually protects her from the kind of disapprobation that she routinely undergoes as a masculine woman without her own income.*
> (Halberstam 1998)

Most of my academic friends view my claiming butch as an eccentricity. They overlook it because they love me and they think I'm smart, which means, at least partly, that we move in the same intellectual circles. They prefer to understand my seeing myself this way as an offbeat and somewhat déclassé avocation, as if I followed mud wrestling or roller derby. They find my insistence that I am butch mildly titillating, but mostly embarrassing. This is even, or especially, true of professional women who themselves might be called butch behind their backs. It's sort of okay to *be* masculine as long as it's not named as such. I resent this lesbian version of Don't ask, don't tell.

If I were working class, there is more of a chance that my being butch might be taken for granted among my friends, and with luck, celebrated, as key to what is distinctive and maybe even good about me. Butch and femme have been central to working-class lesbian life at least since the 1950s.[3] My own research in Cherry Grove suggests that there was more working-class resistance to the total denigration of these identities under the influence of lesbian-feminist ideology in the 1970s and 1980s.

I was born in Manhattan, the privileged child of professional people. My butch body bears the marks of access, opportunity, and a life lived with papers and books. The confidence with which I usually enter stores and bureaucratic offices, my multisyllabic vocabulary, the intact teeth and gums that only life-long dental work makes possible, all express the physical safety of my family's home, their comfortable income and good educations, and the fact that my own life has been lived approximately at their level.

What have I in common with working-class butches, then? My butch body recognizes the claims of our common tomboy origins and overlapping destinies. Yet privilege has always allowed me to get over in places where they mostly couldn't; it has always softened the edges of my butchness, because "masculinity" too is an abstract. In life, masculinity inhabits particular people with contrasting histories. Among men, the masculinity of most college professors looks effete compared to that of most plumbers. Yet no one debates that college professors are "men" (although who is "more of" a man or a "real" man is subject to debate), and to me, butch is a queer identity that cannot transcend but does cut across classes and races, thereby gaining immensely in resonance and richness. Most middle-class put-downs of butches and femmes are class stereotypes and prejudice, conscious or unconscious.

My class became a problem during freshman year in college, when I was seduced by Phyllis Green, a bohemian wildcat of an art student who knew how to find other gay people via New York City bar life. In the summer of 1959 I followed her into a world that thrilled and terrified me with its frankly erotic slow dancing, johns looking to pay lesbians for sexual "freak shows," pot smoking, and an edgy threat of violence. My girlfriend there was Nannette, a former synchronized swimmer turned chorus girl at the Club 82, a drag club on East Fourth Street. At 4 A.M. I'd pick my way through cigar-smoking gangsters to meet her after work. How glamorous she was in theatrical makeup, blue eye shadow-for-days and inch-long false eyelashes! Nannette was the first person I ever touched who died her hair—I vividly recall its orangy color and paperlike texture. A proud femme, Nannette boasted that no man had ever fucked her.

All the butches I met—one who was also dating Nannette threatened to carve up my college kid face with her knife—looked and mostly were tough. Their peroxided d.a. haircuts were slicked back into the same styles the hoody boys from the wrong side of the freeway had worn in my high school. Their most precious asset was pride. "I have no dignity left," my drag queen mentor and friend Skip Arnold told me, "but I do have my pride." Butch pride was expressed by short tempers, fists, and broken bottles. As much as I loved the flash of these butches, and admired their courage, their rugged masculinity and tough talk made me seem wimpish. And the truth is, those bar butches were incompatible with my life plans.

Professional is not the same as rich. I didn't have an independent income like Gertrude Stein, the painter Gluck, or Radclyffe Hall, women who, though not called butches or bull dykes, were the wealthy version of the same impulse, as Radclyffe Hall made perfectly clear in *The Well of Loneliness*. Their friends called them by men's names, they wore masculine clothing, and they paired with feminine women. That they got away with it and were called eccentric or even dashing was thanks to their refuge in bohemian artiness, made possible by money. These mannish wealthy women, like the bar dykes, functioned as the "magical sign of lesbianism" partly because their gender inversion made them so visible. Rich lesbians were not answerable to the work world's feminine gender code to keep a roof over their heads. They paid the price for their visibility in expatriatism and social ostracism. On the other hand, working-class butches paid the price of their visibility with unemployment, beatings, or having to pass as men, as Leslie Feinberg showed in *Stone Butch Blues*.

Middle-class women, floating between Radclyffe Hall's Stephen Gordon and Leslie Feinberg's Jess Goldberg, experience cultural and economic conditions that severely limit the expression of gender deviance. A woman of my class who was probably queer and wouldn't have a husband to depend on was going to have to work. It's important to be precise: for Americans, money and class are more taboo than sex. Slinging boxes onto a truck or waitressing: I was brought up to think that work like that wasn't for people like me. Even being a secretary, work my mother had done—it seemed like a life sentence to boredom, fake smiles, and bringing men coffee. More opportunities were opening up for college-educated women as the 1960s began. I clung tenaciously to my half-formed ambitions; someone who looked like a butch bar dyke, which is to say, someone who looked so obviously gay, could forget about a career.

I left the bars and returned to college, where I had kind of a breakdown. Out of panic, I got engaged to a man with the unconscious intention of getting pregnant. An illegal abortion in Tijuana, Mexico, nearly finished me off. This negative limit proved my biological femaleness once and for all, and the moralistic lecture of the male doctor at Stanford Hospital who saved my life—"I hope you realize, young lady, that you brought this on yourself"—was perfectly consistent with the shame and disgust with which I had always perceived femaleness and femininity in relation to myself. I am never unaware of the vulnerability of this female body of mine.

I retreated in disarray, trying intermittently, with the "help" of a therapist, to be straight for the next seven years, years whose false starts and wasted efforts I regret bitterly. My butch self took refuge in a fantasy world dominated by the figure of Gertrude Stein, about whom I read everything I could find. Stein was to me a mannish ego ideal who had somehow created a domestic and intellectual life in a Parisian setting of dazzling appeal. Her story was like my favorite fairy tale or masturbation fantasy, the only version of butch that appealed to me in every way as I slogged my way through college and graduate school confused, conflicted, and in the closet.

Still, Nannette's friends, the femmes and butches who were strippers and post office clerks, had left their lipstick marks and their back slaps all over me. I saw those uptown ki-ki dykes through their resentful eyes. They made me smell and taste the smugness of women with money and education, and the bitterness of those without. And working-class bar dykes were the first to show me how to be butch, which means they showed me how to have a style. Postmodernism and consumerism have given style a bad name, it is not necessarily superficial. Adrift in a sea of hostility, drowning in shame, the strong little kid I was had grown into an angry, slump-shouldered lump of teenage flesh, and my secrets made me a loner even with friends. Being butch was the first identity that had ever made sense out of my body's situation, the first rendition of gender that ever rang true, the first look I could ever pull together. Butches may have been laughable to straight people and an embarrassment to the uptown dykes, but in the bar life they were citizens, they were mensches, and they were hot.

Power, power: butch dykes had it, Gertrude Stein had it. Not power over femmes, who were as likely to be the seducers or to make more money or to lay down the law. And not worldly power, of course—we still don't have that. Of necessity butches used weapons of the weak, the terrorism of attitude and imagination. Butches had the confidence to take space from the straight world where none had existed, and the power of artists to make new forms out of cultural clay, the impact of the intended word and fabulous gesture. "I am a genius," Gertrude Stein declared, and I for one believed her.

A PERVERTED DESIRE

I spent much of my childhood trying to distinguish identification from desire, asking myself, "Am I in love with Julie Andrews, or do I think I am Julie Andrews?"

(Koestenbaum 1993)

My butch body is more like a gay man's than a straight woman's in this respect: it is perverted, and I say that with pleasure. Many women who came out in the seventies via feminism think of themselves as having chosen, perhaps quite happily, to be lesbian, but not me. If women were like horses, I'd be a horse with stripes, a zebra, and the stripes go clear through me. Life-long gender dysphoria and coming out ten years before Stonewall have made me into a pervert onto whom feminist convictions were successfully grafted. How lively and romantic—compared to girlhood—being a pervert was back in the fifties and sixties! Despite the self-hate, the lies. I told myself that if I could take a magic pill (that was the formulation) I'd choose to be "normal," of course. But try as I might to straighten out, my body always inclined like a landslide toward the valley of perverted desire.

I began to look at myself with some pleasure in the full-length mirror in the gym after my girlfriend Holly said she thought I looked sexy running on the treadmill. If I mention my girlfriends, past and present, a lot, that is partly because, from the days of Phyllis Green and Nannette, the impossible gender of my imagination was reflected back to me only in the lustful or loving gaze of the girly girl dykes to whom I was mostly attracted. I first saw what they saw—that is myself as a sex object—in a series of photographs taken by Nancy Smith, my first great love. Sophisticated and ten years older than me, Nancy, like many of my girlfriends, was a visual artist. Her painterly eye revealed an image the mirror had never shown me: that of a desirable pervert. In her photos my body was beginning to make sense as I stopped trying to be straight and gave up the attendant awkwardness and pretenses. When Picasso painted Gertrude Stein she objected that the portrait wasn't a good likeness. "It will be," he stated.

My girlfriends have told me I'm good-looking so often that, even though they are almost the only ones who say so, I'm finally starting to believe it. At the camp where my parents had sent me to become more feminine the girls had exclaimed, "Oh, you're so good-looking, you'd make such a good-looking boy! Just like Cornel Wilde." As a ten- year-old, what could I do with this? The question How do I look? transcends my own vanity and points toward what Sue-Ellen Case (1993) famously called, in an essay I both admire and critique, "a butch-femme aesthetic."

HELP FROM MY FRIENDS

> *Lived identities are complicated fictions essential to our social function.*
> (Munt 1998)[4]

Gradually evolving from 1950s stone butch to a 1960s graduate-student-in-the-closet, 1970s lesbian-feminist, and then, by the 1980s, back to a larger, more generous vision of being butch, I welded what inner strength I had onto the structures gay people had already built, to become a civilized human being.

What I mean is, like the songs says, I did it *with a lot of help from my friends*. My butch career has been made possible by gay people who have fought to create an alternative vision, a freer cultural space for gender and sexuality. With the exception of my beloved anthropological mentor, the late David Schneider, the straight academic world has hindered me more than helped; respect has come to me mostly from queers without whom I would have published nothing and gone nowhere. Why do I claim this butch identity? Because, to paraphrase

Stuart Hall, to claim an identity is to place oneself in a narrative of history. Or as anthropologist Edward Sapir put it: "The individual is helpless without a cultural heritage to work on. . . . Creation is a bending of form to one's will, not a manufacture of form *ex nihilo*" (1962:102).

Maybe you thought I wasn't going to acknowledge any of the antibutch insults and polemics. The one that the butch is nothing more than "a failed, emasculated, and abjected man." The one that asserts that butch-femme relationships are just pathetic imitations of heterosexuality. Or the more sophisticated apologias that press butchness into the service of some kind of "more interesting" theory, that might valorize butch as a tortured form of feminist protest, or as a masquerade or performance, or as a transvestic challenge to the social order. All of them flatten a lived identity into an abstract and imply that everyday butches in the gay community, who can be notoriously recalcitrant and rigid, are just too too . . . unhip.

I'll engage just one of the charges made against butches, the accusation that we are ugly, that in fact we epitomize the ugliness imputed to all lesbians. This charge of ugliness contains a partial truth, I think. Besides the ugliness stamped on us by the hatred we endure and the shame lodged in our own hearts, butches have the awkwardness of something partly formed, the rough edges of a work in progress.[5]

> *The terms of a different construction of gender also exist, in the margins of hegemonic discourses.*
>
> (de Lauretis 1987)

Because we embody the contradiction of femaleness with masculinity, we stand for and are part of the evolution out of old-fashioned, biology-bound gender. Because our looks are read as obviously sexual, we symbolize and advance the modernist elaboration of nonprocreative desire.

Yet I am hostile to representations of queerness as antithetical to all order, to all categories, to queerness pressed into the service of romantic individualism. My queerness is for my own pleasure in loving and living, something that is impossible without being part of Communities (capital c), imaginatively connected via books and art, conferences and politics, and also community (small c) that comes to my birthday party or answers the telephone when I need someone. Being butch for me is all mixed up with everyday survival. As Wayne Koestenbaum put it, butch and femme and queenliness are "style[s] of resistance and self-protection, a way of identifying with other queer people across invisibility and disgrace."[6] Butch and femme are historic *and* present forms of queer culture, deeply meaningful to many, many lesbians.

Beauty and style give pleasure, and they are fundamental elements of queer ideas and queer art, which are among our most powerful resources (our enemies understood this in their campaign to suppress them). We lesbians must not allow our community sensibility to be anti-aesthetic, antisensual, or antisex. The better butches look—and I don't mean homogenized or slick or, worst of all, prettified versions, but rather masculine lesbians flush with affirmation, verve, and the courage of our sexual convictions—the more we build the queer tribes, the more we affirm diversity and the bigger contribution we make to American culture's half-assed struggle to move into the twenty-first century.

CIVILIZED DESIRE (TONI)

> *Cops called me "boy," boys called me "sir," and the ladies . . . well, the ladies just called me.*
>
> (Hughes 1996)

While still in graduate school, I had the incredible good luck to meet a female impersonator named Skip Arnold who taught me many useful things and gave me the material for my doctoral dissertation and a book about gender in American culture called *Mother Camp*. Skip showed me a way of representing queenly being and queer desire that captured my fancy from the first time I saw his huge bejeweled form on stage.

It was in the gay resort of Cherry Grove, years later, that I was seduced by another drag queen in front of a cheering gay audience. I had gone to the Sunday night drag talent search as usual and found a seat pretty close to the front of the stage. There was a "guest hostess," a big tall queen named Toni in a sequined evening gown and strawberry blonde curls that doubled the volume of his head. I liked him right away, remembering meeting him on the dock on Friday, a middle-aged, obvious drag queen—swaying hips, wrist bent, shaved eyebrows—dragging hat boxes and bulky suitcases, and how he had stopped to admire my standard poodles.

When this maybe sweet but colorless person burst onto the stage as a towering dynamo of a sex goddess, the old thrill—what the hell is it? —shot through me. And he saw it. From the moment he came out for his second number, "And I Am Telling You I'm Not Going" from *Dreamgirls*, his eyes were on me. As he came down off the stage, I held out a dollar, but instead of taking it he pulled me onto the stage.

All I had to do was follow his lead—it was so easy. Bankston, the kid who videotaped it, said admiringly, "You weren't scared of him at all!" No, of course not. I wasn't afraid of him, because I loved *her*. She turned my back to the audience and forced me to my knees. I could have protested like I would have in real life, but on stage I didn't want to. At first her hand guided me. Later I was going with her so easily I couldn't say how I knew what I should do. People were sure we had rehearsed it. No. She had thought it all out and I followed her thought. On my knees looking up at her, the screams of the crowd behind my back—in real life, it happens something like this, between eyeblinks or heartbeats, the look with which she appoints me her butch for a week or for years. Toni could back away then, sure of her conquest, the better to work the crowd: "I don't want to be free . . ." This was no dream. Watching the video later with Bankston, he said, "You looked so right, like the man I've always wanted!" Toni pushed me over on my back and lowered herself over me. Her whole gowned body was big and stiff, like a cardboard tube the size of a tree, because of the girdle and padding, but moving and hot. Above my face the lipsticked open mouth, close-set blue eyes, false lashes, makeup, and the strawberry blonde wig. Laughing, I threw my arms around her neck, and she laughed—the act was working—and we rolled around in a mutual bump and grind, she still mouthing the words to the song, "And you, and you, and youuuu're gonna LOVE me."

Then she turned me toward the screaming, cheering crowd. She curtseyed and I bowed. We were both still laughing and it was perfect, all that art or ritual should be and do in front of a queer crowd plugging right into the spectacle of a metafemme and a metabutch making it. We are hetero, homo, mother and son, father and daughter. This huge masterful mother who isn't really, who wanted me, recognized me, was hot for me like I dreamed she should be, had to be, never was. She who took over and made it all easy, who ran the show in which we starred as mutually adored and adoring: emblems of civilized desire.

Do what you want with me, I said to the queer audience and to Toni, to her. Just let me kiss you. And I did kiss her, and was kissed. Back home the mirror showed red marks of great big lips all over my face.

NOTES

1. "Secondary genders" is the term used by anthropologist Jennifer Robertson (1998: II), who writes about the Japanese all-woman *Takarazuka Revue* troupe that includes both "female" and "male" players. Incoming students are assigned which gender they will play "based on both physical (but not genital) and socio-psychological criteria; namely, height, physique, facial shape, voice, personality, and to a certain extent, personal preference."
2. The American Psychiatric Association's *Diagnostic and Statistical Manual of Mental Disorders*, 4th ed. As listed in a recent exposé of gender correctional programs aimed at children (P. Burke 1996:29).
3. See Kennedy and Davis 1993.
4. "However seemingly intransigent, however poignantly experienced, lived identities are complicated fictions essential to our social function. Pragmatically speaking, this means an equivocal response to identity is required: that we tender our theoretical skepticism with an unaffected respect for the way individuals have negotiated their own desire through the swamp of sexual uncertainty" (Munt 1998:83).
5. "The stone butch has made the roughness of gender into a part of her identity. Where sex and gender fail to match (female body and masculine self), where appearance and reality collide (she appears masculine and constructs a real masculinity where there should be a 'real' femininity), this is where the stone butch emerges as viable, powerful, and affirmative" (Halberstam 1996:7).
6. Koestenbaum 1993:85. "Geraldine Farrar dared to tell Arturo Toscanini, 'You forget, *maestro*, that *I* am the star.' One need not be a star to relish Farrar's concise way of gathering a self, like rustling skirts, around her. . . . No single gesture, gown or haughty glissando of self-promotion will change one's actual social position: one is fixed in a class, a race, a gender. But against such absolutes there arises a fervent belief in retaliatory self-invention; gay culture has perfected the art of mimicking a diva—of pretending, inside, to *be* divine—to help the stigmatized self imagine it is received, believed, and adored" (133).

WORKS CITED

Bannon, Ann. 1983. *I Am a Woman.* Tallahassee, FL: Naiad Press.

Burke, Phyllis. 1996. *Gender Shock: Exploding the Myths of Male and Female.* New York: Doubleday.

Case, Sue-Ellen. 1993. "Toward a Butch/Femme Aesthetic." In *The Lesbian and Gay Studies Reader,* ed. Henry Abelove, Michele A. Barale, and David M. Halperin. New York: Routledge. 294–306.

de Lauretis, Teresa. 1987. *Technologies of Gender: Essays on Theory, Film and Fiction.* Bloom-ington: Indiana University Press.

Halberstam, Judith. 1998 *Female Masculinity.* Durham, NC: Duke University Press.

——— 1996. "Lesbian Masculinity, or Even Stone Butches Get the Blues." *Women and Performance: A Journal of Feminist Theory* 8 (2).

Hughes, Holly. 1996. *Clit Notes: A Sapphic Sampler.* New York: Grove Atlantic.

Kennedy, Elizabeth L., and Madeline D. Davis. 1993. *Boots of Leather, Slippers of Gold: The History of a Lesbian Community.* New York: Routledge.

Koestenbaum, Wayne. 1993. *The Queen's Throat: Opera, Homosexuality and the Mystery of Desire.* New York: Poseidon Press.

Munt, Sally R. 1998. *Heroic Desire: Lesbian Identity and Cultural Space.* New York: New York University Press.

Robertson, Jennifer. 1998. *Takarazuka: Sexual Politics and Popular Culture in Modern Japan.* Berkeley: University of California Press.

Sapir, Edward. 1962. "Culture, Genuine and Spurious." In *Edward Sapir: Culture, Language and Personality,* ed. D. G. Mandelbaum. Berkeley: University of California Press.

1997

JOAN NESTLE
EDMUND WHITE
BARBARA SMITH
MONIQUE WITTIG
ESTHER NEWTON

SAMUEL R. DELANY

EVE KOSOFSKY SEDGWICK
JOHN D'EMILIO
CHERRÍE MORAGA
JUDITH BUTLER

SAMUEL R. DELANY

Samuel R. Delany is a novelist and critic who lives in New York City and teaches at Temple University, in Philadelphia. He is the author of *Dhalgren* (Bantam Books, 1975), *Hogg* (Black Ice Books, 1995), *The Mad Man* (Voyant Publishing, 1995), and the four books collectively known as Return to Nevèrÿon (Wesleyan University Press, 1993). The lecture included here became the basis for his best-selling *Times Square Red, Times Square Blue* (New York University Press, 1999).

... 3, 2, 1, CONTACT

But I tell you, my lord fool, out of this nettle, danger, we pluck this flower, safety.

(Shakespeare, *Henry IV, Part I 2.3*)

My primary thesis is simply that, given the mode of capitalism under which we live, life is at its most rewarding, productive and pleasant when the greatest number of people understand, appreciate, and seek out interclass contact and communication conducted in a mode of good will.

My secondary thesis is, however, that the class war raging constantly and often silently in the comparatively stabilized societies of the developed world, though it is at times as hard to detect as Freud's unconscious or the structure of discourse, perpetually works for the erosion of the social practices through which interclass communication takes place and the institutions holding those practices stable, so that new institutions must always be conceived and set in place to take over the jobs of those that are battered again and again till they are destroyed.

My tertiary thesis, to which now and again I shall return, is that, while the establishment and utilization of those institutions always involves specific social practices, the effects of my primary and secondary theses are regularly perceived at the level of discourse. Therefore, it is only by a constant renovation of the concept of discourse that society can maintain the most conscientious and informed field for the establishment of such institutions and practices—a critique necessary if new institutions of any efficacy are to develop. At this level, in its largely stabilizing/destabilizing role, superstructure (and superstructure at its most oppositional) *can* impinge on infrastructure.

LANDLORD/TENANT RELATIONS

We are all aware that landlords and tenants exist in a fundamentally antagonistic relationship with one another. Generally speaking, throughout most of what we might call the middle classes of our society, landlords tend to be somewhat better off financially than their tenants. Certainly the class war is as strong there as between any groups save, perhaps, workers and employers.

With that in mind, here is a tale:

A black woman born in Nottaway, Virginia, my maternal grandmother came from Petersburg to New York City at age eighteen, in 1898, and moved to Harlem in 1902 when it was still a German neighborhood. With my grandfather, an elevator operator in a downtown office building and later a Grand

Central Terminal redcap, she took rooms in the first house in Harlem open to blacks, on 132nd Street, between Seventh Avenue and Lenox Avenue. Owned by a black man married to a white woman, the house rented to men and women working as servants in the neighborhood. My grandmother told of returning to her rooms after work, while the Germans, sitting in front of their houses along Seventh Avenue played zithers through the evening.

On Morris Avenue in the Bronx, on Mount Morris Park in Manhattan, on Macdonnah Street and Carroll Street in Bedford Stuyvesant, and on Seventh Avenue and LaSalle Street in Manhattan again, my grandparents lived up through my grandfather's death at 72 in 1952 until Grandma's own death at 102 in 1982.

A number of times in the sixties and seventies, Grandma spoke of the social practice in the twenties, thirties, and, in a few places, into the forties, of the landlord's annual or sometimes semiannual visit to her apartment: my sense was that these visits were notably different from the monthly visits *to* the landlord to pay the rent—in the days before universal banking.

Expected by both tenants and landlords, the visits allowed tenants to point out directly to the building's owner any breakages, or repairs that were needed. The owner got a chance to see how the tenant was treating his or her property. By opening the door for less formal ones, these visits established an arena for social interchange. From them, landlords gained a sense of the tenants as individuals. Tenants got a sense of the landlord as a person.

In no way did this social practice obviate the socio-economic antagonism between the *classes*. But it tended to stabilize relationships at the personal level and restrict conflict to the economic level itself—keeping it from spilling over into other, personal situations.

Yes, there might be a spate of cleaning in the apartment in the days before the landlord came. Certainly there might be a rush of painters and plumbers in that same month—so that, during the visit itself, everyone might come off at his or her best. But the visits meant that in those situations in which there were problems on either side that could be resolved only by the greater forces of the class war itself (an eviction, a suit against a landlord for a major dereliction of necessary repairs), there was nevertheless a social field in which either side could ask for leniency or at least understanding from the other; and often it could be granted. Similarly, either side could personally entreat the other to straighten up and fly right. Many times this was enough to avert major confrontations.

What eroded this practice of landlord visits were, first, the economic forces of the Depression. Pressures on tenants (from the exhaustion of having two or three jobs to the anomie of having no job at all) became such that they began housing extra materials or extra people in their apartments, to the point where a good weekend's cleaning could not cover over the evidence. Models for bourgeois living standards became less available, as did the time and energy to implement them.

Landlords found themselves unable to afford keeping the facilities in the first-class shape tenants expected.

Tenants began to see the visits as prying.

Landlords began to see the visits as a formal responsibility empty of content and—finally—an unnecessary nuisance, in which they had to listen to demands they could not afford to meet.

Repair work was now delegated to a superintendent, whose job was to carry out those repairs as inexpensively as possible. While more stringent rules were instituted to restrict property-damaging wear and tear, in practice tenants were now allowed greater leeway in what they might do to the house. Older tenants saw the failure of the landlord to visit as a dereliction of responsibility. But younger tenants cited the "privilege" of better-off tenants in more lavish properties, often paying far higher rents, to forego such visits. Why shouldn't the privilege of the better off be a right—the right of privacy—for all?

For the last twenty-one years, I have lived in a fifth-floor walk-up, rent-stabilized apartment at the corner of Amsterdam and 82nd Street. In that time, the owner of the building has *never* been through my apartment door. Once, five years ago, he shouted threats of legal action against me from the landing below—threats which came to nothing when, in retaliation, I hired a lawyer. This past February, when what became a four-alarm fire broke out in the building at five in the morning, he visited his property for a brief half hour at 7:30 A.M. and, standing out on the street among the fire engines, declared how grateful he was that no one had been hurt, then—in his shako and (the only man I've ever seen wear one) fur-collared overcoat—left. But those are the only two times I have ever seen him in person—or he has ever, I assume, seen me.

On the one hand, when repairs have been needed, and even more so after that brief shouting match in the hall, occasionally I've thought that the more personal relations my grandmother maintained with her landlord during the early decades of this century might well have made things go more easily. Were my landlord someone with whom, twice a year, I sat over a cup of coffee in my kitchen, I might have been able to negotiate speedier, and better quality, repairs—repairs for which, often, I would have been willing to share the financial weight; repairs which would have benefited the property itself. And certainly we both might have bypassed the emotional strain of the aforementioned shouting match.

On the other hand, I try to imagine my landlord's response if he had visited during the first ten months after I had to collapse my Amherst apartment with my New York digs (when I was under precisely the same sort of socio-economic pressures that had eroded away the practice of visits in the first place), and my apartment's back three rooms looked more like an over-full Jersey warehouse space than a home with people living in it. What if he had come during the previous five years when, regularly, I let friends use the place, two and three times a month, as an Upper West Side party space? (More than half a dozen years after the fact, I still meet people who tell me they have been to "great parties" at "my" house, when I wasn't in attendance.) During the same period, I let a succession of friends and acquaintances stay there during the 130-odd days a year I was in Amherst, teaching at the University of Massachusetts. Such visits would have curtailed such practices severely—though, in neither case, on my side or on his, was the *letter* of the law violated.

At the rhetorical level, traces of the social practice my decade-and-a-half dead grandmother spoke of linger in the language, as tenants in the Upper West Side still speak of our landlords' "seeing to" certain repairs—even though the landlord will not and does not intend to set eyes on anything within the front door of the building—just as the term "landlord" is, itself, a rhetorical holdover from a time and set of social practices when the *important* things the owner was "lord" over were, indeed, "land," and the "tenants to the land," rather than the buildings erected on it.

The betraying signs that one discourse has displaced or transformed into another is often the smallest rhetorical shift: a temporal moment (and a sociological location) in the transformation between a homosexual discourse and a gay discourse may be signaled by the appearance in the 1969 Fall issues of the *Village Voice* of the locution "coming out to" one's (straight) friends, coworkers, and family (a verbal act directed toward straights) and its subsequent displacement of the demotic locution "coming out into" (gay) society—a metaphor for one's first major gay sexual act. Between the two locutions lie Stonewall and the post-Stonewall activities of the gay liberation movement. Equally such a sign might be seen to lie at another moment, at another location, in the changeover from "that's such a camp" to "that's camp." The intervening event there is Susan Sontag's 1964 *Partisan Review* essay, "Notes on Camp." I have written of how a shift in postal discourse may be signed by the rhetorical shift between "she would not receive his letters" and "she would not open his letter." What intervened here was the 1840 introduction of the postage stamp, which changed letter writing from an art and entertainment paid for by the receiver to a form of vanity publishing paid for by the sender. (There *was* no junk mail before 1840.) One might detect a shift in the discourse of literature by the changeover from "George is in literature" to "George's library contains mostly history and literature." The explosion of print in the 1880s, occasioned by the typewriter and the linotype, intervenes. The shift from landlord visits to superintendents in charge of repairs is signaled by the rhetorical shift between "the landlord saw to the repairs" as a literal statement and "the landlord saw to the repairs" as a metaphor. I say "shifts," but these rhetorical pairings are much better looked at, on the level of discourse, as rhetorical collisions. The sign that a discursive collision has occurred is that the former meaning has been forgotten and the careless reader, not alert to the details of the changed social context, reads the older rhetorical figure as if it were the newer.

As are the space of the unconscious and the space of discourse, the space where the class war occurs as such is, in its pure form, imaginary—imaginary *not* in the Lacanian sense but rather in the mathematical sense. (In the Lacanian sense, those spaces are specifically Symbolic.) Imaginary numbers— those involved with i, the square root of minus-one—do not exist. But they have measurable and demonstrable effects on the real (i.e., political) materiality of science and technology. Similarly, the structures, conflicts, and displacements that occur in the unconscious, the class war, and the space of discourse are simply too useful to ignore in explaining what goes on in the world we live in, unto two men yelling in the hall, one a landlord and one a tenant, if not mayhem out on the streets themselves, or the visible changes over a decade or so in a neighborhood like Times Square or, indeed, the Upper West Side. Often, like many contemporary theorists, I have wondered if all three spaces aren't in their fundamental form, the same.

An important point: I do not think it is, in any way, shape, or form, nostalgic to say that, under such a social practice as my grandmother knew, both landlord and tenant were better off than I am today. The practice was a social arena of communication which, when utilized fully, meant that both landlord and tenant had to expend more time, energy and money in order to maintain a generally higher standard of living by the tenant and a generally higher level of property upkeep by the landlord, restricting the abuse of that property, from which both landlord and tenant benefited. On both tenant and landlord, greater restrictions obtained as to what was expected and what was not. The practice eroded when the money was no longer there, when the time and energy had to be turned, by both, to other things, and when practices formerly unacceptable to both had, now, to be accepted, so that the visits finally became a futile annoyance to both sides and were dropped.

The establishment of tenant associations—at which landlords are occasionally invited to speak and meet with their tenants—*begins* to fulfill the vacuum in the array of social practices that erosion leaves.

But they do not fill it in the same way.

To repeat: given the mode of capitalism under which we live, life is at its most rewarding, productive and pleasant when the greatest number of people understand, appreciate, and seek out interclass contact and communication conducted in a mode of good will. The class war raging constantly and often silently in the comparatively stabilized societies of the developed world militates for the erosion of the social practices through which interclass communication takes place and the institutions holding those practices stable, so that new institutions must always be conceived and set in place to take over the jobs of those that are battered again and again till they are destroyed. While the establishment and utilization of those institutions always involves specific social practices, the effects of my primary and secondary theses are regularly perceived at the level of discourse. Thus, it is only by a constant renovation of the concept of discourse that society can maintain the most conscientious and informed field for the establishment of such institutions and practices—a critique necessary if new institutions of any efficacy are to develop. At this level, in its largely stabilizing/destabilizing role, superstructure (and superstructure at its most oppositional) *can* impinge on infrastructure.

So stated, these points appear harmless enough. Over the last decade and a half, however, a notion of safety had arisen, a notion that runs from safe sex (once it becomes anything more than using condoms when anally penetrated by males of unknown—or, of course, positive—HIV status, whether you are male or female) and safe neighborhoods, to safe cities, and committed (that is, safe) relationships, a notion that currently functions much in the way the notions of "security" and "conformity" did in the fifties. As, in the name of "safety," society dismantles the various institutions that promote interclass communication, attempts to critique the way such institutions functioned in the past to promote their happier sides are often seen as, at best, nostalgia for an outmoded past and, at worst, a pernicious glorification of everything dangerous—unsafe sex, neighborhoods filled with undesirables (read "unsafe characters"), promiscuity—and an attack on the family and the stable social structure, with dangerous, non-committed, "unsafe" relationships (i.e., those not modeled on the bourgeois notion of monogamous marriage) held up in their place.

CONTACT/NETWORKING

The practice of landlord visits to tenants in the twenties, thirties, and forties can be looked at as sitting directly between two modes of social practice today. The two modes of social practice I shall discuss and the discourse around them that allow them to be visible as such I designate as "contact" and "networking." Like all social practices they create/sediment discourses even as discourses create, individuate and inform with value the material and social objects that facilitate and form the institutions that both support and contour these practices.

Contact is the conversation that starts in the line at the grocery counter with the person behind you while the clerk is changing the paper roll in the cash register. It is the pleasantries exchanged with a neighbor who has brought her chair out to take some air on the stoop. It is the discussion that begins with the person next to you at a bar. It can be the conversation that starts with any number of semi-officials or service persons—mailman, policeman, librarian, store clerk or counter person. It can also be two men watching each other masturbate together in adjacent urinals of a public john—an encounter which—later—may or may not become a conversation. For contact—very importantly—is also the intercourse, physical and conversational, that blooms in and as "casual sex," in public rest rooms, sex movies, public parks, singles bars, sex clubs and on street corners with heavy hustling traffic, and the adjoining motels or the apartments of one or another participant, from which non-sexual friendships and/or acquaintances lasting for decades or a lifetime may spring, not to mention the conversation of a john with a prostitute or hustler encountered on one or another sidewalk, street corner, or in a bar. Mostly, these contact encounters are merely pleasant chats, adding a voice to a face now and again encountered in the neighborhood. But I recall one such supermarket-line conversation that turned out to be with a woman who'd done graduate work on the Russian poet Zinaida Hippius, just when I happened to be teaching Dmitri Merezhkovsky's Christ and Anti-Christ trilogy in a graduate seminar at the University of Mas-sachusetts: Merezhkovsky was Hippius's husband, and I was able to get some interesting and pertinent information about the couple's wanderings in the early years of the century.

I have at least one straight male friend who, on half-a-dozen occasions, has gotten editorial jobs for women he first met and befriended as they were working as topless dancers in various strip clubs that put them on the fringe of the sex workers' service profession.

Another supermarket-line conversation was with a young man who was an aspiring director, looking for some science fiction stories to turn into teleplays; I was able to jot down for him a quick bibliography of young writers and short stories that he might pursue. Whether or not it came to anything, I have no way of knowing. But it was easy and fun.

Still another time, it was a young woman casting director who needed someone to play the small part of a fisherman in a film she was working on, who decided I would be perfect for it. And I found myself with a weekend acting job.

Contact encounters so dramatic are rare—but real. The more ordinary sorts of contact yield *their* payoff in moments of crisis: when there is a fire in your building, it may be the people who have been exchanging pleasantries with you for years who take you into their home for an hour or a day, or even overnight. Contact includes the good Samaritans at traffic accidents (the two women who picked me up and got me a cab when my cane gave way and I fell on the street, dislocating a finger), or even the neighbor who, when you've forgotten your keys at the office and are locked out of your apartment, invites you in for coffee and lets you use her phone to call a locksmith; or, as once happened to me in the mid-sixties when my then-neighborhood, the Lower East Side, was at its most neighborly and under the influence of the counter-culture, a London guest arrived on Wednesday when I was out of town and expecting him on Thursday. Someone living across the street, who didn't know me at all, saw a stranger with two suitcases on my apartment stoop looking bewildered, invited him in to wait for me, then eventually put him up for a night until I returned.

And finally: my lover of eight years, Dennis, and I first met when he was homeless and selling books from a blanket spread out on Seventy-second Street. Our two best friends for many years now are a gay male couple, one of whom I first met in a sexual encounter, perhaps a decade ago, at the back of the now closed-down Variety Photoplays Movie Theater on Second Avenue just below Fourteenth Street. Outside my family, these are among the two most rewarding relationships I have: both began as cross-class contacts in a public space.

Visitors to New York might be surprised that such occurrences are central to my vision of the City at its healthiest. Lifetime residents won't be. Watching the metamorphosis of such vigil and concern into considered and helpful action is what gives one a faithful and loving attitude toward one's neighborhood, one's city, one's nation, the world.

I have taken "contact," both term and concept, from Jane Jacobs's instructive 1961 study, *The Death and Life of Great American Cities*. Jacobs describes contact as a fundamentally urban phenomenon and finds it necessary for everything from neighborhood safety to a general sense of social well-being. She sees it supported by a strong sense of private and public in a field of socio-economic diversity that mixes living spaces with a variety of commercial spaces, which, in turn must provide a variety of human services if contact is to function in a pleasant and rewarding manner.

Jacobs's analysis stops short of contact as a specifically stabilizing practice in interclass relations—signaled by her (largely understandable in the pre-Stonewall 1950s when she was collecting material for her book, but nevertheless unfortunate) dismissal of "pervert parks" as necessarily social blights—though she *was* ready to acknowledge the positive roles winos and destitute alcoholics played in stabilizing the quality of neighborhood life at a *higher* level than a neighborhood would maintain without them.[1] She also confuses contact with community. Urban contact is often at its most spectacularly beneficial when it involves members of different communities. I would recommend her analysis, though I would add that, like so much American thinking on the left, it lacks not so much a class analysis as an *interclass* analysis. But let's go back to my primary thesis; that's where the action is.

There is, of course, another way to meet people. It's called "networking." Networking is what people have to do when those with like interests live too far apart to be thrown together in public spaces through chance and propinquity. Networking is what people in small towns have to do to establish any complex cultural life today.

But contemporary "networking" is notably different from "contact."

At first one is tempted to set contact and networking in opposition: networking tends to be professional and motive driven, it crosses class lines only in the most vigilant manner, and it is heavily dependent on institutions to promote the necessary propinquity (gyms, parties, twelve-step programs, conferences, reading groups, singing groups, social gatherings, workshops, tourist groups, classes) where those with the requisite social skills can maneuver.

The benefits of networking are real and can look—especially from the outside—quite glamorous. But I believe that, today, such benefits are fundamentally misunderstood. More and more people are depending on networking to provide benefits that are far more likely to occur in contact situations—and that networking is specifically prevented from providing for a variety of reasons.

I shall now abridge a set of hysterically funny anecdotes about examples of networking that would leave you rolling in the aisles, concerning the various attempts I have seen by young writers at various writers' conferences to get the attention of the people whom they perceived as powerful, attempts that ranged from displaying real talent in unusual ways to crawling into bed with various and sundry people they feel might do well by them. The final point of all the anecdotes is: none of these efforts worked.

I attend writers' conferences regularly—and science fiction conventions even more so. The clear and explicable reasons for my attendance *are* networking's epistemological benefits. Those networking benefits result from the particularly dense field produced by the networking situation in which knowledge—*not* social favors—moves with particular speed. (The desire for social favor *is* the fuel—or the form—which propels that information through the networking field.) At both formal sessions and informal gatherings, I find out about new writers and interesting books. As well I learn about new publishing programs and changes in the business much more quickly than I would without them. By the same token, people find out about what I'm doing and get a clearer picture of my work. Because I'm comparatively comfortable appearing in public and discussing a range of topics from a podium or from behind a panel table, people can get a taste of the sort of analysis I do and can decide whether they want to pursue these thoughts in my nonfiction critical work. Since I am an academic critic as well as a fiction writer—and a fiction writer who works in several genres—this is particularly useful and promotes, in a small group of concerned readers at least, a more informed sense of my enterprise.

I feel my career benefits regularly from the results of my networking. My ultimate take on networking is, however, this: no single event in the course of my career has been directly *caused by* networking. Nevertheless, the results of networking have regularly smoothed, stabilized, and supported my career and made it more pleasant than it would have been without it.

In general I would say (and I would say this to young writers particularly): rarely if ever can networking make a writing career when no career is to be made. Regularly, though, it can support and make a career function more easily and smoothly.

One does not get publication by appearing in public.

One gets further invitations to appear in public.

Above and beyond its epistemological benefits, networking produces more opportunities to network—and that's about all.

The writer will do best if he or she has a clear sense of the two different processes.

Briefly, what makes "networking" a different process from "contact" is that the networking situation, unlike the contact situation, is one in which the fundamental competition between all the people gathered together in the group within which the networking is supposed to occur is far higher than it is in the population among which contact occurs.

The competition may be only barely perceptible at any given moment, or, under the camaraderie and good will of the occasion, all but invisible—it *is* the class war. Like the overriding economic forces of the class war and its effects on the individuals whose lives are caught up in and radically changed by it, they are seldom experienced *as* a force. That competition is pervasive nevertheless. Because of this the social price tag on the exchange of favors and friendly gestures is much higher here than it is in contact situations.

The people in line with you at the grocery counter are rarely *competing* with you for the items on the shelves in the way that young writers are competing for the comparatively rare number of publishing slots for first novels that can, under the best of conditions, appear each year. And they are not—at the moment—in competitive relations at all for the favors (whether of data or material help) that the established writer might be able to offer.

I'm now going to summarize another anecdote, famous in the science fiction field, of how in the mid–1950s, Ray Bradbury first came to the attention of readers beyond the boundaries of the science fiction "ghetto" (as it has been called).

Having been published the year before, Bradbury's second hardcover collection of stories, *The Martian Chronicles* (1951), was on a remainder table in Brentano's Bookstore, then on Eighth Street in Greenwich Village. In the bookstore to buy up a few of the volumes, the young Bradbury struck up a conversation with a man standing next to him. Bradbury pointed out that, at the same time, newspapers and literary magazines ignored *all* SF books that came in, leaving them unread, giving them, at best, a "Books Received" mention. His volume had gotten almost no reviews in the course of its shelf life.

Bradbury was articulate enough about the situation that the man—who turned out to be the writer Christopher Isherwood—was struck by his argument. A few issues on, in the weekly the *Saturday Review of Literature*, Isherwood (a regular reviewer for the magazine, who happened to have some say in what books he covered—a rare situation) took it upon himself to review Bradbury's book of poetic SF tales, so unlike the usual pulp fare of the day. The review was more or less favorable. In the same review Isherwood also mentioned the situation that Bradbury had outlined. The review and the position it adopted became somewhat notorious, and, as the first SF writer to be reviewed in the *Saturday Review of Literature* (and the last for *quite* a while!), Bradbury's career moved to a new level, from which it has never really retreated.

The first thing to realize in the rehearsal of such a mythic tale, is that, in all its elements—the chance meeting in a bookstore, the happenstance conversation with a stranger over the remainder table—quintessentially it's a tale of "contact," *not* "networking." Also, the contact brought about the *reviewing* of a book already in print, not the *publication* of one still in manuscript—as most of the attendees at writing conferences are hoping for.

For precisely the competition reasons I outlined before, this is the sort of occurrence not likely to happen at a writers' conference, i.e., in a situation set up for networking. Though in the case of science fiction, often with the tale of Bradbury and Isherwood burning brightly in their imaginations, young unpublished hopefuls flock to science fiction conventions in the muffled hope that something like that will happen to them.

In such a networking situation there might well be a panel presentation on the difficulties or impossibilities of science fiction securing good review venues. Such a panel might mean that, instead of flickering as a vague and passing notion, now and again, in the minds of one or three writers specifically faced with it, the problem would, for the next few months be a subject known about by an entire population of writers and readers, who were now also aware of the forces keeping the problem in place. Thus, if a chance to break through it arose, that chance would occur in a field that has been primed to a greater awareness of, if not sympathy for, the problem. (*That* is the benefit of networking.) Unfortunately today, unclear on the difference between the results each mode fosters, too many people go into networking situations expecting or hoping for the results of contact. Too many people shy away from contact, or condone the destruction of social forms that promote contact because they feel networking will compensate for it. It can't.

The reason the networking situation is not likely to produce the sometimes considerable rewards that can come from contact situations is because the *amount* of need present in the networking situation is too high for the comparatively few individuals in a position to supply the material boons and favors *to distribute them in any equitable manner.* The pleasant and chatty cash bar reception at the end of the first day of panels and workshops at the writers conference, may *look* like a friendly and sociable gathering, but at the socioeconomic level, where the class war occurs, the situation is analogous to a crowd of seventy-five or a hundred beggars pressed around a train station in some underdeveloped colonial protectorate, while a handful of bourgeois tourists make their way through, hoping to find a taxi to take them off to the hotel before they are set upon and torn to pieces.

As with the practices described by my grandmother of tenant and landlord in the kitchen over a cup of coffee, the social practices and friendly interchanges that not only appear to, but *do*, fill the writers' conference reception halls, work to stabilize, retard and mitigate the forces of the class war. In no way, however, can they halt or resolve that war. They can allow it to proceed in a more humane manner, maintaining "war" merely as a metaphor. In such situations, stabilization mitigates for *less* change in the power relations at the infrastructure level than might happen in a less concentrated and less competitive situation, even while existing social relations, happenstance, and sometimes even merit might appear to be producing the odd "star" or lucky social "winner."

Two orders of social force are always at work. One set is centripetal and works to hold a given class stable. Another set is centrifugal and works to break a given class apart.

The first set runs from identity, through familiarity, to lethargy, to fear of difference—all of which work to hold a class together. These are the forces that the networking situation must appeal to, requisition, and exploit.

The second set has to do with the needs and desires that define the class in the first place: hunger, sex, ambition in any one of a dozen directions—spatial to economic to aesthetic or intellectual. These forces militate toward breaking up a class, driving it apart, and sending individuals off into other class arenas. This is the level at which, in a democracy, contact functions as an anti-entropic method of changing various individuals' material class groundings. The reason these forces work the way they do is simply because when such desires and needs concentrate at too great a density in too small a social space over too brief a time, they become that much harder to fulfill—even when you pay generous honoraria to people who might help fill them, to move briefly into that crowded social space and dispense data about the process, without dispensing the actual rewards and boons that those involved in the process seek.

Recently when I outlined the differences between contact and networking to a friend, he came back with the following examples: "Contact is Jimmy Stewart; networking is Tom Cruise. Contact is complex carbohydrates. Networking is simple sugar. Contact is Zen. Networking is Scientology. Contact can effect changes at the infrastructural level; networking effects changes at the superstructural level."

Amusing as these examples are, it's important to speak about the very solid benefits of both forms of sociality. Otherwise we risk falling into some dualistic schema, with wonderful, free-form, authentic, Dionysian contact on the one side, and terrible, calculating, inauthentic, Apollonian networking on the other.

Such would be sad and absurd. The way to do this is not to install the two concepts in our minds as some sort of equal, objective and unquestioned pair of opposites. Rather we must analyze both, so that we can see that elements in each have clear and definite hierarchical relations with elements in the other, as well as what other elements are shared. But this sort of vigilant approach alone will produce a clear idea of what to expect (and not to expect) from one and the other—as well as produce some clear knowledge of why we should not try to displace one *with* the other and ask one to fulfill the other's job.

In terms of the Bradbury tale, Greenwich Village in the 'fifties was, for example, a neighborhood in which the chance of two writers running into one another at a bookstore remainder table were far higher than they would have been, say, three miles away across the river in a supermarket in Queens.

The same could be said of the Upper West Side, where I managed to snag the information about Zenaida Hippius or, indeed, the Variety Photoplays Theater, where I met my long-term social friend, standing as it did, between the East and West Village.

Were we so naïve as to assert that in networking situations *there were* selection procedures while in contact situations *there were none*, we would only be rushing to set up false and invalid oppositions.

But while contact may be, by comparison, "random" (but doesn't one move to—or from—a particular neighborhood as part of a desire to be among, or to avoid—certain types of people, whether that neighborhood be Greenwich Village, Bensonhurst, or Beverly Hills?), and while networking may be, by comparison, "planned" (yet how many times do we return from the professional conference unable, a month later, to retain any useful idea?), it is clear that contact is contoured, if not organized, by earlier decisions, desires, commercial interests, zoning laws and immigration patterns. The differences seem to be rather matters of scale; the looser streets of the neighborhood versus the more condensed hotel or conference center spaces and the granularity that allows others to dilute the social density with a range of contrasting needs and desires, as well as differences in social skills and, yes, institutional access.

Contact is likely to be its most useful when it is cross-class contact. Bradbury and Isherwood were, arguably, in the same profession, that is, both were writers. But they were also clearly at different class levels: beginning genre writer and established literary writer. Contact begins to be perceived as bad with the suspicion that the person standing next to you at the remainder table or on the supermarket line or at the corner is not another writer, but is probably homeless or notably poorer than you are; that is, someone whose needs are too great to be handled by personal interchange.

Two modes of social practice: I call them contact and networking. They designate two discourses that, over the range of society, conflict with and displace each other, re-establish themselves in new or old landscapes, where, at the level of verbal interaction, they deposit their rhetorical traces . . .

In one nineteenth-century novel that I've recently been teaching, Flaubert's *L'Education sentimentale*, the two most important relationships for the protagonist, Frédéric Moreau, are definitely contact relationships. Foremost is his relation with Monsieur and Madame Arnoux: In the first chapter he is attracted to Madame Arnoux as she sits on the deck of a ferry leaving Paris for the countryside along the Seine. The meeting is impelled wholly by desire, and Frédéric must put out a good deal of energy to make the contact occur, and stabilize it as a social friendship across class boundaries (provincial bourgeois youth/urban sophisticate adults). The other relation is with Dussardier, whom he meets in a street demonstration, when he and a Bohemian friend, Hussonet—also just met—decide, all-but-arbitrarily, to rescue the young worker from the clutches of the police. Both these relationships have elements of the tragic about them: Frédéric's inability to possess Madame Arnoux causes him a pain that pervades and contaminates every subsequent love relationship of his life. And Frédéric uses and abuses Dussardier in a positively shameful manner: Frédéric tells his bourgeois friends that Dussardier has committed a 12,000–franc theft (which Frédéric uses as an excuse to borrow a like amount to bail out M. Arnoux's family) and, because the young man is working class, none of Frédéric's friends thinks to question this. But when one compares *these* relationships to two that Frédéric has acquired through networking, they come off pretty well. Compare them with his relationship to Madame Dambreuse, the fantastically avaricious and vicious widow whom Frédéric barely escapes marrying: Frédéric knows her because he is given a letter of introduction by M. Rocque to her husband, the business tycoon M. Dambreuse—pure networking. The other distinctly networking relation is Frédéric's deeply vexing friendship with Sénécal, the mathematician who believes in a purely scientific politics—to whom Frédéric is first sent by his school friend Charles Deslauriers. In short, his networking ends up aligning him with extremely—even lethally—vicious men and women. Frédéric's fiancée-through-networking, Madame Dambreuse, delights in the destruction of the social standing of his love-object through contact, Madame Arnoux, when the Arnoux's personal belongings are sold at auction.

At the book's end, Frédéric's networking friend Sénécal runs his contact friend Dussardier through with a sword during a military encounter. Confronted with Madame Dambreuse's viciousness, Frédéric escapes. But his own ability to love has been sadly, permanently injured. Nevertheless, because the allegory of contact relations vs. networking relations plays out identically with both a man *and* a woman, it's hard to avoid the suggestion that the antipathy between friends or lovers acquired by networking and those acquired by contact may well have been a part of Flaubert's complex structure.

THE TIMES SQUARE DEVELOPMENT

Starting in 1985, in the name of "safe sex," New York City began to criminalize every individual sex act by name, from masturbation to vaginal intercourse, whether performed with a condom or not—a legal situation that has catastrophic ramifications we may not crawl out from under for a long, long time. This is a legal move that arguably puts gay liberation, for example, back to a point notably before Stonewall—and doesn't do much for heterosexual freedom either.

This is a rhetorical change that may well adhere to an extremely important discursive intervention in the legal contouring of social practices whose ramifications, depending on the development and the establishment of new social practices that promote communication between the classes are hard to foresee in any detail—though it is not hard to foresee them as, generally and overall, detrimental.

The legal changes were set in place to facilitate the Times Square takeover by the Times Square Development Association.

At a conference at Columbia University sponsored by the Buell Architecture Center ("Times Square: Global, Local," March 1997), organized by Marshal Blonsky on the renovation of Times Square, the keynote speaker was Marshall Berman. The general sense I received (though it would be stunningly incorrect to call it a consensus) extended from, on the one hand, the view that, outside the general difficulties involved in going ahead with the project, there was no problem at all because the developers and architects were supremely sensitive to the needs of the city and its populace (a position put forward by spokesperson-architect Robert Stern) to, on the other hand, an only slightly less sanguine view (put forward by Berman) that, if there *was* a problem, we might as well go along with it, since there was nothing we could do about it anyway.

At the Buell Conference a young sociologist countered my suggestion that there were some serious losses involved in the renovation process with the counter suggestion that the new Times Square would at least be safer for women. This is a point I shall return to. But I begin by noting a smaller point she made and the context in which she made it. During the question period after her presentation, she was speaking of the history of New York City's subway system. She said: "When the subway system first opened, your subway token only cost you a nickel, and the price of a subway token remained a nickel for almost fifty years."

When in 1904 the Times Square Station of the IRT subway opened, no subway tokens, of course, were used at all. The nickel fare, for which the city was so long famous, went directly into the slot of the subway turnstile.

> And down beside the turnstile pressed the coin
> Into the slot . . .
> "fandaddle daddy don't ask for change—*IS THIS*
> *FOURTEENTH? . . .*"

wrote Hart Crane, in "The Tunnel," in 1927, the penultimate section of his great poetic mosaic of American sensibilities, *The Bridge*. Well, the coin was a nickel and the place you got it was the change booth. I didn't correct the sociologist when she made her error; my question here, however, a prologue to my discussion of still another venue where networking is eroding contact, is what would the status of such a correction have been, had it been made? What is the status of the failure of someone with the available facts to offer it? Would stating the fact have been a simple and unencumbered rectification of an

Queer Ideas

inadvertent error, and by extension, my failure to state it simply another such error? Would it have been a gesture of nostalgia to an earlier vision of the transportation system? Would it have been the assertion of an authentic image of the past in place of an inauthentic image and thus the failure to state it a momentary triumph of such inauthenticity? Or was it a mild, momentary slip of no particular consequence, so that pointing it out would have been an equally mild moment of embarrassment, which I sidestepped by overlooking it with no harm to the general social good? Or was it a case of a hard-edged objective truth and an equally hard-edged objective falsity, the replacement of one by the other another case of the evanescence of knowledge of the past and the displacement by ignorance based on our assumption of a universal present? Frankly, I believe all of these would have been the case, and what's more, inescapable. But I also maintain that none of these, for the purposes for our discussion here, are particularly interesting. What interests me, is that the encounter of the two facts represents a rhetorical detail and a rhetorical collision, which is a moment in the process by which one material discourse can be seen to give way to another, to have been revised by, and to have eroded away, another.

The Times Square problem I perceive entails the economic "redevelopment" of a highly diversified neighborhood, with working class residences and small human services (groceries, drugstores, liquor stores, dry cleaners, diners, and specialty shops ranging from electronic stores and tourist shops to theatrical memorabilia and comic book stores, interlarding a series of theaters, film and stage rehearsal spaces, retailers of theatrical equipment, from lights to make-up, as well as inexpensive hotels, furnished rooms, and restaurants at every level, also bars and the sexually-orientated businesses that, in one form or another, have thrived in the neighborhood since the 1880s) giving way to an upper middle class ring of luxury apartments around a ring of tourist hotels clustering around a series of theaters and restaurants in the center of which a large mall, and a cluster of office towers, is slowly but inexorably coming into being.

Let's speak a bit about the four great office towers that will be the center of the new Times Square.

The generally erroneous assumption about how new buildings make money is something like this: a big company acquires the land, clears it for construction, and commences to build. After three to five years, when the building is complete, the company rents out the apartments or the offices. If the building is a success and all the spaces are leased and the site is a popular one, then and only then does the corporation that owns the building begin to see profits on its earlier outlays and investments. Thus the ultimate success of the building as a habitation is pivotal to the building's future economic success.

If this were the way new office buildings were actually built, however, few would even be considered, much less actually begun.

Here is an only somewhat simplified picture of how the process *actually* works. Simplified though it is, it gives a much better idea of what goes on and how money is made, nevertheless:

A large corporation decides to build a building. It acquires some land. Now it sets up an extremely small ownership corporation, which is tied to the parent corporation by a lot of very complicated contracts—but is a different and autonomous corporation, nevertheless. That ownership corporation, tiny as it may be, is now ready to build the building. The parent corporation also sets up a much larger construction corporation, which hires diggers, subcontracts construction companies, and generally oversees the building proper.

The little ownership corporation now borrows a lot of money from a bank—enough to pay the construction corporation for constructing the building proper. The small ownership corporation also sells stock to investors—enough to pay back the bank loan. The tiny ownership corporation (an office, a secretary and a few officers who oversee things) proceeds to pay the parent construction corporation with the bank funds to build the building. It uses the stock funds to pay back the bank. Figured in the cost of the building is a healthy margin of profit for the parent corporation—the large corporation which got the whole project started—while the investors pay off the bank, so that *it* doesn't get twisted out of shape.

Yes, if the building turns out to be a stunningly popular address, then (remember all those contracts?) profits will be substantially greater than otherwise. But millions of dollars of profits will be made by the parent corporation just from the construction of the building alone, even if not a single space in it is ever rented out. (Movies are made in the same manner, which is why so many awful ones hit the screen. By the time they are released, the producers have long since taken the money and, as it were, run.) Believing in the myth of profit only in return for investments, public investors will swallow the actual cost of the building's eventual failure—if it fails—while the ownership corporation is reduced in size to nothing or next to nothing: an office in the building on which no rent is paid, a secretary and/or an answering machine, and a nominal head (with another major job somewhere else) on minimal salary who comes in once a month to check in . . . if that.

Two facts should now be apparent:

First Fact: the Times Square Development Corporation *wants* to build those offices towers.

Renting them out is secondary, even if the failure to rent them is a major catastrophe for the city, turning the area into a glass and aluminum graveyard. A truth of high-finance capitalism tends to get away from even the moderately well-off investor (the successful doctor or lawyer, say, bringing in two- to four-hundred thousand a year), though this truth is, indeed, what *makes* capitalism: in short-term speculative business ventures of (to choose an arbitrary cut-off point) more than three million dollars, such as a building or civic center, (Second Fact) the profits to be made from dividing the money up and moving it around over the one to six years, during which that money must be spent, easily offset any losses from the possible failure of the enterprise itself as a speculative endeavor, once it's completed.

The interest on a million dollars at 6.5 percent is about 250 dollars a *day*. On a good conservative portfolio it will be 400 dollars a day; and the interest on ten million dollars is ten times that. The Times Square Corporation is determined to build those buildings. The question is: how long will it take to persuade investors to swallow the uselessness of the project for them?

Far more important than whether the buildings can be rented out or not is whether *investors think the buildings can be rented out*. In the 1970s, three of the four office towers were tabled for ten years, because a few years ago, enough people pointed out the impossibility of renting them, that investors were wary and the project had to be put off. The ostensible purpose of that ten-year delay was to give economic forces a chance to shift and business a chance to rally to the area. The real reason, however, was simply the hope that people would forget the arguments against the project, so clear in so many people's minds at the time. Indeed, the crushing arguments against the whole project from the middle 1970s were, by the middle 1980s, largely forgotten, the forgetting of which has allowed the project to take its opening steps over the last ten years. Public relations corporations have been given another decade to make the American investing public forget the facts of the matter and convince that same public that the Times Square project is a sound one. Right now, it looks to me as if we can forget how the nickel fare functioned, we can forget anything. The interim plan, which we should also take a look at now claims to gamble on the possibility that the economic situation might be better—at which point the developers will go ahead with those towers, towers which, Mr. Stern has told us, *will* be built.

Berman's article in *Dissent*, which I will refer to, concludes with a P.S.: it begins, "I have just read in the *Times* of August 1 [1997], about a deal in the works to bring Reuters to Times Square. It wants to build an 800,000–square foot office tower on Seventh Avenue and Forty-second Street." He goes on to say that Reuters is an interesting company (as if it would have anything more to do with the building than, perhaps, rent 10 percent, or less, of its space) and he seems appalled that the awful Philip Johnson plan, designed over a decade ago will be utilized for the construction—as if, for a moment, *anyone* in a position of power involved in the deal cared. (Millions were paid for it; it must be used.) He concludes by suggesting that people who care about the square raise the roof before the deal gets done. Well, this is a networking situation: consider my roof raised.

CROSS-CLASS CONTACT

From here I want to survey three topics—topics I will look at as systems of social practice related by contact: (1) the public sex practices that have been attacked and so summarily wiped out of the Times Square area; (2) crime and violence on the street: (3) the general safety of the neighborhood—and the problem of safety for women.

First, the street-level public sex that the area was famous for, the sex movies, the peep-show activities, the street corner hustlers and hustling bar activity were overwhelmingly a matter of contact.

Call-boy and call-girl networks, not to mention the various forms of phone sex, follow much more closely the "networking" model. But what *I* see lurking behind the positive foregrounding of "family values" (along with, and in the name of such values, the violent suppression of urban social structures, economic social and sexual) is a wholly provincial and absolutely small-town terror of cross-class contact.

A salient, stabilizing factor that has helped create the psychological smoke screen behind which developers of Times Square and every other underpopulated urban center in the country have been able to pursue their machinations in spite of public good and private desire is the small-town fear of urban violence. Since the tourist to the big city is seen as someone *from* a small town, the promotion of tourism is a matter of promoting the image of the world—and of the city—that the small town is assumed to hold.

Jane Jacobs has analyzed how street crimes proliferate in the city: briefly, lack of street-level business and habitation diversity produces lack of human traffic, lack of contact, and a lack of those eyes on the street joined in the particularly intricate self-policing web Jacobs claims is our greatest protection against urban barbarism on the street. Many people have seen Jacobs as saying merely that the *number* of eyes on the street do the actual policing. But a careful reading of her arguments shows that these "eyes" must be connected to individuals with very specific and intricate social relations of both stability and investment in what we might call the quality of street life. Too high a proportion of stranger to indigenes, too high a turnover of regular population, and the process breaks down. Such lacks produce the dangerous neighborhoods: the housing project, the park with not enough stores and eating spaces bordering on it, the blocks and blocks of apartment residences without any ameliorating human services.

Many non-city residents still do not realize that their beloved small towns are, per capita, far more violent places than any big city. New York has an annual rate of one murder per 108,000 inhabitants. Some large cities have as few as one per 300,000.

In 1967, however, I spent the winter months in a Pennsylvanian town, which had a cold-weather population of under 600. That winter the town saw five violent deaths, homicides or manslaughters.

If New York City had five murders per 600 inhabitants per winter, it would be rampant chaos! The point, of course, is that the *structure* of violence is different in cities from the structure of violence in small towns. Three of those small-town violent deaths, with their perpetrators and victims, occurred within two families who had a history of violence in the town going back three generations—along with a truly epic rate of alcoholism. A social profile of those families would yield one not much different from the stereotyped pictures of the Hatfields and the McCoys of early sociological studies. The other two violent deaths that winter came when three adolescent boys from comparatively "good" families, bored out of their gourds during two solid weeks of snow, on a February evening's adventure pushed a car over a cliff. In the car a young couple was necking. The two young people died, but they were from out of town—strangers, not residents and from another town twenty-five or thirty miles away. That particular incident produced an ugly and finally very sad court trial; one

of the boys was sent to reform school. The other two got off with strong repri-
mands. But the town's general sense was that the victims shouldn't have been
there in the first place. You stay in your own locality. Shut them in too long by
the snow like that with nothing to do, and boys will be boys . . .

In a small town the majority of the violence that occurs (say, three out of
five cases) does not really surprise anyone. People know where it's going to
occur and in which social units (that is, which two families) 60 percent of it
will happen. They know how to stay out of its way. Your biggest protection
from the rest of it is that you're not a stranger to the place; and you should
probably stay out of places where you are. Comparatively speaking, the violence in cities is random. No one knows where it's going to fall, who the next
mugging victim, house breaking victim, rape victim, not to mention victim of
an apartment fire or traffic accident, will be.

Small towns control their violence by rigorously controlling—and often all
but forbidding—interclass contact, except in carefully controlled work situations. The boys of good families who killed the young couple (people in the
town would be appalled that today I describe the incident in such terms,
though few of them would argue with me that that's what happened) did not
associate with the sons and daughters of the local Hatfield/McCoys. When
small towns are beautified and developed, their development generally proceeds in ways that make easier the location, unofficial segregation, and separa-
tion of the classes.

Because our new city developments, such as Times Square, are conceived
largely as attractions for incoming tourists, they are being designed to look safe
to the tourist, even if the social and architectural organization laid down to
appeal to them is demonstrably inappropriate for large cities and promotes
precisely the sort of isolation, inhumanity and violence that everyone abhors.

The traditional way that cities keep their violence rate monumentally
lower than in small towns is by the self-policing practices that come from
"eyes on the street" *supported by a rich system of relatively random benefits
and rewards that encourage pleasant sociality based entirely on contact.* That
system of random rewards from contact results in everything from basic
intra-neighborhood "pleasantness" to the heroic prizes of neighborly assis-
tance in times of catastrophe. But even more important, in a society that
prides itself on the widespread existence of opportunity, interclass contacts
are the site and origin of a good many of what can later be seen as life opportunities, or at least the site of many elements that make the seizing of such
opportunities easier and more profitable.

The small-town way to enjoy a big city is to arrive in town with your family, your friends, your school group, your church group, or—if you are really
brave—your tour group, with whom you associate (these are all pre-selected
network groups) and have fun, as you sample the food and culture and see the
monuments and architecture. But the one thing you do not do is go out in the
street alone and meet people. The fear of such an activity in New York City is,
for most out-of-towners, one with the fear of bodily contagion from AIDS
coupled with the equally bodily fear of hurt and loss of property.

Around 1990, I was returning on a plane to New York from a reading in Boston, with the Russian poet André Vosnesensky. Vosnesensky was staying at the Harvard Club, just a block or two north of Grand Central Station, and was unaware that one could take a bus directly there from the airport and save considerably on the taxi fare.

When we got off at Grand Central, I suggested that he might want to use the facilities at the station. Very worriedly, he told me: "Oh, no. I don't think we better do that."

Naively, I asked: "Why not?"

"Because," he told me, leaning close, "I don't want to catch AIDS."

Used to dealing with people who were afraid of touching people with AIDS or eating after them, I was nevertheless so surprised to discover someone who thought he would be at the risk of contagion from using a public urinal, that I was non-plussed. We were to part less than five minutes later—and I have not seen him since.

But rather than take this as a spectacular example of misinformation and/or information, I think it is more interesting to see it as a cross section of the process by which AIDS functions, on an international level, as a discursive tool to keep visitors to the city away from all public facilities and places where, yes, one might, if so inclined, engage in or be subject to any sort of interclass contact.

Paradoxically, the specifically gay sexual outlets—the sex movies that encouraged masturbation and fellatio in the audience, the rougher hustler bars, the particular street corners that had parades of active hustlers—are or were locales where the violence that occurs is closer to the high small-town level than it is to the overall lower big-city level: but, there, to complete the paradox, that violence tends to be structured, rather, *like* small-town violence. If you frequent the place, quickly you learn from where and/or from whom it is going to come. A stranger or first-time visitor is probably far more vulnerable than a long-time, frequent habitué of the facility: the hustler bar, the sex theater, or the low-life street corner. Someone who visits such places two or three times a week, or monthly, is likely to be pretty clear which person—or prejudicial as it sounds, which kind of person—will likely be the source of violence. That is why prostitutes can work the streets and neighborhoods they do. That is why, gay and straight, so many middle-class and working-class men feel perfectly safe visiting such urban spaces on a regular basis, often several times a week over years, even when, from statistics or just their own observation, they know perfectly well that every couple of weeks or months—in extreme cases two or three times a day—some sort of robbery or fight happens, or bodily injury is done to a customer. In such places, however, the violence is not random. It follows more or less clear patterns that are fairly easily learned. Thus habitués feel—and, indeed, usually are—as safe as most people in any other small-town-*structured* violent environment. And of course—the one thing Jacob's analysis leaves out—during the times of non-violence, which *still* make up the majority of the time, in such locations the same principles of traffic, social diversity, and self-policing hold sway, yes, even here.

Another point that people forget is: public sex situations are not Dionysian and uncontrolled but are rather some of the most highly socialized and conventionalized behavior human beings can take part in.

The sexual activity of the Times Square area (and by that I mean both commercial and non-commercial) has been hugely decried, called awful and appalling by many—including architect Robert Stern. We do *not* want a red-light district there, is the general cry of planners and organizers. People who utilized, or worked in it, however, are sometimes a bit more analytical than those issuing blanket dismissals. A good deal of what made the situation awful, when it was awful, was not the sex work *per se* but the illegal drug traffic that accompanied it, that worked its way all through it, and that, from time to time, controlled much of it. The middle 1980s saw an explosion of drug activity, focusing particularly around crack, that produced some of the most astonishing and appalling human behavior I personally have ever seen. Its extent, form, and general human face have yet to be chronicled.

In 1987 I had a conversation with an eighteen-year-old Dominican, who was indeed hustling on the strip. He was worried because he was living with a seventeen-year-old friend—another young crackhead—in a project further uptown.

The younger boy had been regularly selling all the furniture in the apartment, and, when his mother had objected, he had killed her.

Her body, the other boy told me, was still in the closet. The older boy did not know what to do.

I suggested that he tell his younger friend—whom I did not know and had not met—to go to the police.

Some days later, when I ran into the older boy, he told me that is indeed what his young friend had done. The older boy was now homeless.

One would have to be a moral imbecile to be nostalgic for such a situation.

Indeed, the major change in the area over the period between 1984 and 1987 was that professional prostitutes and hustlers—women generally between, say, twenty-three and forty-five, and the men somewhat younger, asking (the women among them) thirty-five to seventy-five dollars per encounter (and the men ten to fifteen dollars less)—were driven out of the area by a new breed of "five dollar whore" or "hustler," often a fifteen-, sixteen-, or seventeen-year-old girl or boy, who would go into a doorway and do *anything* with anyone for the four-to-eight dollars needed for the next bottle of crack. Some of that situation is reflected in the scream that ends Spike Lee's film *Jungle Fever*.

It was that appalling.

It was that scary.

I hope we can look even on that period of human atrocity, however, with a clear enough vision to see (as was evident to anyone who walked through the neighborhood during those years, who lingered and spoke to and developed any concern for any of these youngsters) that this activity clotted in the area, that it grew and spread from there to other neighborhoods, that it reached such appalling dimensions *as a direct result* of the economic attack on the neighborhood by the developers, Robert Stern's employers, in their attempt to destroy the place as a vital and self-policing site, as a necessary prelude to their sanitized site.

The old Times Square and Forty-second Street was an entertainment area catering largely to the working classes who lived in the city. The middle class and/or tourists were invited to come along and watch or participate if that, indeed, was their thing.

The New Times Square is envisioned as predominantly a middle-class area of entertainment, to which the working classes are welcome to come along, observe and take part in, if they can pay and are willing to blend in.

What controls the success (or failure) of this change are the changes in the city population itself—and changes in the working- (and middle-) class self-image. Sociologists will have to look at this aspect and analyze what is actually going on.

Let's return to the question of Times Square as a safe space for women—which some, looking at the new development, have somehow managed to see it as. The first thing one must note is that there have always been women in Times Square, on Forty-second Street, and on its appendage running up and down Eighth Avenue. They were bar-maids. They were waitresses. They were store clerks. They were ticket takers. I do not know much about the female work population of the twenty-story Candler office building on the south side of Forty-second Street at number 220, between the former site of the Harris and the Liberty theaters, but for many years I regularly visited a friend who worked at a translation bureau run by a Mrs. Cavenaugh on the nineteenth floor: and I will hazard that at least 40 percent of the workers there were women. Also, women lived in the neighborhood. Until the end of the 1970s it was a place where young theater hopefuls—more men, yes, than women; but women, neverthe-less—lived in a range of inexpensive apartments and furnished rooms around Hell's Kitchen (renamed, somewhat more antiseptically, "Clinton" a few years back). The vast majority of these women are not there now. And the developers see themselves as driving out (the minuscule proportion of) those women who were actual sex workers.

To see such a development, which makes a city space safe for one class of women by actively driving out another class, as having any concern for women *as* a class is at best naïve. The Times Square developers' concern for women and women's safety extends no further than seeing women as replaceable nodes with a certain amount of money to spend in a male-dominated economic system.

Some of what was in the old Times Square worked. Some didn't work. Often what worked—about, say, the sexual activity (and, despite the horror of the planners, much of it did: we have too many testimonials to that effect by both customers *and* the sex workers themselves), worked by accident. It was not planned. But this does not mean it was not caused, analyzable, and (thus) instructive.

The new Time Square is simply not about making the area safe for women. It is not about supporting theater and the arts. It is not about promoting economic growth in the city. It is not about reducing the level of AIDS or even about driving out perversion (that is, non-commercial sexual encounters between those of the same sex who can find each other more easily in a neighborhood with sex movies, peep show activities and commercial sex) nor is it about reducing commercial sex, hustling and prostitution.

The new Times Square is about developers doing as much demolition and renovation as possible in the neighborhood, and as much construction work as they possibly can. Some old-fashioned Marxism might be useful here: infrastructure determines superstructure—not the other way around. And for all their stabilizing or destabilizing potential, discourse and rhetoric are superstructural phenomena.

SUPERSTRUCTURE/INFRASTRUCTURE

There is, of course, an important corollary for late-consumer media-dominated capitalism—which is largely absent from classical Marxism: "Superstructure stabilizes infrastructure."

Briefly and more dramatically, superstructural forces (personal relations, the quality of life in the neighborhood, the passage of time) may make a small business decide to shut down and vacate to Queens (as my local drycleaners, Habanna San Juan, is currently doing after twenty-five years in three different locations in the Upper West Side—each location smaller than the space before, and the last further from the main thoroughfare than the previous two: there are fewer Hispanics here than before, the Spanish owner is older, he lives in Queens and has been commuting into this neighborhood at seven in the morning for more than two decades and is tired of it). But infrastructural forces will determine whether *his* landlord has three bids from white-owned businesses for the same space two months before this long-term Puerto Rican dry cleaner tenant leaves—or whether the same space will sit vacant for the next eighteen months with a crack across the glass behind the window gate.

That is to say, infrastructural forces will determine whether most of the neighborhood perceives Habanna San Juan's closing as another Puerto Rican business going as the neighborhood improves—or as another business-in-general folding as the neighborhood declines.

One of the problems with getting people to accept the first tenet of Marxism (infrastructure determines superstructure) is that we can look around us and *see* superstructural forces feeding back into the infrastructure and making changes in it. Because we are the "political size" we are (and thus have the political horizons we do), it's hard for individuals to see the extent (or lack of it) of those changes—we have no way to determine by direct observation whether those changes are stabilizing/destabilizing or causative. And when we are unsure of (or wholly ignorant of) the infrastructural forces involved, often we assume that the superstructural forces that we have seen at work are responsible *for* major (i.e., infrastructural) changes. Infrastructural forces, however, often must be ferreted out and effects disseminated by the superstructure.

Infrastructure makes society go. Superstructure makes society go smoothly (or bumpily).

In 1992 we emerged from twelve years of a national Republican administration that favored big business—with the result that we now have some very strong big businesses indeed. The argument which the Reagan/Bush leaders used to convince the public that this was a good thing was the promise of tax cuts and the "trickle-down" economic theory. The "trickle-down" economic theory, you may recall, was the notion that somehow big business (especially if deregulated) would be helpful and supportive to small businesses.

It has taken a half dozen years for New Yorkers to learn, at least, what anyone over thirty-five could have told them in 1980 when Reagan was elected: big businesses drive out small businesses. Left unsupervised, big businesses stamp out small businesses, break them into pieces, devour the remains, and dance frenziedly on their graves. Now that we have watched Barnes & Noble destroy Books & Company on the East Side and Shakespeare & Company on the West and, in my own neighborhood, seen the Duane Reade Pharmacy chain put Lasky's and Ben's and several other small drugstores out of business, people have some models for the quality of service and the general atmosphere of pleasant interchange to be lost when big businesses destroy small ones.

Small businesses thrive on contact—the word-of-mouth reputations that contact engenders: "You're looking for X? Try Q's. It's really good for what you want."

Big businesses promote networking as much as they possibly can. "Shop at R's—and be part of today!" vibrating over the airwaves in a three-million-dollar ad campaign.

In one sense, the Times Square takeover is one of the more visible manifestations of the small having been obliterated by the large. We are in a period of economic growth, we all know. But most of us are asking: why, then, isn't *my* life more pleasant? The answer is because "pleasantness" is controlled by small business diversity and social contact; and in a democratic society that values social movement, social opportunity, and class flexibility, interclass contact is the most rewarding, productive and, thus, the privileged mode of contact.

Big business is anti-contact in the same way that it is anti-small business. But there are many jobs—like bookstores and, often, drugstores—that small businesses can fulfill more efficiently for the customers and more pleasantly (that word again) than can big business.

Again, certain benefits from contact, networking simply *cannot* provide.

An academic who heard an earlier version of this argument told me that it explained a family phenomenon which, in his younger years, had puzzled—and sometimes embarrassed—him.

"Whenever we would go with my grandfather to a restaurant—my grampa had been born and grown up in Italy—within ten minutes, he had everybody in the restaurant talking not only to him but to everybody else."

The question in his grandson's mind: "Why do you always have to *do* that, Gramps?"

The answer he realized, from my talk: how else could an unlettered laborer such as his grandfather, in the 1930s and 1940s, go into a new neighborhood, a new area, and get work?

A reasonable argument might be made that a notable percentage of the homeless population in our cities today is comprised of men and women who grew up in social enclaves that counted on contact relations to provide the prized necessities, jobs, shelter, and friendship—a social practice at which we can still see that they were often quite good—but who were unsuited, both by temperament and education, for the more formal stringencies of networking relations, which include securing work and necessary housing through want ads, resumés, job applications, real estate listings; a mode of social practice which, in urban venue after urban venue, has displaced contact relations ("You want a job? Show up tomorrow morning at six-thirty: I'll put you to work . . . I've got an apartment you can have, in a building I own, for two hundred a month") till there are hardly any left. Indeed, it is my deep suspicion that the only consistent and ultimately necessary learning that occurs across the field of "universal higher education" toward which our country leans more and more is the two-to-four years of acclimation to the bureaucratic management of our lives that awaits more and more of the country's working classes—and that goes along with (if it is not the institutional backbone of) Richard Gordon's analysis of the "homework economy" and the "feminization of poverty," that Donna Haraway brought to our attention more than a decade ago in her widely read, *A Cyborg Manifesto*.

Because isolated, low-level, optionless poverty that shifts between poor homes and the very bottom of the job system (where the "system" itself is seen as a fundamentally bureaucratic network phenomenon) has been called "feminized," one is tempted to call "masculinized" that homeless poverty where one has dropped through the system's very bottom into a world where ever-shrinking contact opportunities are the only social relations available. One of Gordon's points was that more and more men find themselves caught up in "feminized" poverty structures. Well, many, many women and children are on the streets barely surviving, suffering, and dying in "masculinized" poverty. I think that the gendering of such states merely overwrites and erases the contextual power divisions and questions of wealth deployment with vague suggestions of a wholly inappropriate, bogus, and mystifying psychologization (men choose one kind of poverty; women choose another; when poverty is precisely about lack of choices)—and so should be discouraged, however well-intentioned it all first seems.

URBAN CONTACT

Here's a composite entry from my last Spring's journal (1997).

After a trip to the Thirty-fourth Street Central Post Office to mail a book to a friend, I walked up Eighth Avenue to the Port Authority, where I stopped to speak to Todd—of the spectacularly missing front tooth. His clothes were clean and his shirt was new, but he is still homeless, he explains. (In his middle thirties, he *has* been for over a decade.) Just come from a stint sleeping on the subway, he asked me for some change to get something to eat. I gave him a handful that probably totaled about $1.75. "Oh, thanks, man," he said, "now I can go get me some chicken wings."

I was in the city to participate in a three-day conference at the Center for Lesbian and Gay Studies at the CUNY Graduate Center: "Forms of Desire." It's April, and after the snowstorm on the first, warmer weather seemed to have doubled the daytime Times Square traffic. Ben, gone to vacation with his wife in Germany for the winter, was back setting up his shoeshine stand behind the subway kiosk on the northwest corner. To the southeast, under the Port's marquee, Mr. Campbell was taking the afternoon shift. And Christos was there, among the pretzel and hotdog vendors, with his shishkebab wagon. (More and more these days he leaves the actual running of the stand to a Pakistani assistant.) Hustlers Darrell and David have not been in evidence awhile now. Back in January and February, I'd run into Darrell a few times, however, either on the corner or coming out of the peep-shows further up Eighth Avenue. Street life wasn't so good for him, he admitted. But the long-awaited publication of his picture in *OUT Magazine*, he told me, had opened up some model work for him with *The Latin Connection*.[2] Months ago, someone introduced him to some film makers (pure networking), but the *OUT* photo (pure contact) apparently pushed them to act on his application a lot more quickly.

I hope things go well for him.

Back in January I saw David over on Ninth Avenue, running after drugs. ("Hey, there—man! Hey, there! So long!") But not since.

There on the crowded corner, however, Jeff and Lenny and Frank were still hanging out—even while a scuffle between two young men created a widening circle under the Port's marquee, till a sudden surge of police tightened it into a knot of attention. A policeman sped past me into the crowd, while the woman beside him shrieked. Then, for a solid minute, the knot pulled tight enough to become impenetrable to sight. Moments later, however, the same policeman led away a white kid in a blue checked shirt with a backwards baseball cap and a bleeding face (as he stumbled in the policeman's grip, he bumped against Christos's stand), while a Hispanic kid in a red jacket, shaking his head, talked to another policeman. Beside me, tall Frank tells me, "Wow! They *got* him. They actually caught him. Man, that was cool. I didn't think they were going to get him. But they caught him!" Like Jeff, Frank, a long-time hustler on that corner, has no brief for violence that might keep his customers away.

The third evening after the conference, at the back of the 104 Broadway bus, half a dozen riders (four middle-aged women, two middle-aged men), each with his or her copy of *Playbill*, spontaneously began to discuss the matinees they'd seen that afternoon.

In the full bus, the conversations wound on, and I found myself talking to a woman sitting next to me, from Connecticut, who had just come from the theater. It is spring, and New York is full of contact—though I note the conversation in the back of the bus is not cross-class contact, but pretty well limited to folks who can afford the sixty or seventy dollars for a Broadway ticket, and so partakes a bit more of the economic context of networking—the *Playbills* acting as signs of the shared interest (and shared economic level) characteristic of a networking group. Also, characteristic of networking groups, what circulated among them was knowledge about which actors were good, which plays were strong or enjoyable, which musicals had good voices but weak songs, and which just did not seem worth the time or money to attend.

Let me be specific. In the ten years I've known Todd, I'm sure the handouts I've given him, a dollar here, two dollars there (say, once a month), easily total 180 dollars or more—that is, over twice the price of a Broadway show ticket. If, on the bus, however, one of the *Playbill* wavers were to ask me or one of the others with whom she had been chatting amiably, "Say, here's my name and address. The next time you're going to the theater, just pick up an extra ticket and drop it in the mail to me," it would bring the conversation to a stunned halt; and however the theater-going passengers might have dealt with it in the public space of a twenty minute bus ride, certainly no one would have seriously acceded to the request.

That is to say, once again, the material rewards from street contact (the quintessential method of the panhandler) are simply greater, even if spread out over a decade, than the rewards from a session of networking—which rewards take place (I say again) largely in the realm of shared knowledge.

That evening, around 7:20, I got home to comet Hale-Bopp, bright and fuzzy-bearded above the west extremity of Eighty-second Street, against an indigo evening only a single shade away from full black. At the corner, I phoned up to Dennis in the apartment (one payphone was broken; I had to cross over to use the one on the far corner), who hadn't seen it yet, to come out and take a look. Two minutes later he was down on the stoop; to prepare him, I pointed out a couple of diamond-chip stars overhead. "Now that's a star. And *that's* a star. But if you look over there—"

Without my even pointing, he declared: "Wow, *there* it is!"—the fuzzy star-like object with it gauzy beard of light fanning to the east (I'd first seen it on my birthday, two nights before, in Massachusetts).

Dennis dashed back up to get his binoculars and to check it out from our roof; I turned up the street to make a quick trip to the supermarket. On my way back down Eighty-second Street, Hale-Bopp created a veritable wave of contact.

First an overheard father and two kids, son and daughter: "Hey, do you see the comet up there . . .?"

"Yeah, I saw it last week."

Moments later, I pointed it out to a heavy, white-haired plain-clothes policeman lounging in jeans and a blue sweat shirt by the gate at the precinct, who responded: "Do I see it? Sure. It's right up there, isn't it?"

Which turned two women around in their tracks, one in a brown rain coat, both in hats. "Is *that* it? Oh, yes."

"Yes, right there. *My* . . . !"

"You can really see it, tonight! Maybe we should go down to the river and look."

I left the policeman explaining to them why they *didn't* want to do that.

Thirty yards further down the block, I pointed it out to a stocky young Hispanic couple who passed me hand in hand: "Yeah, sure. We already seen it!"

And a minute later I pointed it out again to a homeless man in his twenties with blackened hands and short black hair, who'd set his plastic garbage bag down to dig in a garbage container for soda and beer cans. "Oh, wow! Yeah—" slowly he stood up to rub his forehead—"that's neat!" While I walked on, a moment later I glanced back to see he'd stopped an older Hispanic gentleman in an overcoat with a pencil-thin moustache, who now stood with him, gazing up: "There—you see the comet . . . ?"

With my cane, I walked up my stoop steps, carrying my groceries and my notebook into the vestibule, where I unlocked the door and pushed into the lobby.

How does this set of urban interactions beneath a passing celestial portent differ from similar encounters, on the same evening 100 or 500 miles away, on some small-town street? First, these encounters are in a big city. Second, over the next eight months, I have seen none of the people involved in them again— neither the homeless man nor the Hispanic gentleman, the young couple nor the pair of women, nor the policeman (one among the seventy-five-odd officers who work out of the precinct at the far end of my block, perhaps fifteen of whom I know by sight). Their only fallout is that they were pleasant—and that pleasantness hangs in the street under the trees and by the brownstones' stoops near which they occurred, months after Hale-Bopp has ellipsed the sun and soared again into solar night. That fallout will remain as long as I remain comfortable living here.

MECHANICS OF DISCOURSE

Not a full year after the CLAGS "Forms of Desire" conference that took place under the auspices of Hale-Bopp and provoked the journal entry above, at the February '98 OutWrite Conference of Lesbian and Gay Writers in Boston, Massachusetts, one of the Sunday morning programs began with two questions:

"Why is there homophobia?" and "What makes us gay?"

As I listened to the discussion over the next hour and a half, I found myself troubled: rather than attack both questions head on, the discussants tended to veer away from them, as if the questions were somehow logically congruent to the two great philosophical conundrums, ontological and epistemological, that ground Western philosophy—"Why is there something rather than nothing?" and, "How can we know it?"—and, as such, could only be approached by elaborate indirection.

It seems to me (and this will bring the multiple arguments of this lengthy discussion to a close under the rubric of my third thesis: the mechanics of discourse) there are pointed answers to be given to both questions, answers that are imperative if gays and lesbians are to make any progress in passing from what Urvashi Vaid has called, so tellingly, "virtual equality" (the appearance of equality with few or none of the material benefits) to a material and legally based equality.

During the 1940s and 1950s my uncle (my mother's brother-in-law) Myles Paige, a black man who had graduated from Tuskegee, was a Republican and a

Catholic, and a respected judge in the Brooklyn Domestic Relations Court. By the time I was ten or eleven, I knew why "prostitutes and perverts" (my uncle was the first to join them for me in seductive alliteration; it is not without significance that, in the 1850s in London, "gays," the plural term for male homosexuals today, meant female prostitutes) were to be hated, if not feared. I was told the reason repeatedly during half a dozen family dinners, where, over the roast lamb, the macaroni and cheese, the creamed onions and the kale, at the head of the family dinner table my uncle, the judge, held forth.

"Prostitutes and perverts," he explained, again and again, "destroy, undermine and rot the foundations of society." I remember his saying, again and again, if he had his way, he "would take all those people out and shoot 'em!" while his more liberal wife—my mother's sister—protested futilely. "Well," my uncle grumbled, "I *would* . . ." The implication was that he had some arcane and secret information about "prostitutes and perverts" that, while it justified the ferocity of his position, could not be shared at the dinner table with women and children. But I entered adolescence knowing that the law alone, and my uncle's judicial position in it, kept his anger, and by extension the anger of all right-thinking men like him, in check—kept it from breaking out in a concerted attack on "those people," who were destroying, undermining and rotting the foundations of society—which meant, as far as I understood it, they were menacing my right to sit there in the dining room in the Brooklyn row house on Macdonnah Street and eat the generous, even lavish Sunday dinner that my aunt and grandmother had fixed over the afternoon . . .

These were the years between 1949 and 1953, when I—and, I'm sure, many others—heard this repeatedly as the general social judgment on sex workers and/or homosexuals. That is to say, it was about half a dozen years after the end of World War II. Besides being a judge, my Uncle Myles had also been a Captain in the U.S. Army.

What homosexuality and prostitution represented for my uncle was the untrammeled pursuit of pleasure; and the untrammeled pursuit of pleasure was the opposite of social responsibility. Nor was this simply some abstract principle to the generation so recently home from European military combat. Many had begun to wake, however uncomfortably, to a fact that problematizes much of the discourse around sadomasochism today. In the words of Bruce Benderson, writing in the *Lambda Book Report 12*: "The true Eden where all desires are satisfied is red, not green. It is a bloodbath of instincts, a gaping maw of orality, and a basin of gushing bodily fluids." Too many had seen "nice ordinary American boys" let loose in some tiny French or German or Italian town where, with the failure of the social contract, there was no longer any law—and they had seen all too much of that red "Eden." Nor—in World War II—were these situations officially interrogated, with attempts to tame them for the public with images such as "Lt. Calley" and "My Lai," as they would be a decade-and-a-half later in Vietnam. Rather, they circulated as an unstated and inarticulate horror whose lessons were supposed to be brought back to the States while their specificity was, in any collective narrativity, unspeakable, left in the foreign outside, safely beyond the pale.

The clear and obvious answer (*especially* to a Catholic Republican army officer and judge) was that pleasure must be socially doled out in minuscule amounts, tied by rigorous contracts to responsibility. Good people were people who accepted this contractual system. Anyone who rebelled *was* a prostitute or a pervert—or both. Anyone who actively pursued prostitution or perversion was working, whether knowingly or not, to unleash precisely those red Edenic forces of desire that could only topple society, destroy responsibility, and produce a nation without families, soldiers or workers—indeed, a chaos that was itself no state, for clearly no such space of social turbulence could maintain any but the most feudal state apparatus.

That was and will remain the answer to the question, "Why is there hatred and fear of homosexuals (homophobia)?" as long as this is the systematic relation between pleasure and responsibility in which "prostitution and perversion" are seen to be caught up. The herd of teenage boys who stalk the street with their clubs, looking for a faggot to beat bloody and senseless, or the employer who fires the worker who is revealed to be gay or the landlord who turns the gay tenant out of his or her apartment, or the social circle who refuses to associate with someone who is found out to be gay, are simply the Valkyries—the *Wunschmadchen*—to my uncle's legally constrained Wotan.

What I saw in the conversation at OutWrite was that the argument exists today largely at the level of discourse, and that younger gay activists find it hard today to articulate the greater discursive structure they are fighting to dismantle, as do those conservatives today who uphold one part of it or the other without being aware of its overall form. But discourses in such conditions tend to remain at their *most* stable.

The overall principle that must be appealed to in order to dismantle such a discourse is the principle that claims desire is never "outside all social constraint." Desire may be outside one set of constraints or another; but social constraints are what engender desire; and, one way or another, even at its most apparently catastrophic, they contour desire's expression.

On the particular level where the argument must proceed case by case, incident by incident, before it reaches discursive (or counterdiscursive) mass, we must look at how that principle operates in the answer to our second question: "What makes us gay?"

There are at least three different levels where an answer can be posed.

First, the question might be interpreted to mean, "What do we do, what qualities do we possess, that signal the fact that we partake of the preexisting essence of 'gayness' that gives us our gay 'identity' and that, in most folks' minds, mean we belong to the category of 'those who are gay'?" This is, finally, the semiotic or epistemological level: how do we—or other people—know we are gay?

There is a second level, however, on which the question might be interpreted as: "What forces or conditions in the world take the potentially 'normal' and 'ordinary' person—a child, a fetus, the egg and sperm before they conjoin as a zygote—and 'pervert' them (that is, turn them away) from that 'normal' condition so that now we have someone who does some or many or all of the things we call gay—or at least wants to, or feels compelled to, even if she or he would rather not?" This is, finally, the ontological level: what makes these odd, statistically unusual, but ever-present, gay people exist in the first place?

The confusion between level one and level two—the epistemological and the ontological—is already enough to muddle many arguments. People who think they are asking question two are often given (very frustrating) answers to question one—and vice versa.

But there is a third level where the question can be interpreted, which is often associated with queer theory and academics of a poststructuralist bent. Many such academics have claimed that their answer to (and thus their interpretation of) the question is the most important one, and that this answer absorbs and explains what is really going on at the first two levels.

This last is not, incidentally, a claim that I make. But I do think that this third level of interpretation (which, yes, is an aspect of the epistemological, but might be more intelligibly designated today as the theoretical) is imperative if we are to explain to a significant number of people what is wrong with a discourse that places pleasure and the body in fundamental opposition to some notion of a legally constrained social responsibility, rather than a discourse that sees that pleasure and the body are constitutive elements of the social as much as the law and responsibility themselves.

One problem with this third level of interpretation of "What makes us gay?" that many of us academic folk have come up with is that it puts considerable strain on the ordinary meaning of "makes."

The opposition to our interpretation might begin like this (I start here because, by the polemic against it, the reader may have an easier time recognizing it when it arrives in its positive form): "'To make' is an active verb. You seem to be describing a much more passive process. It sounds like you're describing some answer to the question 'What allows us to be gay?' or 'What facilitates our being gay?' or even 'What allows people to speak about people as gay?' Indeed, the answer you propose doesn't seem to have anything to do with 'making' at all. It seems to be all about language and social habit."

To which, if we're lucky enough for the opposition to take its objection to this point, we can answer back: "You're right! That's *exactly* our point. We now believe that language and social habit are much more important than until now, historically, they have been assumed to be. Both language and social habit perform many more jobs, intricately, efficiently and powerfully, into shaping not just what we call social reality, but even what we call reality itself (against which we used to set social reality in order to look at it as a separate situation *from* material reality). Language and social habit don't simply produce the appearance of social categories: rich, poor, educated, uneducated, well-mannered, ill-bred— those signs that, according to Henry Higgins in *My Fair Lady*, can be learned and therefore faked. They produce as well what until now were considered ontological categories: male, female, black, white, Asian, straight, gay, normal and abnormal . . . as well as trees, books, dogs, wars, rainstorms and mosquitoes.

"Because we realize just how powerful the socio/linguistic process is, we *insist* on coupling it with those active verbs, 'to make, to produce, to create'—

although, early in the dialogue, there was another common verb for this particular meaning of 'make' that paid its due to the slow, sedentary and passive (as
well as to the inexorable and adamantine) quality of the process: 'to sedi-
ment'—a verb that fell away because it did not suit the polemical nature of the
argument, but which at this point it might be well to retrieve: 'What makes us
gay?' in the sense of, 'What produces us as gay? What creates us as gay? What
sediments us as gay?'"

The level where these last four questions overlap is where our interpretations of the question—and our answer to it—emerges.

Consider a large ballroom full of people.

At various places around the walls there are doors. If one of the doors is
open and the ballroom is crowded enough, after a certain amount of time
there will be a certain number of people in the other room on the far side of
the open door (assuming the lights are on and nothing is going on in there to
keep them out). The third-level theoretical answer to the question "What
makes us gay?" troubles ordinary men and women on the street for much the
same reason it would trouble them if you said, "The open doors is what makes
people go into the other room."

Most folks are likely to respond, "Sure, I *kind* of see what you mean. But
aren't you just playing with words? Isn't it really the density of the ballroom
crowd, the heat, the noise, or the bustle in the ballroom that drives (i.e., that
makes) people go into the adjoining room? I'm sure you could come up with
experiments where, if, on successive nights, you raised and lowered the tem-
perature and/or the noise level, you could even correlate them to how much
faster or slower people were driven out of the ballroom and into the adjoining
room—thus proving crowd, heat, and noise were the causative factors, rather
than the door, which is finally just a facilitator, *n'est-ce pas*?"

The answer to this objection is "You're answering the question as though it
were being asked at level two, the ontological level. And for level two, your
answer is fine. The question I am asking, however, on level three, is, 'What
makes the people go into *that* room rather than any number of other possible
rooms that they might have entered, behind any of the other *closed* doors
around the ballroom?' And the actual answer to that question really *is*, 'That
particular *open* door.'"

It's time to turn to the actual and troubling answer we have come up with
to the newly interpreted question, "What makes us gay?" The answer is usually
some version of the concept "We are made gay because that is how we have
been interpellated."

"Interpellate" is a term that was revived by Louis Althusser in his 1969 essay,
"Ideology and Ideological State Apparatuses." The word once meant "to interrupt with a petition." Prior to the modern era, the aristocrats who comprised
many of the royal courts could be presented with petitions by members of the
haute bourgeoisie. These aristocrats fulfilled their tasks as subjects to the king
by reading over the petitions presented to them, judging them, and acting on
them in accord with the petition's perceived merit. Althusser's point is that "we
become subjects when we are interpellated." In the same paragraph, he offers

the word "hailed" as a synonym, and goes on to give what has become a rather notorious example of a policeman calling out or hailing, "Hey, you!" on the street. Says Althusser, in the process of saying, "He must mean me," we cohere into a self—rather than being, presumably, simply a point of view drifting down the street.

That awareness of "he must mean me" is the constitutive *sine qua non* of the subject. It is the mental door through which we pass into subjectivity and selfhood. And (maintains Althusser) this cannot be a spontaneous process, but is always a response to some hailing, some interpellation by some aspect of the social.

In that sense, it doesn't really matter whether someone catches you in the bathroom, looking at a same-sex nude, and then blurts out, "Hey, you're gay!" and you look up and realize "you" ("He means me!") have been caught, or if you're reading a description of homosexuality in a textbook and "you" think, "Hey, they're describing me!" The point is, rather, that anyone who self-identifies as gay must have been interpellated, at some point, as gay by some individual or social speech or text to which he or she responded, "He/she/it/they must mean me." That is the door opening. Without it, nobody can say proudly, "I am gay!" Without it, nobody can think guiltily and in horror, "Oh my God, I'm gay!" Without it, one cannot remember idly or in passing, "Well, I'm gay."

Because interpellation only talks about one aspect of "making"/ "producing"/ "creating"/"sedimenting," it does not tell us the whole story. It is simply one of the more important things that happens to subjects at the level of discourse. And, in general, discourses constitute and are constituted by what Walter Pater, in *The Renaissance*, called "a roughness of the eye." Thus, without a great deal more elaboration, the notion of interpellation is as reductive as any other theoretical move. But it locates a powerful and pivotal point in the process. And it makes it clear that the process is, as are all the creative powers of discourse, irrevocably anchored within the social, rather than somehow involved with some fancied breaking out of the social into an uncharted and unmapped beyond, that only awaits the release of police surveillance to erupt into that red Eden of total unconstraint.

What the priority of the social says about those times in war where that vision of hell was first encountered by people like my uncle, possibly among our own soldiers: "Look, if you spend six months socializing young men to 'kill, kill, kill,' it's naïve to be surprised when some of them, in the course of their pursuit of pleasure, do. It is not because of some essentialist factor in 'perversion' or 'prostitution' (or sexuality in general) that always struggles to break loose."

While one thrust of this essay is that catastrophic civic interventions such as the Times Square Redevelopment Program are incorrectly justified by the assumption that interclass contact is somehow unsafe (it threatens to unleash the sexual, crime, mayhem, murder . . .) and its benefits can be replaced by networking (safe, monitored, controlled, under surveillance . . .), a second thrust has been and is that social contact is of paramount importance in the specific pursuit of gay sexuality: The fact is, I am not interested in the "freedom" to "be" "gay" without any of the existing gay institutions or without other institutions that can take up and fulfill like functions.

Such "freedom" means nothing. Many gay institutions—clubs, bars of several persuasions, baths, tea-room sex, gay porn movie houses (both types), brunches, entertainment, cruising areas, truck stop sex, circuit parties, and many more—have grown up outside the knowledge of much of the straight world. But these institutions have nevertheless grown up very much *within* our society, not outside it. They have been restrained on every side. That is how they have attained their current form. They do not propagate insanely in some extra-social and unconstrained "outside"/ "beyond," apart from any concept of social responsibility—and that includes what goes on in the orgy rooms at the baths. The freedom to "be" "gay" without the freedom to choose to partake of these institutions is just as meaningless as the freedom to "be" "Jewish" when, say, any given Jewish ritual, or Jewish text, or Jewish cultural practice is outlawed; it is as meaningless as the "freedom" to "be" "black" in a world where black music, black literature, black culture, black language, and all the black social practices that have been generated through the process of black historical exclusion were suddenly suppressed. I say this not because a sexual preference is in any necessary way identical to race, or for that matter to religion. (Nor am I proposing the equally absurd notion that race and religion are equivalent.) I say it rather because none of the three—race, religion or sexual preference—represents some absolute essentialist state; I say it because all three are complex social constructs, and thus do not come into being without their attendant constructed institutions.

Tolerance—not assimilation—is the democratic litmus test for social equality.

The Times Square renovation is not just about real estate and economics, however unpleasant its ramifications have been on that front. Because it has involved the major restructuring of the legal code relating to sex, and because it has been a first step not just toward the moving, but toward the obliteration, of certain business and social practices, it has functioned as a massive and destructive intervention in the social fabric of a non-criminal group in the city—an intervention I for one deeply resent.

If the range of heterosexist homophobic society as a system wants to ally itself to an architecture, a life-style, and a range of social practices that eschew contact out of an ever inflating fear of the alliance between pleasure and chaos, then I think it is in for a sad, unhappy time, far more restrictive, unpleasant and impoverishing than the strictures of monogamy could ever be.

The thousands on thousands of gay men, contingently "responsible" or "irresponsible," who utilized the old Times Square and like facilities for sex, already know that contact is necessary. I would hope that this talk makes clear that it is necessary for the whole of a flexible, democratic society—and I feel it is only socially responsible to say so.

1. Astute as her analysis is, Jacobs still confuses contact with community. Urban contact is often at its most spectacularly beneficial when it occurs between members of different communities. That is why I maintain that interclass contact is even more important than intraclass contact.

2. In another form, parts of this paper first appeared as an article for *OUT Magazine* ("X-X-X Marks the Spot" by Samuel R. Delany, December '96—January '97), which focused on street corner life at 42nd Street and Eighth Avenue. It included photographs of some of the people interviewed by Philip-Lorca diCorscia.

1998

EVE KOSOFSKY SEDGWICK

Eve Kosofsky Sedgwick is Distinguished Professor of English at the City University of New York Graduate Center. Her publications include *Between Men: English Literature and Male Homosocial Desire* (Columbia University Press, 1985), *Epistemology of the Closet* (University of California Press, 1990), for which she was awarded an Honorable Mention for the MLA's James Russell Lowell Prize in 1991, and *Tendencies* (Duke University Press, 1993). She has also published the poetry collection *Fat Art, Thin Art* (Duke University Press, 1994) and the memoir *A Dialogue On Love* (Beacon Press, 1999), which draws on her Kessler Lecture. Her most recent publication, *Touching Feeling: Affect, Pedagogy, Performativity* (Duke University Press, 2003), examines linguistic concepts and the motivations behind performance. Sedgwick is a contributing editor to *MAMM: Women, Cancer, Community,* a health publication for female survivors of breast, ovarian, and other women's cancers.

A DIALOGUE ON LOVE

In the waiting room, do I have a mental image of him at all? The handsome, lean, well-dressed therapists female and male in this large practice filter through the sunny room, greeting their patients, ushering them up or across. . . .

I look expectantly at each of the men.

And I'm trying now to remember it, the grotesque, reassuring shock of Shannon hovering down a few stairs into this view, mild and bristling with his soft gray nap,

> *big-faced, cherubic—*
> *barrel chest, long arms, short legs,*
> *Rumpelstiltskin-like*

and wearing, I've no doubt, a beautifully ironed

> *short-sleeved cotton shirt*
> *the color of an after-*
> *dinner mint, tucked in*

at his rotund waist. If it was as hot as Durham usually is in early September, he had a handkerchief too for mopping his forehead.

There would have been a substantial rumble of genial introduction. My tentative greeting maybe not quite audible in the middle of it. Was this ordinary for him—the first encounter in this familiar room with big, female middle-aged bodies deprecated by the softness of our voices? Maybe in some manual it's the secret definition of "depression."

And yet (I told him, settled in his office upstairs), it's not so clear to me that depressed is the right word for what I am. Depressed is

> *what everyone says—*
> *I'm weeping in a lot of*
> *offices these days*

(and I'm sure the tears slipped over my lids as I said it). But I think I *know* depression, I have my own history of it; and it felt, twenty years ago when I really was subject to it, so much less bearable than this does. So much.

"And yet, you're crying now."

On record, the triggering event was a breast cancer diagnosis eighteen months ago.

Shannon doesn't produce an empathetic face at this, or say "That must have been hard for you." He makes an economical nod.

"I kind of did beautifully with it. I bounced back from the mastectomy, and when it turned out that there was some lymph node involvement too, I tolerated six months of chemotherapy without too many side effects. You know, I *hated* it, and it completely wore me down, but . . . ."

"The saving thing was that for me it wasn't all about dread. I know there are people whose deepest dread is to have cancer, to undergo surgery, to deal with the likelihood of dying." I shake my head many times.

Those are not my deepest dread. I dread

> *every bad thing*
> *that threatens people I love;*
> *for me, dread only*
>
> *I may stop knowing*
> *how to like and desire*
> *the world around me.*

"That's it, what you mean by real depression?"

"Oh, yeah."

In some ways the cancer diagnosis came at the best possible time. —The best time if feeling ready to die is a criterion. It was about two months after a book of mine had come out.

"What kind of books do you write?"

I tell Shannon I'm a literary critic; I work in gay and lesbian studies.

The book was *Epistemology of the Closet*, and the writing, the organization of it had come very hard to me for some reason. "So I was amazed at how satisfying its publication was. As an object, the book itself looked lovely—everyone said so. And for an academic book it got a lot of attention, a lot of praise.

"It was one of those happy times when you say to yourself, Okay, this is good, this is enough; I'm ready to go now. When the diagnosis came I was feeling—as an intellectual—loved, used, appreciated. I would have been very, very content to quit while I was ahead."

"Did it surprise you to be feeling that?"

"No. No."

No.

To feel loved and appreciated—I've slowly grown used to that. And to feel the wish of not living! It's one of the oldest sensations I can remember.

"But you didn't get your wish."

"Oh, no, breast cancer doesn't usually work like that. I *felt* sick, but that was from the treatment, not the illness—if the cancer ever does get me, it probably won't be for years. And the chances of that are something like 50-50."

Probably there's a smile on Shannon's face after I produce this. Certainly not because he wants me sick, and not either because he's glad I could be well. It's because, momentarily, he identifies with the mechanical elegance of the trap this disease has constructed for an anxious and ambivalent psyche. 50-50, I think he's thinking, perfect for turning this particular person inside-out.

Sometime in these early sessions, Shannon says about why he became a therapist: "I've always been fascinated by machines. When I was a kid, I'd take them apart and put them back together just to make sure I knew how they worked. It's still a lot of the reason I like my job."

> First encounter: my
> therapist's gift for guyish
> banalization.

o

I arrive with photos for show-and-tell. Diffidently, but Shannon is game for them. Amazing the mix (I think now) of pride and peevishness behind my choice of these pictures! I was thinking, I guess, of therapy as the place for turning the old twining pains into grownup, full-throated grievances. But also want Shannon to see in us that same

> unbroken circle
> of the handsome, provincial
> Jewish family

the photos all mean to offer evidence of.

o

> We are good-looking.
> All Mediterranean,
> all with fine brown frames
>
> and those sparkling or
> soulful, extravagant-lashed
> eyes of chocolate

—all but a dorkily fat, pink, boneless middle child; one of my worst nicknames is "Marshmallow."

o

It's true, it's hard to see my mother's eyes. Except in a couple of languid shots from her twenties, she suffers from "photo-face," the painful, dissociated clamp-eyed rictus

> *tugging at the cords*
> *of her neck to make her look*
> *like Nancy Reagan*

or a tiny Anne Sexton. Another result of this tension is that any child young enough to be held will be transfixed by the flashbulb at some precarious angle to her body, or seem to pop from her arms as toast from a toaster.

Shannon wonders at whom her photo-face is aimed. I guess at my father, always behind the flash? But really, the audience for these photos is the four New York grandparents—especially her mother, Nanny, who sews all the dresses and will want to see (at least, will be supposed to want to see) how family-like they make the young family appear.

Nina, on the other hand, displays the googly eyes in their platonically ideal form, and at this moment of Western culture that makes her "look like Annette Funicello." Uncanny how frontal, as toddler and child, she always manages to be—whether in the mode of cute or seductive;

> *there's something perfect*
> *about her, something that gives*
> *a snap to snapshots.*

o

I haven't brought teenage pictures. Until one, stylized shot where I'm nineteen, eyes crinkled with laughter and embarrassment as Hal, who's twenty-three, is pushing a morsel of our wedding-cake into my mouth. Empathetically, urgingly, his mouth gapes toward mine like a mother bird's.

> *"Is there any way*
> *this Hal can be sweet as he*
> *looks?" Yeah. And then some,*

as seen a few years later in the small circle of unspeakably tender, slightly sad protection he creates for me in a visit to my parents' house. Those are years of acute depression for me, the years that convince me I can't bear to bring my mind close again to the Kosofsky world.

Recent pictures—professional ones, this time—are from my folks' fiftieth anniversary. Mother sends Daddy her brutal photo-face. Her real face, which turns out to be inquisitive, mischievous, and longing, gravitates helplessly (though she isn't trying to help it) toward the un-made-up, white-framed, down-to-earth visage of W.—the new, cherished intimate. A slightly older, German Jewish photographer and professional woman whose gravely literal aura and round eyes are not so unlike my dad's.

My own eyes, blue with the electric blue of my shirt, are also magnetized: blotting up as if passively, one by one, each of the three.

○

"Yes, we always used
to joke at home about my
mom being a dyke."

"What do you mean, *joke*? For that matter, what do you mean 'always'?"

"Well, as long as I can remember, at least from my teens, it was this family . . . joke. Not that it was treated as something that could really happen. But as a true fact about how my mother *was*, what interested her—sure."

"Like what? How would it sound?"

"*You* sound as if you haven't heard this particular family joke before."

"No, I haven't. Though I might like to! I get the feeling it's very Kosofsky?"

"Yeah, that's true—one of those things that make a girl proud to be Kosofsky."

"Were they mean jokes? Would she make them herself?"

"I don't think they were mean at all. Like, she would come back from swimming at the Y, and there'd be a lot of joking about her hanging around the locker room to ogle naked women."

"And she would say it too?"

"Oh, yeah, of course, it was her own account. Or she would joke about crushes she used to have on her teachers, or on women athletes when she was a kid. I think I heard a lot more about Babe Didrickson than most English teachers' daughters do."

"Was there ever serious talk, or just these jokes?"

"Only the jokes. I promise you, that was how we dealt with everything sexual. At least—until she was almost seventy, and met W."

"Tell me some more of them."

"Oh, it's hard for me to remember. There was a standing routine about how she always wanted her hair shorter, how she could never get her haircutters to believe how short she really wanted it. Then as soon as my father or someone would say her hair looked nice, she'd say it was time for a new haircut."

"But in these pictures she doesn't look mannish, does she?"

"No! She's dainty, dainty."

○

"The best thing," I'm telling Shannon one day, "I think the thing I'd most want somebody to know about how I've lived. . . . Oh, I do seem to be confessing to you that I

have the secret vice
of mentally writing my
obituary!

Do you think you can bear it?"

Shannon mimes invitation.

"What I'm proudest of, I guess, is having a life where work and love are impossible to tell apart. Most of my academic work is about gay men, so it might seem strange to you that I would say that—not being a man, not even, I don't think, being gay. But it's still true. The work is *about* sex and love and desire, to begin with—so it's almost bound to be involving at that intimate level. But beyond that, even—Oh, where to start!

"Well, I should say that one true thing about me is that my love is *with* gay men."

I don't quite understand what the term "fag hag" means. Anyway I don't understand what it could mean nowadays. Fag hag conjures up for me a scene at a bar in the 1950s where a lot of self-hating people are getting very drunk— me, I don't even drink.

Anyway, sometimes I think the term fag hag has a fake specificity. Maybe it does the same work that, say, "nigger lover" did in the 50s and 60s: to punish anyone who just doesn't feel some form of contempt that their society says they ought to feel. So I don't have any sense whether or not the term describes me. And of course "It isn't that I like or love all gay men—naturally I don't. I love the particular people I do love.

"Still . . . still. . . all these aspects of my life are so intimately involved with each other."

"A funny fate for someone who's so shy—as though, if you don't have the talent to fake intimacy a lot of the time, you're *forced* to do the real thing?"

○

TALKS ABOUT THE FEELING OF BEING RESPONSIBLE FOR ME—FOR MY INVOLVEMENT, FOR DRAWING OUT MY BEST INTEREST AND INTELLIGENCE TO INTERACT WITH HER. LIKENS IT TO TRYING TO ENGAGE HER MOTHER WHO WOULD INTERACT WITH HER AS A PERSON, AS IF ADULT FOR A TIME AND THEN ARBITRARILY CUT THAT OFF AND TREAT HER LIKE A CHILD BUT IN AN INAUTHENTIC WAY. "NURSERY SCHOOL TEACHER'S VOICE," SING-SONG, OVER-ENUNCIATED, SACCHARINE.

—some estranging sense,
radiating discomfort,
of "mother" with "child."

Hating that: my first
memory of real hatred.
A blade. A glass wall.

"I'm wondering if you were a holy terror," Shannon says one day. "In certain ways you sound like what parents would perceive as quite a difficult kid. But also some, you sound malleable and passive. Do you have a sense of whether you seemed to your folks like a *good* child?"

"Oh, I hope so!" I'm fervent. "That was absolutely all I wanted to be."

"It *was*?"

"Oh, yeah. Is that queer? I literally can't remember a single time I deliberately made mischief. It's funny, I know I must have been a smart, creative kid—it must have been in my nature somewhere to be active, aggressive, even sadistic." The only actual motives I remember having, though, were almost abject. I'd have done anything on earth to win my parents' love and admiration, and keep far away from trouble.

"—oh, and I guess to keep *everyone* away from trouble.

> *As if "middle child"*
> *were like an identity—*
> *or the lack of one,*

since it seemed the very essence of middle-childness to identify with everyone *but* myself." I remember, in fourth grade, reporting in show-and-tell on my sister's arithmetic homework.

"Oh, *that* syndrome—I think I do know that one," says Shannon, and narrates a *Twilight Zone* plot to illustrate—

But no, I never saw it. I'm thinking of a girl-text: *Little Women.* (This, Shannon hasn't read.) Where the sister I yearned toward was not Jo the bookish butch, not pretty artistic Amy, nor—well, did anyone ever identify with Meg?—but rather

> *slow musical Beth,*
> *called by her father "Little*
> *Tranquility," whose*
>
> *death in late girlhood*
> *sets a seal of peace on her*
> *stormy family.*
>
> *"Birds in their little*
> *nests agree" is her favorite*
> *song—even back then*
>
> *I wondered, reading,*
> *whether she was mentally*
> *retarded or just*

stimulus-averse
like me. But oh, the quiet
around such deathbeds!

How low the price of
love: just that one sister, so
willing, disappear.

○

A moment's realization, startlingly clear. "I've figured out what it means when I complain to you about things," I tell him. "Or to anybody. When I tell you how bad it is, how hard I've worked at something, how much I've been through, there is only one phrase I want to hear.
Which is:

"That's enough. You can
stop now."
        Stop: *living, that is.*
And enough: *hurting.*

"Like, 'I didn't realize how hard it was for you; you've done well; you've been through plenty; you're excused.'"

○

That's enough; you can stop now. Isn't this the blessing into whose enfolding arms every complaint of suffering bounds—in its dreams?
    At least, it means that in my native land.
    Five miles across the border, phrasebooks say, it's different.
    There, it's a way that parents calm their kids.

○

FROM AWHILE AGO E HAS LATCHED ONTO THE CONCEPT THAT SHE IS SOMEONE WHO FEELS NEED TO MAKE OTHERS SMARTER—THIS COMING FROM RECOGNITION THAT SHE FELT RESPONSIBLE FOR ELICITING MY INTELLIGENT INTEREST. SHE HAS ASKED SEVERAL PEOPLE ABOUT THIS AND GOT CONFIRMATION EXCEPT FROM ONE FRIEND WHOM SHE CLEARLY FEELS SHE HAS MADE SMARTER. IS REALLY SHAKEN BY THIS BUT STILL HOLDS ONTO THE CONCEPT OF HERSELF AS MAKING PEOPLE SMARTER. (EVE: "MAKE THEM SMART" = SPANK THEM?) RELATES BACK TO THE EARLY ENGAGEMENT PROBLEMS WITH HER MOTHER. BUT FROM THE DEFLATION BROUGHT ABOUT BY HER FRIEND'S DISCON-FIRMATION, SHE FOCUSES ON THE GRANDIOSITY IN THE CONCEPT. MY COMMENT IS THAT NORMAL DEVELOPMENT SEEMS TO ME TO MOVE FROM GRANDIOSITY TO DISIL-LUSIONMENT, BUT IN HER CASE IT MAYBE MOVES TO HER TRYING TO CONSOLIDATE AND MAKE PRACTICAL HER, SOMEWHAT GRANDIOSE, WAY OF SEEING HERSELF.

When Shannon pushes the story toward adolescence, I love evoking Girl Scout camp, age 12—getting a crush on one of the counselors; cutting my thumb with a knife while whittling soap, and being deliciously fussed over and comforted; being inept at all the camp-type activities but still feeling as if I was making a place for myself with sheer, dorky Evie-ness; unexpectedly and unpreparedly getting my period in the middle of all this, very embarrassed but, again, fussed over, enjoying that; intimacy (trading stories about grownup things: death, sex) with a baby butch in my tent; early experiments with the pleasure of voices—mine silvery—in the dark.

I can contrast this lusciously homosocial space with the strained, puppet-like heterosexual impositions and self-impositions of junior high school.

Shannon remarks, "But it doesn't really sound as if there was anything sexual about this girl scout camp space."

"It *doesn't?*"

"I mean, it wasn't coed or anything, not like your school."

Unmistakable manifestations of impatience from the sofa.

"What you're describing about the camp, it sounds like that has to do with nurturance, really, not with sexuality. . . ."

"Like these have nothing to do with each other?"

"Well, sure. But you need to make it clearer, then, what kind of sexual charge some of this might have had, what it felt like to you."

"It felt like—a good image for it is—I mean, *you wouldn't know about this,* but imagine what it feels like when you're about to get your period. There's an almost-familiar tug, a hand closing, in your abdomen . . . you don't particularly associate it with your cycle, at least if you're really young . . . it feels more like your own self-presence, but more so. Later, of course, it turns into ordinary pain,

> *but before being*
> *cramps, it's this pull, as if of*
> *excess gravity—*

that you *could* read as sexual; but you could also *not.* That's the best image I have for being at camp.

"Whereas what was going on at school—it was (at least for me it was) more like trying to learn a language. And except for English, I'm awful at languages."

I find only half a dozen teenage snapshots to show—and mostly they don't show much. Shannon's words for this body and face are matronly, masklike, and I guess I can see why. But one he connects with, showing me under a tree with my father's dad, whom I look just like, and inimitably out-of-it.

It occurs to me to say: Something I see in that picture we haven't talked about and might sometime—that's the notion of "sweet." I think "sweet" is probably pretty important.

Shannon taking off his thick glasses, staring closely at the snapshot. Then, to my surprise, springing nimbly from his chair.

"I'm kind of knock-kneed, so I'm not sure I can do this, but . . ." he says, and I see he's studying the picture and trying to pretzel into just the same posture—feet in a sort of third position, chin and eyes down to the right, hands clasped in a twist behind the back.

Having done so: "Sweet!" he announces. "Sweet! You're right! It feels sweet! I had no idea, just looking at it, quite how sweet it was! But I can feel it in the tension across my shoulders, all the way down into my back; kind of smiling,

looking off to the
side. Yes, sweet *is what I feel!"*
Shannon bewitching.

○

RETURNS TO ABOVE IN THAT SHE TALKS A LOT ABOUT 7TH GRADE AND THE DISMISSAL OF HER FRENCH TEACHER AFTER BEING ARRESTED FOR SOLICITING IN A MEN'S ROOM. THIS INVOLVES A LOT OF THEMATIC MATERIAL. SHE HAD NOT KNOWN THAT, AS HER MOTHER EXPLAINED IT, THERE WERE MEN WHO LOVED OTHER MEN THE WAY MOST MEN LOVE WOMEN. THIS CAUGHT HER IMAGINATION AND SHE BEGAN READING INSATIABLY IN THE AREA, BUT ONLY ABOUT GAY MEN—IT WAS ONLY LATER THAT SHE LEARNED ABOUT LESBIANS. THIS INTENSITY WAS SOME PROPELLED BY HER CHAGRIN AT HAVING MISREAD THE FRENCH TEACHER SO COMPLETELY—HER PERCEPTUAL ACUMEN HAVING FAILED HER. YET IN THE LOOKING INTO AND LEARNING ABOUT IT HER FASCINATION WITH IMPLICIT THEMES WAS ENGAGED AND SHARPENED. IT ALSO PROVIDED SOMETHING OF AN OUT IN HER STRUGGLE WITH THE HETEROSEXUAL DEMANDS OF ADOLESCENCE—THAT THERE COULD BE SOMETHING OTHER THAN THE TRADITIONAL HETERO RELATIONS, AND MEN WHO MIGHT HAVE AN INTEREST IN WOMEN OTHER THAN THE TRADITIONAL ONE. WHAT STRIKES ME MOST HERE IS EARLY ABILITY TO TURN A SITUATION OF PROHIBITION AND RIGID EITHER / OR INTO A NEW INTEREST THAT IS ELASTIC, PRODUCTIVE, EXCITING FOR E'S VIEW OF WORLD. BUT HOW TO RELATE TO HER JR HS DEPRESSION??

○

CONTINUES ON THE THEME OF THE ANXIETY ATTENDANT ON HER IN THE FAMILY SPACE. MEMORIES OF BEING TEASED / RIDICULED ABOUT NOT BEING ABLE TO TAKE A JOKE, BEING THIN SKINNED, ETC. SHE OFTEN DID NOT FEEL PART OF / BELIEVE SHE WAS PART OF THE FAMILY, AND SO WAS OPEN TO ATTACK FROM VARIOUS MEMBERS. SHE ACTUALLY WAS DIFFERENT IN SKIN FROM ALL OF THE OTHERS IN THE FAMILY AND SO WHEN THEY WENT TO THE BEACH SUMMERS SHE BOTH WAS THE OBJECT OF A LOT OF GREASING AND CREAMING AND CONCERN, AND ALSO ALWAYS BURNED. THE TACTILE SENSE OF PAIN AND THE UNHAPPINESS AND ALIENNESS ARE VIVID IN HER MEMORY. NOW, WHEN SHE GOES TO THE BEACH, SHE STAYS IN DURING THE DAY AND

°

But then when we've gotten up to go after this session and we're confirming our times for the next week or two, suddenly I notice Shannon suspended motionless, gazing dumbly at his appointment book. I wait patient for about half a minute. Then, "Yesss?" I quiz him.

He looks up with a strange smile.

"Well," he says, "I seem to have somebody else's name written down for your time next Friday. And it isn't that I got mixed up and made an appointment with somebody else, either—I knew it was with you. I just wrote down somebody else's name instead."

There's a long, odd silence. I feel vastly amused, I guess at the "psychoanalytic" stylization of this moment. Also funnily touched. Also I suppose ready to feel insulted (who's been eating my porridge?), though not actually feeling so. Want to say something

> like, well, sweetheart, you're
> the shrink, you're supposed to tell
> me what all this means.

But Shannon remains very taken aback—for him it's too early to laugh. I see there's something disproportionate going on, but I've no way of knowing whether it's *all* about me, his feelings for me, or *none*. Or just a little. Is this a joke I'm in on, that I make the pith of—or is there some other intimacy on his docket, so vastly stronger or sweeter than ours that even to associate the two makes a joke?

It feels unexpectedly haimish and familiar, this included / excluded relation to Shannon's inner process.

I'm also noting, the discussion of slips of this kind has formed *no* part of our discourse. I'd looked forward to it in advance, but I've only had reason to feel how resistant he always seems to focusing on the level of the signifier. Yet this mistake really captures him—captures and throws him.

Finally I can gather my wits a little and say, I hope affectionately and lightly (but I'm not sure), "I guess if you really want to see someone else during that hour, it could be arranged."

To which he responds with, again, disproportionate amusement or *something*: still with the appointment book open at his waist, he swings back on his heels in a 360-degree revolution of inarticulacy, to wind up facing me again, laughing heartily—and we say a cheerful goodbye.

Odd little man.

We stumble back to a notation that really struck me as right.

Namely: I envision my bond with my mother as a therapy relationship, in which I am the therapist. Probably I have always related to her in this way.

That is: I've had an
immemorial motive
of eliciting,

supporting, helping
her inhabit and extend
a certain "true self"

rather than a more available false self, that nursery-school "mother."

Shannon likes the idea. But he wants me to feel, too, the important differ-ence from real therapy: that this therapist *needed* and yearned for exposure to that true self of the patient's.

(Maybe all that made it "true" was that it *was* what I needed?)

o

It comes to me, too,
that even though it was my
own, childish needs that

drove the "therapy,"
our practice must also have
required me (or else—

permitted me?) to
learn a rather imposing
habit of silence

about my own needs.
Hasn't that been the major
defense I've mounted

against my mother
all these years?—defense of and
also against her.

o

I'm saying to him one day, "Apparently I see myself as quite a timid person—though also, I guess, brave, in a different register. But sometimes I think you see me as timid in ways I don't even have a clue about."

And he nods seriously.

But he adds: "I don't think timidity is just a trait that lives inside a person, but instead, something relational.

"There are lots of things that are perfectly easy if you're doing them with someone else, but almost impossible if you feel you're doing them alone."

Which is just plain true!
Like going to a party
where no one knows you—

excruciating
by yourself, effortless when
a friend will come too—

o

And at once it's vivid to me again, the bliss of moving within a beloved aegis. It feels more than protective. It feels electrifying.

The pride, in childhood,
of going anywhere with
my older sister!

The extravagant
rightness of it! Intimate
sanction for us two,

to be sealed with my
favorite pronoun: the dear
first person plural.

o

It never surprised *me* that "we," in French, means yes.

Even in adulthood I'm addicted to the word. "Oh, yes, we saw that movie." "Our favorite restaurant." "We figured out—"

Hal, Michael, my family, students, friends find it puzzling. "*We* saw that? Not that I remember."

Secretly this is a matter of pride to me.

Promiscuous we!
Me, plus anybody else.
Permeable we!

o

I want to know, "Don't you ever find yourself *suspicious* when I'm so sanguine about all these intimate relationships of mine—Hal, Michael, friends, students? Don't you wonder, can that much good relating really happen? And where are all the conflicts?"

With some thought, he says, "For a long time I was aware of staying agnostic about it. Not suspicious, but close to that. But over time, I guess I've figured that if you've been systematically misperceiving all these relationships—well, it *is* systematic. Are you asking this because you want to flash me a yellow light about it?"

"No, no, I don't think so. But I sometimes wonder

> *whether you think I*
> *over-idealize my*
> *friends. Kind of wholesale."*

"You think?"

"I think *about* it, sure. Last week Mary described me to myself as 'scattering sequins over us all'—all the people I love. She's right, she and they do seem so glamorous and numinous to me. I always see the light shaking out of their wings. It does shock me when anyone views them in an ordinary light—or worse, when they see each other that way."

Shannon says, "You don't seem so given to *dis*enchantment."

"Only with you!" I have to answer him laughing. "I seem to play that game over and over with you. My Barbie doll to dress and undress.

"Otherwise, really no. Except for very early in relationships. It's as though I want to start out powdering people with fairy dust when I first know them—like there's a working hypothesis that I'll trust them, we're playing the same exciting game, that they're radiant, kind, mysteriously talented, spiritually powerful. With lots of people the sequins naturally drop off soon, quite without melodrama or, really, embitterment. But if people stay numinous to me for a while, then there they are—in the pantheon."

Shannon says, yes, he does see me very given to such idealizations.

There's a long silence.

Often it's sobering to be agreed with.

°

I pick up with the idealizing habit, how it's related to being so depressive. Asking Shannon, "Do you think it's just defending me against a fearful certainty that, if I ever took off my emerald glasses, or stopped hurling sequins, the world around me would be exposed as black-and-white instead of color; or awful; or just plain dead?"

> *Meaning: is all this*
> *Bob Mackie glamour holding*
> *onto one big lie?*

"I see that sometimes that's exactly the feeling," Shannon says. "I've known other people besides you who do this, too. But actually it seems like a pretty wonderful adaptation.

"It makes them happier, and it makes the people around them different and better. It improves the environment."

"You mean it's *nice*."

"Well, yeah. Not *just* nice. But can you keep it in your head how very nice it is, and also that it's a kind of depressive idealization—at the same time?"

"You mean without ontologically ranking the two views of it?"

"Mm-hmm. Because it's the pressure to rank them that's *really* depressive, isn't it?"

○

AT THE END OF THE HOUR SHE SKETCHES A DREAM. SHE IS 10 MINUTES LATE FOR AN APPOINTMENT WITH ME AND ARRIVES AT MY HOUSE, WHERE EVERYTHING IS IN DISARRAY. I AM THERE, A NUMBER OF KIDS WHO KEEP POPPING UP, PEOPLE COMING AND GOING, MY WIFE. E IS INCLUDED IN WHAT IS GOING ON, BUT IS NOT ABLE TO GET MY FULL ATTENTION, ALTHOUGH HER FEELING IS ALSO ONE OF INTIMACY AND PLEASURE. THERE IS A CHILD WHO IS BEING CARED FOR BY A SEEMINGLY RETARDED WOMAN READING TO HIM. KID'S NAME IS DAVID. E WAS LATE BECAUSE SHE HAD TROUBLE GETTING DRESSED, AND HER CLOTHES ARE ON HER BODY IN SOMETHING OF A STUCK ON MANNER. SHE HAS BROUGHT A CHIFFON PIE AND NOTICES THAT HER BRA HAS GOTTEN BAKED INTO A LAYER OF THE PIE. SHE PULLS IT OUT SAYING THAT SOME SCARF HAS GOTTEN IN HERE, TRYING TO CONCEAL THAT IT IS HER BRA. I GO OFF INTO A BATHROOM. SHE FINDS HERSELF UNDER A LAP ROBE WITH ANOTHER PERSON AND MY WIFE, ARMS AROUND EACH OTHER'S SHOULDERS. SHE ASKS ABOUT THE KIDS AND MY WIFE SAYS DAVID IS OUR SHADOW CHILD, AN EXPERIMENT THAT FAILED. SHE REFLECTS ON HAVING COME TO SEE ME BUT ENDING UP CLOSE WITH MY WIFE.

○

DREAM—MEAT COUNTER AND PILE OF TINY, COLORED, DEAD, ADORABLE ELEPHANTS. —WITHOUT MAGICAL THINKING I IMAGINE THE WORLD WOULD BE GRAY, NO COLORS, AIR PUSHED OUT OF IT, LIKE A PILE OF DEAD LITTLE ELEPHANTS—THE HORROR WAS IN HOW CUTE THEY STILL WERE—

○

At first I thought I'd know when therapy was successful because I'd stop feeling the want of being dead.

But, I finally say to Shannon, "This is such a deep, old fact about me that it could be a *terrible* index of what might change. If I waited for that. . . !"

I'm wondering now what else might be different and better—even for someone who remains convinced, with the ancients, that it would be best not to be born.

Yes, Shannon says. He too has assumed this is a likely scenario: many other things changing but the one thing not changing. Also, he says, if such a thing did change it would probably do so imperceptibly slowly.

Then he produces an apparent non sequitur. A story about a patient of his long ago, someone with "not exactly multiple personalities,

> *but I would say that*
> *the parts of her were only*
> *barely holding hands,"*

who after many years—in fact long after the end of therapy—woke up one morning and found she no longer had multiples. Just that suddenly.

Looking back, I think he's produced this story "just in case." Just in case, that is, what my announcement really meant was something different, something like "I think I'm ready to relinquish this stubborn symptom, but I'm scared about what will be left of *me*."

I love his floating the story so coolly *as* a non sequitur—a story about the non-necessity, in therapy, of what "follows." It gives me a clue. I want to be open to the chance that what any clamorous pain

> *wants to tell me, is*
> *that it is ready at last*
> *to bid me goodbye.*

○

After this, in fact, I get very charmed and relaxed by everything that looks like non-necessity. I've started noticing how lots of Shannon's best comments—the ones that change the aspect of things for me—amount to nothing more profound than "It ain't necessarily so."

Nowadays, when students ask me, about one thing or another, "But wouldn't that clearly imply—?" or "Doesn't that have to involve—?", it feels Shannonlike when I can respond,

> *that may not be a*
> *theoretical question.*
> *Just empirical.*

○

THREE HOURS TODAY; E'S MOTHER, THEN HER FATHER, THEN E LATE IN THE DAY. THE STYLE OF THE PARENTS IS QUITE DIFFERENT. RITA IS ALWAYS MOVING; YOU ARE NEVER SURE IF YOU WILL GET A "REAL" ANSWER, OR A "CANNED" ONE, OR AN EVASION.

"I've never met anyone who moves around so much," he tells me—"not physically but in terms of where she *is* in the conversation. It made me think of the old *Starship Enterprise.* 'Yes, I think we're getting a radar fix—*no*, it's *gone*, no, I think we're getting closer. . . sorry, sir, it's drifting—yes *here* it is. . .'"

SHE COMMUNICATES THE PROMISE OF SOMETHING INTERESTING AND REAL AND SOMEHOW EDIFYING, BUT DOES NOT RELIABLY DELIVER. SHE IS QUITE BRIGHT, ERUDITE, AND CREATIVE. THE FATHER IS MUCH WARMER AND KINDER, BUT WITHOUT THE BRIGHT INCISIVE-

NESS OF HIS WIFE. HIS TALK IS ALLUSIVE AND FRAGMENTED—DENSE AND SOMEHOW MELANCHOLY. HE ALSO DWELLS ON THE LATER YEARS EVEN WHEN I TRY TO GET HIM TO TALK ABOUT THE EARLY YEARS.

RITA, IN CONTRAST, STAYS WITH THE PRE-TEEN YEARS. SHE PRESENTS A PICTURE OF A CHILD WHO SPRANG INTO BEING FULLY FORMED. SHE REALIZED EARLY THAT E WAS BRILLIANT AND, DENYING ANY INTIMIDATION BY OR TROUBLE WITH THE BRILLIANCE, SAYS SHE WAS NOT AFRAID OF E AS LONG AS SHE WAS BIGGER THAN E . . . THEN SAYS THAT THAT DIDN'T LAST LONG.

Shannon says the sense of this kid being uncanny or a changeling was stronger than he could have pictured. He mentions several stories they both told, going way back to toddlerhood, that somehow all led to the same punchline: "—and from then on we realized she was going to go her own way." Somehow as if any display of my agency was the same as a full-scale declaration of independence? As if the day I quit nursery school was the day I left for college.

"From what you say I almost wonder if they perceived me as a child at all— whether they had any ordinary enjoyment of me as a kid, or attention to me as one, or worries about me, that weren't organized around the supposed strangeness of this presence."

"I tried and tried to elicit stories like that," he says. "They just wouldn't come up with any. Was she cute? Did you have fun with her? Did she have trouble teething? No."

A long pause.

THROUGHOUT THE INTERVIEW SHE CASTS THINGS IN TERMS OF "AREN'T ALL FAMILIES" OR "MOST CHILDREN ARE." YET SHE IS CLEARLY VERY INVESTED IN THIS GIRL.

ANOTHER TRAIT IS HER USE OF "NOT SOMETHING ONE WOULD ASK, OR TALK ABOUT, OR MENTION" IN A NUMBER OF CONTEXTS. SHE ALWAYS WONDERED WHY E & HAL DIDN'T HAVE CHILDREN BUT WOULD NEVER ASK. ESPECIALLY IN THE AREA OF SEXUALITY SHE SAYS THAT THEY WERE NOT RESTRICTIVE (WE NEVER COVERED THE CHILDREN'S NAKEDNESS) BUT NOT PRONE TO TALK ABOUT IT. BUT THEN SAYS THAT HER STUDENTS HAVE COMMENTED TO HER ON THE AMOUNT OF SEXUAL ALLUSION IN HER TEACHING. THEN SAYS THAT ALL CHILDREN ARE SEXUALLY AWARE AND FEELING EARLY. SHE WAS AWARE OF E'S MASTURBATION BUT, OF COURSE, WOULD NEVER HAVE MENTIONED IT. THE FATHER IS "IN AWE OF" E RATHER THAN BEING AFRAID OF HER.

I TALK WITH E, TELLING HER ALL THIS FOR ALMOST THE WHOLE HOUR. SHE IS QUITE PLEASED AND RELIEVED THAT I SAW THE THINGS SHE HAS BEEN TELLING ME SHE EXPERIENCED. —AFTER THE HOUR, I FEEL SOME DOWN. AS BEST I FORMULATE IT, IT IS THAT WELL, YES IT REALLY WAS LIKE I THOUGHT IT WAS AND SO NOW WHAT. NO SECRETS TO UNCOVER. NOTHING TO FIND OUT TO MAKE IT BE DIFFERENT. WILL SEE IF E HAS ANY OF THIS REACTION.

∘

That night, my folks have a chance to compare notes about their conversations with Shannon. My father remarks on a phrase they both found themselves using: something like,

> *"Eve always knew what*
> *she knew, and knew she knew it.*
> *Whether she was* right. . . ."

o

But over the weekend I get a chance to ask my mother, "Can you bear another psychohistory question? Would you tell me some about what it was like for you to have Nanny as a mother?"

I see her scanning the angles of this question—

> *what particular*
> *damning judgments of herself*
> *mightn't it entail?*

Finally, generously, she doesn't second-guess it. "Mmm. *Pretty* good, I'd say. Certainly, she tried hard. Pretty good–*considering*."

"How's that?"

"Well, of course different people would give you different answers about any parent. For me, the hardest thing about Nanny was her very loud voice. You know that's not something it's easy for me to deal with, and I've developed a very different manner from that, myself. *That* was painful for me.

"Also Nanny was very certain in her judgments; she always knew she was right. She had a hasty temper and she would let you feel her anger."

"Though," Daddy adds, "she never held a grudge."

"No, that's very true, when her anger was over, it was over.

"She was an intensely intelligent woman," my mother is going on, "*intensely*, and she accomplished an amazing amount considering her lack of education—if she'd been educated, she's somebody who would have made a mark in the world."

I pipe up, "It's always been hard for me to imagine Nanny as the mother of babies. I remember when I was little, she used to terrify me—always threatening to *gobble me up* because I looked so *delicious*. As if irony and aggression were her only modes of affection. 'You have such *rough skin*! Such *disgustingly* rough skin! RRRrrrr!' It was years before I could decide whether she actually meant these things: I remember explicitly telling myself she couldn't, because everyone else said I had really soft skin! And even then I found it alarming. Her voice was so raucous, her movements were so startling and abrupt. But was she like that with you too?"

Yes, my mother says, she was.

o

There's a pair of us?
She refined to her quiet
by the long labor

of refusing her
mother's noisy and pointed
wit of the fishwife—

and her own relish
in it—I, the refusal
of a refusal—

o

Refusals everywhere, these corrosive ones–

Also, though: my mother could have felt, early on, somehow that this odd child's presence embodied her own mother. Someone she'd find, at unpredictable moments, really alarming—

the both of us so
quick to be certain that we
knew what we did know.

The dangerous thing about being mistaken by my mother for her own, apparently all-powerful mother, was that she would fantasy me, too, to be competent, powerful, invulnerable.

Me, sobbing and sobbing. But saying,

Okay—my mouth wants
to say she couldn't believe
that, being a child,

I needed care and
attention. But the simple
truth is that I still

identify with
her enough not really to
believe it myself.

o

On a day soon thereafter:

> "I've had in mind the
> conventional terms of the
> family romance
>
> where they think I'm just
> their kid, but I know that I'm
> really the exiled
>
> daughter of the king
> and queen of Mars. But this is
> just the opposite!
>
> Isn't it? Where they
> are convinced that, for better
> or worse, I come from
>
> some other planet—
> and it's I who don't know,
> I who think to be
>
> their own, peasant child,
> to be one of them. —In fact
> who longs to be so."

Shannon makes it sound as though they were apt to treat me as a kind of independent contractor living in the house—or ambassador of a neighboring principality, maybe.

"Do you think that's why their discipline always felt so cataclysmically raw to me?" I suddenly think to ask. "It's not that it was frequent, or especially brutal. But it's children who get spanked, not ambassadors. If I was used to all that inexplicable protocol, then it must have felt like the strangest assault on my dignity. Almost, my national dignity! Mustn't it?

○

The next morning,

> just waking—massive
> as having a stroke—come two
> realizations.
>
> "But," I tell Shannon,
> "like Jeopardy!, the trick here
> is in the question.

"Here's the question: how to relate young Eve's family situation, on the one hand, to her personal / professional / political / academic engagements over the past 15 years, and specifically her relation to queer stuff, on the other?"

"Yeah? I'm listening."

"Okay, in each case, imagine somebody who expends extortionate amounts of energy trying to convince the members of some group (*not* a particularly privileged group, *not* a high-status group, in fact a clannish, defensive, stigmatized, but proud, and above all an interesting group) that she, too, is to be accepted as—and in fact, truly *is*—a member of this group. A kid, a Kosofsky—or later, gay. But each time, it's in the face of some inherent, in fact obvious absurdity about the claim."

"But," Shannon sensibly asks her, "why would she want to do that?"

"Well of course as a kid, because I have no choice about it. But then as an adult because—what, because it 'feels right,' feels productive and *true*, too. Oh, and of course by then, because it's what I'm used to doing."

> *Only visibly*
> more *preposterous this time,*
> *now that I almost*
>
> *know what it is that*
> *I'm claiming or offering—*
> *it's like a big dare,*
>
> *also like a big*
> *allegory about love.*
> *Experimental.*
>
> *And at least to me,*
> *metamorphic (which is how*
> *I recognize love).*

It's as if I can now understand the ineffable happiness—and the fragility and depletion attaching to it, too—that goes, for me, with being accepted and loved (in my personal life, I mean) as an essential, central member of a queer family. Whose ideology, yes, I do a lot of the work of articulating, making new, making compelling to others.

In this small (but not quite circumscribable) context, yes, I can recognize others and be recognized in many aspects that don't, this time around, seem to denegate one another: as loving *and* bright, as included and constitutive, and not too scary. . . .

While on a bigger gay / lesbian scene, what I've maybe helped happen (both for me, and for the self-perception and group-perception of some other people) is so much more partial, iffy, streaky, potentially upsetting, often thrilling, feels completely risky—but it's a recognizable transformation of the same project: trying to convince this family I'm not the daughter of the king and queen of Mars.

○

Next thing I see: it makes so much sense how this adult project of queer community resonates with my old need to "be my mother's therapist," to promote her turning into somebody less anxious and fuller.

Especially, I mean, to the extent that her potential for being different, and happier, was visibly tied up with a lesbian possibility.

Because that lesbian component went in

> *two directions whose*
> *double-vectoring now feels*
> *so familiar and*
>
> *(in a bizarre way)*
> *so "comfortable" to me: first,*
> *as having something*
>
> *obscurely to do with*
> *who I was, woman myself.*
> *But at the same time*
>
> *how much of what she*
> *suffered was a deeply lodged*
> *protest against a*
>
> *life immobilized*
> *in this nuclear scene of*
> *caring for children?*
>
> *So the girl child who*
> *somewhere in the future makes*
> *part of the scene—still*
>
> *has to nonexist*
> *if the beloved is to*
> *materialize.*

○

> *Melodrama of*
> *uncertain agency, called*
> *"Bringing Out Momma."*

FREE FLOATING CREATIVITY LATELY. SUDDENLY LOTS OF ARTS AND CRAFTS FASCIN-
ATION.

It's strange, because I'm excited about writing—at least the one project,
Shannon's. But this thrills me (I don't think I've had quite this feeling before)
because it is so *not* writing.

Writing, my perfectionism gets all over everything. I wrestle and contort to
keep it at bay long enough for words to get onto the screen. Like Michelangelo
knowing what's supposed to emerge from the marble block, my task is to excise
everything that isn't *that*. Maybe it's called "knowing what you're doing"; it
feels less and less good.

But in this other, indiscriminate realm, that conscience has no foothold.
What *am* I doing? Messing with "stuff." Having materials in my hands; seeing,
at an instant of pause and speculation, whether there's something satisfying,
something surprising to me, that they *almost* are.

> *Little to ask! When*
> *they turn into anything*
> *(lovely)—I'm in joy.*

°

It's hard for me to admit to Shannon, around this time, a habit I have on gray
days or early evenings, when I'm sad or ragged, of driving past the corner of
Ninth and Main streets, casting my eyes for solace up four stories to the lit-up

> *honeyed cell of his*
> *availability to*
> *someone—if not me.*

°

DREAM WITH HAL AND ME AND MY MOTHER. HAL AND I HAVING SEX IN A BIG OLD
HOTEL—ENJOYING—BUT I HAVE TO FIND MY MOTHER—LOOKING FOR HER—REAL-
IZE THAT I FORGOT TO NOTICE WHETHER EITHER OF US HAD AN ORGASM—DISCON-
CERTING—HOTEL UNDER RENOVATION AND THERE ARE EXPOSED FLOORS, WHOLE
SIDES OPEN WITH NO WALLS. CANNOT GET TO THE DINING ROOM THAT MY MOTHER
IS IN FROM WHERE I AM: ORIGINALLY TWO DIFFERENT BUILDINGS WITH DIFFERENT
FOUNDATIONS. THEN THERE TURNS OUT TO BE A WAY—IF YOU GO AROUND AND
THROUGH A BACK ENTRANCE. —DREAM LEAVES E DELIGHTED WITH THIS PORTRAYAL
OF HER SEXUALITY AT THIS TIME—THE EXPOSED STRUCTURE, INCOHERENCE OF LEV-
ELS, THE CONFUSION OF HAL AND HER MOTHER; QUESTION OF ORGASM JUST FLOAT-
ING OUT THERE.

It does seem quite a strangeness—the floating downstream with a current that's so, resolutely wordless. As though in all its modesty, its refusal to generate propositions, selves, ideas, this might be a cataclysmic change disguised as an unassuming indulgence. As though if I let my

> *habitual* yes
> *stretch this far there could never*
> *be another no.*

NECK PAIN!! / TEARFUL, FEELING BAD. WILL CONTACT M.D. TODAY.

○

SILK WORK—TURNING FABRIC INTO OTHER FABRIC / CHILDHOOD BLANKET WITH THE SATIN BINDING / SKIN HUNGER / THE FASCINATION EVERYONE HAD WITH HOW SILKY MY SKIN WAS / BRO'S PILLOW "PIFFO," HIS DROOLING, "MAKING FISHES" ON IT / MAY SAY SOMETHING ABOUT HOW HUNGRY OUR SKIN WAS FOR TOUCH; BUT ALSO ABOUT OUR HAVING THE PERMISSION TO DEVELOP AUTONOMOUS RESOURCES / THE DOWNSIDE OF BEING SILKY WAS THAT SOMEHOW I WAS AN OBJECT FOR OTHERS TO SATISFY THEIR TOUCH NEEDS, NOT MINE / TREASURE SCRAPS OF SILK / SOMEHOW THE SILK AND SHIT GO TOGETHER—THE WASTE PRODUCTS, FANTASIES OF SELF SUFFICIENCY, NOT DEPENDENT, SPINNING STRAW INTO GOLD.

○

GOOD WORK ON AN ATTRACTIVE WOVEN SCARF, THE PRODUCT OF THE WEEKEND'S LEARNING HOW TO WORK WITH THE TABLE LOOM. TACTILE, NON-VERBAL, REGRESSIVE, ENJOYABLE. LACKING THE CONSTANT ALERTNESS IN HER WRITING ABOUT BEING OR BECOMING THE RIGHT PERSON TO DO IT. // TWICE E IS IN THE MIDDLE OF PARSING THE THREADS OF INFLUENCES AND MEANINGS OF SOME PART OF THIS OR SOME TOPIC AND THE THREAD OF THE REASONING GETS LOST—NOT SURE WHAT THIS IS, MORE THAN JUST BEING PREOCCUPIED WITH WEAVING. . . .

○

RESISTANCE TO GOING BACK TO THE *DIALOGUE ON LOVE* IS THAT PRODUCTION OF THE FIRST PERSON IS BOTH LABOR INTENSIVE AND FELT TO BE CONSTRAINING, THAT THERE WERE EMOTIONAL REGISTERS THAT WEREN'T AVAILABLE WHILE GENERATING FIRST PERSON. A TEXTURE BOOK WOULDN'T NEED TO HAVE A FIRST PERSON AT ALL, ANY MORE THAN WEAVING ITSELF DOES. THAT RHYMES WITH A LOT OF STUFF FOR ME—THE BUDDHIST STUFF, MANIA FOR MAKING UNSPEAKING OBJECTS, THE CHILDHOOD EXPERIENCE OF TRAVELING IN THE CAR WITH THE FAMILY IN THE DARK . . . EVEN FANTASY OF "SILVERY VOICE."

○

The cars, each of us,
bubbles of the same dark, strung
in a dark necklace.

o

I can't remember if it's Michael or Stephen who first shows me Sogyal Rinpoche's *Tibetan Book of Living and Dying.* Of course I head straight for the chapters on how to die, which feel awfully alien; but as I start to read from the beginning, something else happens.

One assumption I realize, with surprise, I've seen before in Proust: that when

the truth comes to you,
you recognize it because
it makes you happy.

o

HAD SCAN OF NECK FRI. TO RULE OUT ANYTHING MORE THAN MUSCLE STRAIN AS CAUSE OF THE NECK PAIN—TURNS UP A SPINAL METASTASIS OF THE BREAST CANCER OF ALMOST 6 YEARS AGO. I ASK WHAT IT MEANS. SAYS IT MEANS SHE WILL DIE OF THIS—NOT NECESSARILY SOON THOUGH, AS CANCER SEEMS AN INDOLENT ONE AND SO FAR ONLY IN E'S BONES. 2 YRS–5 YRS? SOME LIVE A DECADE OR MORE. REACTION SO FAR IS A LITTLE RELIEF OF THE "OTHER SHOE" VARIETY AND JUST DEALING WITH THE HUGE LOGISTICS OF MORE WORKUPS, NECK BRACE, PLANS FOR RADIATION, WHAT TO DO ABOUT THE SEMESTER'S TEACHING, ETC. IN SOME SENSE THIS STILL A REACTION TO THE DIAGNOSIS, WITH HER REACTION AS IT RELATES TO HER LIFE STILL TO REGISTER.

Phones just outside the
clinic door.
  Impermanence
arrives so quickly!

o

DREAM—MEDICAL CHECKUP IN BUILDING MADE OVER FROM ROMANESQUE CATHEDRAL—E ARRIVES WITH HAL, THEN IS WITH TWO NURSES AND NOTICES SHE IS SEPARATED FROM HAL, CONCERNED THAT HE WILL BE WORRIED AND UNABLE TO FIND THEM—EXAM BY HER ONCOLOGIST AND AN OLDER M.D., HER ONCOLOGIST HAS CANCER NOW AND THE OLDER M.D. HAS HAD IT, HAS SHIRT OFF AND SCARS ON HIS TORSO. —MOVING AROUND IN THE BUILDING EVE CATCHES GLIMPSE OF A HIGH, ROUNDARCHED ATTIC ROOM SOMEONE HAS JUST LEFT, EMPTY NOW BUT FULL OF GOLDEN YELLOW LIGHT FOR READING, AND FEELS A LONGING TO BE THERE—RESULT OF TESTS IS BENIGN, THOUGH, AND SHE IS SORROWFUL WITH SOME OF THE "DO I BELONG IN THIS FAMILY?" FEELING //

DREAM WITH HER IN SESSION AND MY SAYING INSTEAD OF TALKING I WOULD PLAY THE PIANO, A PIECE WRITTEN FOR THE CROWN AND BEING SENT TO THE UNREBELLIOUS DISSIDENTS IN THE NORTH. SHE FINDS THE PIECE RELAXING AND THE CONCEPT OF MUSIC BEING SENT TO THE UNREBELLIOUS DISSIDENTS TO ENFOLD THEM INTO THE SPHERE OF THE CROWN FASCINATING.

○

Humiliating to me, but when mortality gets personal—so suddenly—the thought of hell refuses to go away. I'm a good rationalist, but it hovers around, and a couple of bad nights give me a crash course in how it can colonize, infect the thought of dying.

Worse, though, it just won't make sense to me, hell. It has nothing to do with my belief. There are five of the Ten Commandments, say, that engage my actual sense of the right and the wrong; and to put it mildly, the people and institutions that are insistent about hell engage it a lot less. Could I really suffer eternally for breaking sanctions that can only seem to me like wicked gibberish?

You'd think my heart could dismiss the possibility of a universe so arbitrary

> and at the same time
> so punitive . . .
>   "But wait till
> your father gets home."

That we each die alone and must work out our salvation in our own way— these seem most urgent spurs, no longer truisms at my new juncture.

○

HAD A BREAKDOWN, LOSING IT, IN THE WAITING ROOM ABOUT THE POSSIBILITY OF BECOMING PHOBIC ABOUT IVS (WHICH WOULD MAKE HER LIFE HELL GIVEN ALL THE IVS SHE IS BOUND TO GET). FEAR OF FEAR OF PAIN: IVS A FOCAL POINT FOR UNEXPRESSED FEELINGS ABOUT THE WHOLE EXPERIENCE. BUT SOME OF IT IS THE PUNCTURING OF ONE BODY LAYER AND THEN ANOTHER LAYER OF PAIN INSIDE, VEINS ROLLING AROUND RUBBERY AND BRITTLE FROM CHEMO, INESCAPABLE, BEING UNABLE TO JUST BE PASSIVE, LET IT WASH OVER HER (HER USUAL RESOURCE FOR DEALING WITH PAIN).

○

Meanwhile the question of wanting things—being able to want and inhabit the life, the time and loves I have—focuses acutely, and I'm not surprised that the organ where it seems to have taken up dwelling, at this moment, is the fingers.

Not that I think of arresting the thread of life as it draws through them, but there's this hunger, that feels like a skin-hunger, to handle every rough or silky twist of its passing. I understand it as

> enjoining care to
> the material senses,
> and to making stuff.

○

MEANWHILE—*THE TIBETAN BOOK OF THE DEAD*. THE MODEL OF A TRUE AND REVE-LATORY RELATIONSHIP IS THE GRATITUDE AND TENDERNESS BETWEEN MOTHER AND CHILD / TEACHER AND STUDENT—THE UNIQUE IDEA THAT YOU CAN TELL IF IT'S TRUE BY THE FEELINGS OF TENDERNESS AND GRATITUDE (NOT OEDIPAL-STYLE ENVY, LACK, VIOLENCE)—THAT THIS IS ALSO THE RELATIONSHIP BETWEEN YOU AND THE UNIVERSAL LUMINOSITY WHICH IS (ALSO) YOU. SOME TENSION AS THE MODELS USED ARE INTER-SUBJECTIVE (E.G., TEACHER / STUDENT) BUT NON-DUAL. BUT E: "NON-DUALISM IS MOTHER'S MILK TO ME." THE POSSIBILITY THAT SOME PASSAGE OF DISCONTINUITY LIKE DEATH CAN BE THE OCCASION OF ENLIGHTENMENT, IF YOU DO IT RIGHT, I.E., IF YOU CAN BE IN A PLACE TO RECOGNIZE A LOVE THAT IS YOU AND IS ALSO TOWARDS YOU. — THOUGHT OF THE PANDA AS EMBLEMATIC OR SOMEHOW SYMBOLIC OF BUDDHA FOR E—A STYLIZED FIGURE, NOT INDIVIDUALIZED, SOMETHING THAT ENABLES THE RECOG-NITION OF PERSONALLY SPECIFIC THINGS IN, E.G., HAL AND ME THAT ARE LOVABLE, BUT IT ALSO DEINDIVIDUATES US , MOTHER AND/OR CHILD—SUBJECT AND/OR OBJECT . . .

With my puritanical modernist aesthetic I used to think it was embarrass-ing, in a religion like Buddhism, to have images of divinity scattered all over the landscape. It had that whiff of idolatry.

"But I was reading this book, and I happened to look up around my living room, and what was there? Like, twelve or fifteen stuffed pandas and pictures of pandas."

Not because I view them as gods! Not because I believe, even, in god—like my belief mattered.

But because to see them makes me happy. Seeing self and others transmo-grified through them—the presence, gravity, and clumsy comedy of these big, inefficient, contented, very endangered bodies. With all their sexual incompe-tence and soot-black, cookie-cutter ears. It seems so obvious that the more such images there are, the happier.

And it means a lot, to be happy.

It may even mean: to be good. Ungreedy, unattached, unrageful, unigno-rant. Far different from the pharisaism that says, "I am lucky and happy because I am good," a modest occasional knowledge: I'm good, if I am, because I'm lucky enough to be happy (if I am).

It never seems sensible to pass along moral injunctions. I sometimes think that beyond the Golden Rule,

the only one that
matters is this: If you can
be happy, you should.

○

WONDERS IF SHE IS SHUTTING DOWN SOME AFFECTS, BUT FEELS MORE THAT SHE IS FEELING GOOD, NOT ANXIOUS, READY FOR THESE NEW PROJECTS, TRYING TO HONESTLY RELATE TO THE FUTURE OF HER DEATH. HAD A VERY SOFT, GOOD FEELING DREAM— THE GROWING WEB OF CONSCIOUSNESS AROUND THE LIMBS, BRANCHES, LEAVES OF TREES ON THE FIRST FEW PAGES OF NEWEST BOOK.

○

TESTS SHOW NO NEW CANCER; TESTS SHOW SAME OLD CANCER. SPINAL PAIN REMAINS BUT SOME LESS. E WORKING ON HOW TO LIVE IN RELATION TO AN INCUR- ABLE, NOT PRESENTLY DEBILITATING ILLNESS. TALKING ABOUT THE NUMBER OF PEO- PLE WHO ASK IF HER NEWS IS GOOD OR BAD—THAT IS NOT A FLEXIBLE OR PRODUCTIVE WAY OF THINKING ABOUT THIS. AN AIM NOT TO HOPE OR FEAR A LOT, NOT LEAD OTHERS TO.

○

Here's a Buddhist meditation I've read about. I can even do it.

It happens in a public place; the substance of it is to recognize that every other person there, one by one, male and female and young and old, has been, in some earlier life, your mother.

Or more likely, in many lives.

And regarding the people one by one, you learn to understand how this could have been so. One by one as you gaze, you can see what kind of mother they were to you; you can see as well, slowly, what kind of a child you were to them.

Over and over and over

> *you're like Aeneas*
> *encountering a stranger,*
> *Venus, and guessing,*
>
> *just from the rosy*
> *glow of their neck and their feet*
> *and the stately step,*
>
> *though too late, "Surely,*
> *stranger, you are a goddess.*
> *Surely, my mother."*

Shy as I am, I'm pretty good at this meditation.

In almost every face I can find the curve of a tenderness, however hidden. The place of a smile or an intelligence—a shared one.

Even in a skinhead without any lips to speak of; or in a girl who's anxious, anorexic, half crazed with all her narcissistic burden—even from her I can elicit and nurture it, the sense of her possible, beautiful care of me. Indeed, of a compassion; of her imagination, or his.

Of course, with babies it's easy.

In a roomful of my students—I can find it.

◦

It's a therapy day and I've driven up to the gray building early for our hour. Early enough to clamber across the parking lot, across the parking lot of the bank next door, across Ninth Street, to ask someone at the BP station on the corner a question about my car.

But the shrubby border between the two parking lots is unexpectedly steep, mulched with its slippery pine needles. Typically clumsy, I tumble, almost fall. Then collecting myself, move on

> *through the bank's parking*
> *lot with all a fat woman's*
> *disavowing haste.*

After my errand, I'm walking back from the gas station when I notice Shannon rounding the corner toward the gray building. He's crossing the bank parking lot ahead of me and doesn't see me.

When Nina and I were in the same high school, she bitterly accused me of embarrassing her by walking around alone looking as if I was *thinking*. I don't know if that's how Shannon looks; I notice more the calm buoyancy with which he is able to steer his round, large, light body, like a float in a Macy's Thanksgiving Day parade.

Even if he is thinking, he's alert to his surroundings. When he gets near the bottom of the shrubby border, suddenly the balloon makes a graceful, low dip: I see him gather up from the pavement the clumps of pine mulch I kicked down as I was teetering on the brink. Then bobbing up gently, he pats it back into place, his hands briefly smoothing it in with the other mulch.

Me hanging back, wanting not to be seen.

◦

> *This little, spied-on*
> *scene: how does it endow me*
> *with hidden treasure?*

Why do I feel afterwards as if, whatever my frustration or fear, I'm carrying with me an object of reflection: if I turn inward toward it, it will make me smile?

I'm wary of such sudden condensations of sweetness, the kind that, in the past, have made me fall in love.

But I don't resist, either, secretly fingering this enigmatic pebble. I can't quite figure out what makes its meaning for me.

Diffident, I write to my friend Tim that there may be something inexhaustibly pleasing in the tight, light knot of space, time, and seeing. How the small extent of Ninth Street, our wide-skied, midwestern-feeling little college town, turns into a time-lapse graphic that lets Shannon occupy the place where I was, encountering my ghost without recognition, unmaking my mistake—me, turning back, seeing it. And I love that his care for me was not care for *me*.

Tim writes back, "Far from tedious I find the image of Shannon bending over to pick up mulch—the same that you had dislodged, in falling, if I understood you—not knowing it was you who had dislodged it, to have the power of something in De Quincey—or perhaps the film noir version of De Quincey, that I carry around in my head.

"An immediate, involuntary substitution: anonymous shrinks, doing reparative work—in their spare time."

○

Over weekend, E got a call from woman she has known here who just found out she too has breast cancer. E describes this woman as already having a significant depression. She describes someone driven to keep working even if she has no enjoyment in the labor. To me this has something of the sound of how E used to be in her not "being able to stop." She remembers telling me how she waits for someone to tell her she can "stop now"—e.g., die. She imagines me doing this sometime in the future. She also talks about having come to be able to hear a voice like my voice inside herself when it is quiet that she can trust and have confidence in. I can imagine the voice telling her she can stop.

JOHN D'EMILIO

John D'Emilio is a professor of history and director of the Gender and Women's Studies Program of the University of Illinois at Chicago, where he teaches courses in gay and lesbian studies. He is the author or editor of half a dozen books, including *Sexual Politics, Sexual Communities: The Making of a Homosexual Minority in the United States* and *Intimate Matters: A History of Sexuality in America* (with Estelle Freedman). A collection of his essays, *The World Turned: Essays on Gay History, Politics, and Culture*, received the 2003 Editor's Choice Award of the Lambda Literary Foundation. He has served as co-chair of the Board of Directors of the National Gay and Lesbian Task Force (NGLTF) and was the founding director of NGLTF's Policy Institute. He has won numerous awards and honors, including fellowships from the National Endowment for the Humanities and the Guggenheim Foundation. His biography of civil rights leader and pacifist Bayard Rustin, *Lost Prophet: The Life and Times of Bayard Rustin*, was published in summer 2003.

A BIOGRAPHER AND HIS SUBJECT

Wrestling with Bayard Rustin[1]

Four years ago, the Center for Lesbian and Gay Studies at the City University of New York sponsored a conference on the state of gay and lesbian history. I was one of several presenters in a session on biography. None of us on the panel had consulted beforehand. But by the beginning of the third or fourth presentation, a common pattern had emerged, and the audience erupted with laughter. Each one of us had opened our remarks with a mixture of apology and denial: we each were not, we assured the audience, writing a biography!

At the time the motives behind the denial seemed pretty obvious to me. Most of us on the panel would have defined ourselves as activist-scholars. We saw the work we did as intellectual endeavors closely tied to a project of social change. In writing about Bayard Rustin, for instance, I was much less interested in recounting the life of an individual than I was in exploring a period of radical social movements. To see my purpose as the telling of one man's life story seemed unworthy of the years of effort that a biography takes. Beyond that, gay and lesbian scholarship in the '90s was falling under the sign of the queer. Its methods were those of the intellectual avant-garde while biography was as traditional and boring a genre as one could imagine. From the obligatory opening about the grandparents of the subject to the closing at the memorial service, biographies unfold in a fashion too linear and predictable for the end of the millennium.

Some time after the conference, I began to have dreams about Rustin. This invasion of my psyche gave me another angle for understanding the refusal to own up to my status as a biographer. I have cared passionately about everything that I have researched and written, but for the most part, I have been able to write history from a comfortable emotional distance. Yes, I can remember feelings of disgust as conservative gay men in the McCarthy era stole the Mattachine Society from my beloved Communist founders. But this was a short-term encounter with characters and episodes that I left behind quickly as I moved on to the next chapter in the story. Not so with Rustin. We have been living together now for most of this decade. He's there when I wake up in the morning and when I go to bed at night. We have a long-term committed relationship, and I haven't been able to treat his life and his experience with the kind of detachment that I've brought to the study of history.

In our postmodern world, where fractured selves and fluid identities somehow keep peskily asserting themselves, it is hardly original to acknowledge that biography is never just about the life whose story gets told. The experience, the concerns, the identities—the subjectivity—of the author are also always present, weaving their way into the structure, presentation, and content of the biography, even when invisible. Biography fails when this dual subjectivity goes unacknowledged—when we delude ourselves into believing that we can reconstruct another life uncontaminated by our own. But it can succeed amazingly well when the passions of the biographer are thoughtfully mobilized, when identity and difference, empathy and incomprehension, work dynamically with and against each other to produce flashes of insight and sparks of tension on the page.

Last spring, when CLAGS's director Jill Dolan let me know that I had been selected to give this year's Kessler lecture, it came not only as an honor, but as an opportunity. I don't want to go so far as to claim that Rustin and I had been engaged in mortal combat. But the easy part of his life—easy at least for me—was over. As I approached the period that had most drawn me to the project in the first place, I found myself stuck in a way that is unusual for me. I was trapped in a place for which "writer's block" is not an accurate description.

My dreams about Rustin, which had stopped long before this, offered something of a clue to what was going on. The setting was always a rattily furnished, frenetically busy activist office. The emotional tone was one of urgency. The plot line was always the same. Bayard and I were both there, he was engaged with something, and I was desperately trying to get his attention.

My reaction to the first dream was something like "Oh, Jesus. What kind of biography will I write if I'm this obsessed with pleasing my subject?" But by the third or fourth replay, it became clear that approval was not the issue. Rustin and I were in struggle. I am trying to force *him* to stop and pay attention to *me*. The urgency, the desperation is about my perception that something is terribly wrong.

All of the research I've done has grown from very immediate concerns. My projects have mixed political and personal interests that have struck close to home. I decided to write about the pre-Stonewall movement because of the experience of being an activist here, in New York City, in the early and mid-1970s. Those days were thrilling, but also bewildering. The excitement of reimagining and, in the process, reinventing our lives was balanced at times by a sense of being rudderless, of having not a clue as to what we were doing or where we were going, of having no history or tradition in which to anchor our activities.

Bayard Rustin captured my interest because of how his life and his career seemed to speak to issues that were absorbing me at the turn of the last decade. At the end of the 1980s, something fairly remarkable—and almost never commented upon—was happening in the lesbian and gay movement. The executive directors, the key staff, and sometimes the board leadership of many major organizations were men and women who, if asked, would have identified themselves as of the left. Yet there they were, running large community centers that provided social services and were dependent on government contracts, or at the helm of organizations that lobbied legislatures and worked through the courts.

To paraphrase a nineteenth-century homosexual emancipationist, they were radical souls trapped within the bodies of reformers. At a time when American civic culture left little room for an oppositional politics, here was a serendipitously creative effort by an assortment of movement types to experiment strategically. Women and men committed to a transformative social vision were engaging institutional structures in ways that seemed, at quick glance, as traditional as one could imagine. But look more closely, and you would have noticed a more complicated scenario. For instance, in the context of the National Gay and Lesbian Task Force, whose board I chaired, it seemed that insider and outsider tactics were intentionally being played off one another. Street activists and lobbyists, the Stonewall generation and its successor, were in dialogue, and were choreographing a new kind of social movement dance. They were mobilizing and insinuating, rabble-rousing and negotiating, dreaming boldly and plodding methodically, simultaneously. And it seemed to me that there weren't many models for this kind of movement activism. Instead, the history of social movements more often reflected the tensions that erupted when self-defined radicals and reformers squared off against one another.

Meanwhile, my teaching had been evolving so that half of what I was doing was connected to the 1960s. If any of you have worked with students on the '60s, you know how exciting the classroom can become. Undergraduates who gravitate toward these courses tend to be young women and men who are in some way at war with contemporary America. They are struggling to resist the conservative times in which we live. They are looking for any handle they can grasp to support their desire to care. They love the optimism, passion, and hopefulness of the '60s. They love the sense of community. They love the idea that students like themselves were making history.

But pedagogy alone wasn't drawing me to the '60s. The trajectory of my own life was forever altered by those times. The personal transformations set in motion by the radical politics and culture of the '60s were what made me receptive later to the message of gay liberation.

My awakening happened here at Columbia. I arrived on Morningside Heights in 1966, an overly intellectual boy from the Bronx soaked in the patriotism of Cold War Catholicism. My first week here I learned from the Protestant campus minister that God was dead. The senior who was assigned to orient me to campus life turned out to be a Dorothy Day–style Catholic who took me on retreats filled with renegade priests and nuns contemplating marriage and agonizing over the war in Vietnam. Before long I was booing Selective Service representatives who visited the campus, and had eggs thrown at me by campus jocks who were angry for different reasons. In this building I learned conversational Italian with an instructor who had us talking about student strikes in Rome and factory takeovers in Turin. Meanwhile, late at night in what passed for the campus coffeehouse, I met and talked with men who wanted men. In the corridors of Butler Library I cruised the man who became my first lover. I made my first gay friends on the sixth-floor corridor of John Jay Hall where I was living. When students shut down the university for several weeks in 1968, I divided my time between heated political discussions in the dorms, and equally heated explorations of the West Village, which I was discovering for the first time. Becoming gay and becoming a political radical are inseparably linked in my experience—and completely bound up for me with the 1960s.

If my imagination presents the '60s to me as a moment of awakening, the classroom exposed a different subterranean emotional drama. No matter how I planned the course, somehow what emerged was a story of loss and devastation, a declension narrative that took my students through the rise—and then fall—of hope and optimism. The "good '60s" of sit-ins, freedom rides, and a war to end poverty were followed by the "bad '60s" of burning cities, Watergate, and a war in Asia. The good '60s are uplifting, while the bad '60s are wrenchingly demoralizing—even as they also thrill.

This is not a narrative that I invented. It defines much of the historical writing on the 1960s, and is the story that a subset of my generation has spun out over and over and over. In my work on gay history I have certainly proven that I can disrupt other "traditional" or well-established narratives. But the means to disrupt this one was eluding me.

And so I came upon Rustin with a set of hopes and expectations. At the time I began researching his life, almost nothing historical had been written about him. Mostly he had a brief walk-on part as the man who organized the historic 1963 March on Washington. But he was the centerpiece of one chapter in a journalistic account of protest in the '60s, and what was there intrigued me. Rustin's life looked to be the ideal material for constructing a different narrative of the '60s at the same time that his career resonated with the contemporary concerns of the queer movement. Rustin bridged two generations of radicalism in the United States. To the new youth activists of the late '50s and early '60s, he brought the experience of having organized during the heady years of the 1930s. His activism was suffused by deep moral conviction. He wove Quaker traditions and Gandhian principles into a seamless ethical system that shaped his dealings with Southern sheriffs, American military officers, and restaurant owners in northern cities. Rustin, more than anyone, brought Gandhi to the United States. He presided over the transformation of direct action tactics from the cherished possession of a few initiates to its embrace by masses of Americans.

Of most interest to me was the way Rustin's concerns shifted in the 1960s. He had spent almost two decades refining direct action *tactics* until they perfectly comported with a moral philosophy of how human beings should be treated. Now he was turning his attention to questions of strategy: how to make the tactics of protest serve a grander design of political, economic, and social revolution. At the moment when the "good '60s" were at a crossroads, Rustin was addressing to his comrades in the peace, civil rights, and economic justice struggles a strategic manifesto that broke dramatically with the orthodoxy of these social movements.

If an interest in the 1960s drew me to Rustin, his early life is what captivated me. A biographer—or at least this biographer—could not ask for a more compelling subject. His story is heroic and harrowing. It abounds with triumphs and trials. It combines the narrative contours of the saint and the sinner.

Many young white boys today are coming of age immersed in the fictional world of Harry Potter. The stuff of prepubescent fantasies of masculine courage and strength are wizards and potions and magic wands, and broom-sticks that race through the air. I, on the other hand, was nurtured on the lives of the saints. I ingested the stories of Francis of Assisi, of Ignatius Loyola, of Xavier and Augustine. They were men of passion, talent, and intellect, and they all led oversized lives. They perfectly embodied a Catholic plot line that inverted the Puritan declension narrative. These were accounts of a fall and then a rise. In Catholic storytelling, even the grisliest deaths transmuted into heroic events, victories in a cosmic struggle.

Of course, a good Catholic—and believe me, I was a good Catholic boy—reads these stories not with a sense of identification, but with yearning. The reader of these lives does not get to claim sainthood, but instead must pray and wish for the moment when the power of temptation yields to an almost gentle decision to follow a path of goodness. Though Rustin came from a different religious tradition, through the first four decades of his life one can see played out a grand struggle—between a desire for greatness and the troubles brought upon him by his sexual yearnings.

His desire for greatness was not conventional. It was not for fame or fortune or success as American society normally measures such things. It emerged and took shape gradually, as a Black adolescent of extraordinary talents came face to face with the constraints of white racism. A personal, individual decision to resist gradually evolved into something larger—to be like an Old Testament prophet leading his people to freedom.

Southeastern Pennsylvania, where Rustin grew up, resembled much of the North in the first third of this century. While it lacked the South's solidly built edifice of Jim Crow laws and customs, it practiced segregation nonetheless. Many times the racist practices of the North must have seemed even more infuriating because of the inconsistency of their application. In Rustin's home-town of West Chester, the elementary school was segregated, but the high school was not. The public library was open to everyone, but the gymnasium at the YMCA and the downtown soda fountain were for whites only.

Rustin excelled in high school. He won just about every honor the school offered—prizes for essays and oratory, his poetry in the school magazine, county and state honors in football, track, and tennis. His grandmother reminded readers of the local press that he was "the first colored youth to have won [the school oratory prize] in forty years." The town's newspaper often featured on its front page his exploits on the football field. When Bayard graduated, he was a speaker at commencement, and his yearbook shows him with a longer list of awards and activities than any other senior. But while his best friend, who was white, graduated with a scholarship to an Ivy League college, Bayard closed his triumphal high school career with *no* college prospects.

Despite the fame that Rustin later achieved, reconstructing the early life of an African American from a working-class family in a provincial town is not easy. The Chester County Historical Society flows over with meticulously accumulated files about white Quaker families whose doings were significant only to themselves. Not so for the Rustin clan.

And yet, despite the paucity of evidence, I *know* that sometime in high school, a decision formed, a moral resolve was made, *never* to accept from white America the restrictions it sought to impose on his person. Rustin would go where he pleased. He would claim any one he chose as his friend and intimate. He would have access to the intellectual traditions and the cultural resources that the world had to offer. In high school he enacted this determination through the friendships he formed, through his refusal to leave a restaurant that denied him service, through his challenge to the authority of his athletic coach.

Although I am framing this resolve in racial terms, because this was the context in which it evolved, Rustin was an equal opportunity flayer of tradition. "He did not suffer fools gladly," more than one of his associates told me. Anyone or anything could become his target. Many who encountered this side of Rustin have spoken to me of his arrogance, a quality that does not sit well with a Quaker or Gandhian. I prefer to think of it as a suit of armor that protected him against the racist and, later, the homophobic assaults, that came at him early and often.

Let's jump ahead a decade and change our locale. In the early 1940s, Rustin was living in Harlem, socializing in the Village, attending Quaker meetings on the East Side, and working on the Upper West Side. As a field secretary for the Fellowship of Reconciliation, a Christian-pacifist organization whose office was located three blocks from here on Broadway, he traveled from coast to coast. He lectured and organized not only in large cities like Philadelphia, Chicago, and San Francisco, but in the small towns of the plains, the mountain states, and the south. He was an apostle of world peace in the midst of a global war, and of racial justice before the civil rights movement commanded national headlines.

There is something about beginnings that entrances me: the beginnings of a life before its direction is firmly set, of a career before it peaks, of a social movement before it can claim many successes. How else can I explain the fact that I devoted seven years of my life to studying a homophile movement whose adherents barely exceeded in number the audience in this room! So it is with the Rustin biography. I could rummage through the 1940s forever, turning up another memory, another set of notes from one of his lectures, another clipping from a small-town newspaper.

The Rustin of those years is extraordinary. The folks who knew him then, no matter what happened in later years, recall him with awe. Norman Whitney, one of his Quaker mentors from this era, was reported to have said of Rustin that "if ever he doubted the existence of God, he always thought of Bayard." "An electrifying presence," another informant told me. "Such charisma that you cannot imagine," said a third. "A prophetic type." "There was a magic about Bayard."

Above all, in stories that tumbled from their mouths, they talk about his courage. A courage called forth because of the decision *never* to collude with racism by acquiescing to its demands. Courage on a bus trip through Tennessee when he refused to sit in the back, and was dragged off alone and beaten by police. Courage as he walked down the main street of a Montana town with a white pregnant woman. Courage when he was trapped in a house in Chapel Hill, North Carolina, surrounded by cars filled with angry white men who were armed with clubs and throwing rocks. Courage as he stood eyeball to eyeball with a screaming Cold Warrior on Times Square during the height of the Korean War, and displayed not an impulse to defend his person.

These stories circulated through the peace and Northern civil rights movement, making Rustin seem larger than life. Meeting him, one woman told me, "was like being in the presence of history." Young activist wannabes encountering Rustin for the first time would imitate his speech, his gait, his gestures, as if by doing so they could absorb some of his powers. And yet in all these stories is the unmistakable sense that he always remained eminently reachable— especially to the young students whom he mentored. Rustin made a commitment to social justice seem natural, an understanding of political economy accessible, and courage as something to be found inside everyone.

Twenty-plus years ago, when I interviewed Harry Hay and corresponded with Chuck Rowland about the founding of the Mattachine Society, I fell in love with each of them. As a young gay man trying, somehow, to be a gay socialist, I was touched beyond words to know that, a generation earlier, gay Communists in Los Angeles were plotting the liberation of a little boy in the Bronx who would one day be gay. Now I encounter the Rustin of the 1940s, and I yearn for him. I want him in my life. But not in the life of a fifty-something man who gives Kessler lectures, writes books, and teaches gay studies.

As I work on this biography I find myself time traveling emotionally to an earlier me. I want Rustin in the life of the fragile adolescent who came to this campus more than a generation ago and found himself confronted by unexpected challenges, without any of the usual moorings. An adolescent who needed a mentor and needed, badly, to borrow someone's courage. I want him with me at the one and only meeting of SDS that I ever attended, across the street in Fayerweather Hall, and that I fled feeling stupid and inadequate. I want him with me as I sat down in the middle of West Forty-seventh Street, protesting a speech by the Secretary of State, praying that the charging police horses will stop before they reach me. I want him with me as I leafletted army recruits in front of the Whitehall Induction Center and an angry crowd gathered across the street. I want him as a reassuring presence during the hair-raising, ear-splitting fights with my god-and-country, Cardinal Spellman–style Catholic parents over my decision to file as a conscientious objector. I want him near as I sat quivering in front of the members of my draft board on Arthur Avenue in the Bronx, trying to persuade them to grant me CO status while they signed induction orders.

The gays-in-the-military debate of the '90s has obscured a different kind of military drama of a generation ago, when many young men were searching for ways to stay out of the military. Desperation was rife, and a cottage industry of draft counseling grew up to help them. I remember one teenager I counseled at the center here on campus asking me without blinking an eye how many knuckles he needed to lose in order to be draft-exempt.

Most conscientious objectors and draft resisters in those years, sexually speaking, were straight as an arrow. And my own relationship to the draft certainly had roots in a Catholicism that was getting reconfigured because of my experiences on Morningside Heights. But it was also being shaped, in ways that were both cliché-ridden and not, by my rapidly accumulating gay experiences. Warfare was revolting to the emotional sensibilities that drove me toward men. But it was also petrifying to imagine myself in the military's domain during wartime. I couldn't tell if it was more terrifying to imagine doing what they wanted me to do, which was to kill, or doing what I knew they didn't want me to do. Then there were the terrors of being denied CO status—the prospect of jail, the overheated melodramatic visions of prison: not the fantasies of Jean Genet, but the violence of *Fortune and Men's Eyes*, which was playing in New York in those years.

A generation earlier, Rustin had embraced terrors of a magnitude that made mine seem inconsequential. Early in 1944, he surrendered himself to federal marshals to begin serving twenty-seven months for refusing to cooperate with the Selective Service system. This was in the middle of "the good war." There was no mass movement to support his resistance. As a Quaker, he could easily have qualified for alternative service as a religious pacifist, but he chose instead to have no truck with military authority at all.

For Rustin, as a Black man, to *choose* prison flew in the face of the logic of African American experience. After emancipation, incarceration became the successor institution to slavery. If the plantation could no longer serve as a prison-without-walls, the prison could become a forced labor camp. State legislatures revised their criminal codes to make it easier to lock up Black men for petty offenses, and then used them on forced labor gangs. Jails were also places that Black men sometimes did not leave alive. They were institutions where racist brutality could be enacted with almost no constraints. Rustin was sent to a federal prison in Kentucky, south of the Mason-Dixon Line, at a time when the penal system enforced racial segregation.

And, of course, he was also a gay man. "Triple jeopardy" barely suggests how dynamics of race, sexuality, and political identity played themselves out during Rustin's incarceration. He was physically attacked by white Southern inmates for his challenge to prison segregation. He was resented by guards because of the perceived moral superiority he projected. He was despised by just about everyone—including himself—for the sexual desires he could not suppress and which brought him disgrace.

Rustin's time in prison was a nightmare of harrowing proportions. He spent long stretches in solitary confinement. He suffered through hunger strikes and forced feedings. He fought with guards. He faced the humiliation of confinement in a psychiatric prison facility. He felt the shame of his exposure as a deceitful homosexual before the community of pacifist militants. The photographic evidence from these years is striking. A picture of him taken before the start of his sentence records a sweet tranquillity which is captivating. Another taken midway through his ordeals reveals him bitter, resentful, and sullen.

Yet he came out of prison not broken but toughened, not weakened but determined, the courage he displayed earlier now so magnified that he knew he could face anything. He would have to summon up this fortitude often over the succeeding years. Cold War America was not a propitious time for a Black Gandhian militant, publicly branded a sex pervert, to be agitating for world peace, racial justice, and a socialist vision of economic democracy.

Let's jump ahead again, this time to the mid-1960s, the moment of my awakening to a radical politics of dissent, and the historical moment that has led me to Rustin's life in the hope that it will illuminate the mysteries of how to make change.

In the years between his wartime incarceration and the flowering of '60s protest, Rustin and his political comrades had lived through what, for shorthand, we can call McCarthyism. The isolation that they experienced politically was compounded for Rustin by the controversies that kept erupting around his sexuality. From the late 1940s through the mid-1960s, Rustin's homosexuality rarely receded from the consciousness of the peace movement and the civil rights struggle. He was jailed for it once, and arrested a number of other times. He lost one job, and had his services rejected by organizations he loved. He found himself abandoned by one mentor, A. J. Muste, and by a man whom he had mentored, Martin Luther King, Jr. Politicians as different as Adam Clayton Powell and Strom Thurmond deployed Rustin's sexuality to discredit him. Right-wing organizations like the American Legion, the Minutemen, and the John Birch Society seemed at times to be trailing him, making his speaking engagements flash points for homophobic panics.

But by 1964, Rustin's world was very different. The grim years of the early Cold War and the witch hunts of the McCarthy era seemed to be in the past. Protests over atmospheric testing, intercontinental missile systems, and civilian defense drills had brought the peace movement out of the shadows. Dramatic events in the South—from the sit-ins of 1960 to the battle of Birmingham in 1963—had made racial equality the most insistent social and political issue of the times. Through the vehicle of the 1963 march on Washington, Rustin, too, was able to move out of the shadows. The success of the march made his place no longer seem tenuous or contingent.

In the expansive freedom that his newly found status brought him, Rustin experienced a season of strategic creativity. He was shaping ideas about politics and change that were new both to the civil rights movement and the peace movement. They grew out of his assessment of what the March on Washington and the civil rights movement meant for America. Despite the sarcasm of Malcolm X's description of the march as the "farce on Washington," Rustin believed that the march had legitimized mass action. Organizations like the NAACP and the Urban League, which looked askance at collective action, had endorsed and supported it. The march also broadened the coalition of forces engaged in the struggle for racial equality by drawing to it white-dominated religious denominations and labor unions. At the same time, Rustin believed the civil rights movement was changing the whole political climate of the nation. The insistent demand for freedom and justice had broken the logjam to progressive change created by Cold War anticommunism. Rustin saw in the civil rights movement an engine powering the nation toward the kind of social and economic programs that the Johnson Administration was soon to propose.

Rustin's strategic perspective, which he expounded in speeches, movement gatherings, and writing, revolved around a few simple propositions. The first was the belief that the historical moment was both propitious and transitory. For the first time since the 1930s, enough Americans were mobilized around calls for equality and justice that the possibilities for change were expansive. But moments like this were evanescent, and all around him Rustin could see the signs of incipient backlash. The second proposition, addressed to Black America, was that success in the freedom struggle would come only through espousal of a program of change far more substantial than the demand for legal equality; Rustin used the word "revolution" when he spoke of this. The third proposition was that revolutionary change will only come to Black America through a process of securing allies and building coalitions; it could not come through the efforts of African Americans alone. Rustin also urged movement activists to push beyond their reliance on protest tactics which, no matter how successful, kept them perpetually reproducing outsider status, and instead pressed them to directly engage the institutions and structures of the American political system. Finally, and most concretely, Rustin urged the elements of the progressive coalition he was calling for to see the Democratic Party as the institution they needed to transform.

Depending on the setting, Rustin's proposals today can seem boring, controversial, or naive. For contemporary progressives, who regularly work with the Democratic Party, the only thing the party has going for it is that it is not the Republican party. The idea that it might be the vehicle to take us to a paradise of social and economic justice seems ludicrous. But 1999 is not 1964. When Rustin was writing, the Democratic Party was pushing past the edge of the centrist agendas that have typified two-party politics. He was saying: "Let's push harder. Let's make it ours. Let us be the ones to redefine its soul."

For progressives today, especially those located in identity-based movements, the call for coalition politics has become normative. But that wasn't always so. When Rustin was arguing for what we might call a multi-issue agenda, neither the NAACP, nor Martin Luther King and the Southern Christian Leadership Conference, nor the militants in SNCC and in CORE thought that minimum wage legislation, or a full employment bill, or the right of workers to bargain collectively belonged on the agenda of the civil rights movement. If multi-issue coalition politics now seems foundational to some of us, that conviction pays tribute to the power of Rustin's historical legacy, whether we know it or not.

And yet, at the same time, these ideas are still controversial and are fought over every day. They are fought out in a gay movement that seems to have no trouble seeing that the military exclusion policy is a gay issue, but that can't seem to grasp, for instance, that the demonization of immigrants damages to the core the well-being of our community.

In proposing this course correction, Rustin was implicitly arguing against several distinct, but powerfully related, strands of thought in the world of

American dissent. He was rejecting romanticized leftist notions of a seizure of the state, a moment of dramatic crisis when control over the levers of power shifts suddenly and decisively. He was rejecting a long tradition of American perfectionism that privileged the unbending adherence to absolute moral principle, that defined being right as more important than—and at odds with—being effective. He was rejecting a culture of marginality that took pride in being on the outside, one in which radical dissenters could not imagine themselves doing anything other than protest. He was rejecting the single-issue politics that characterized much of the peace and civil rights movements in this era.

Despite the fact that historians rewrite history all the time, the trajectory of past events doesn't shift simply because we find new ways of looking at them. But as I investigated Rustin's life, there was something tremendously comforting about the way he was trying to rethink radical politics in the heat of struggle. Just when these times were at the cusp of shifting from the "good '60s" to the "bad '60s," Rustin was proposing a strategic reevaluation that promised to build rather than fracture an inchoate progressive coalition. Rustin was challenging the orthodoxy of his political world. He was opening a door to let me revisit what happened in the '60s. He was making his biographer happy, satisfied, and fulfilled.

But subjects can't be counted on to cooperate so neatly with their biographer's wishes. They especially can't be counted on when those wishes are embedded in subterranean veins of emotion. I said at the beginning of this talk that the life of the biographer inevitably informs the biography he or she writes. Let me take that one step further. For me, the work of biography has become most difficult where my subject's history most challenges the unexamined assumptions of my own life. I have gotten stuck in the places where Rustin's life and mine are in conflict. And nowhere is this clearer than in relation to the war in Vietnam.

From what I've said earlier, it must be abundantly clear that the antiwar movement served as my coming of age ritual. It figures as powerfully in my self-definition as my sexual coming out in those same years. In the three decades since then, I have never seen a need to look with detachment at the antiwar movement and reevaluate it. It has always seemed self-evident that the only questions to ask were whether we all worked tirelessly enough to end that abomination, and whether more effort would have brought more results sooner.

Scan the key public events associated with Vietnam era protests—scan the antiwar movement's greatest hits—and you will not see the figure of Bayard Rustin. The pacifist who chose jail as D-Day was approaching in 1944 was not on the platform in front of the United Nations in April 1967 when Martin Luther King gave an impassioned speech against the war; he was not present at the confrontation at the Pentagon in October 1967; he did not participate in the moratorium protests in 1969; he was not engaged with the turmoil unleashed by the American invasion of Cambodia.

To hear some of my informants tell it, Rustin was more than absent from these events. The pain and resentment of what long-time pacifists experienced as his apostasy during the Vietnam era have transmuted over time into a belief that he actively supported the war. With the anger over his defection has come a search for explanations. I've been told that he became the paid help of the AFL-CIO labor aristocracy. I've been told that he became a captive of the Shachtmanites, a tiny group of leftists with roots in the Trotskyist movement of the 1930s. I've been told that he was in the thrall of a young former lover, Tom Kahn. I've been told that he became a shill of the CIA.

How they've come to make and believe these claims is a whole other story about how the American left constructs identities and exclusions. Their claims evoke underground strands of class, race, and sexual prejudices that infected the peace movement of these decades. For now let me do the short response: it's not true that Rustin supported the war. In fact, in 1965, as opposition to the war began to crystallize, Rustin was articulating a vigorous pacifist response. At a major rally in Madison Square Garden, Rustin gave a speech that one member of the audience described as "by far the most inspired, principled denunciation of our foreign policy. . . . It brought sharply into focus the connections between the struggle for civil rights and the need for an end to militarist actions abroad." During that summer and fall, he worked closely with King and the Southern Christian Leadership Conference to craft an antiwar stance for King whose stature made his voice particularly critical for the peace movement. But as the war escalated, and the antiwar movement mushroomed, Rustin distanced himself from it.

Rustin's reservations came in a complicated package. Some of them were framed in purely moral terms. The pacifism that he and others tried to craft in the 1940s blended Gandhi and Jesus in ways that made means and ends, words and actions, inseparable. If the evil of violence was that it ruptured the wholeness of the human community, opposition to violence always had to repair the damage. Respect for the perpetrator was as important as the demand to stop the violence. Motive and process were as critical as outcome. These were the beliefs that shaped Rustin's pacifist agitation in the '40s, and his insinuation of nonviolence into the heart of the civil rights movement in the '50s.

Rustin looked at the antiwar movement after 1965, and saw it polluted by an anti-American rhetoric. He saw it morally corrupted by its endorsement of the violence of the National Liberation Front and North Vietnam. He saw a movement compromised by the unmediated rage of its leaders and participants, a movement that had little in common with the pacifism that once made him choose jail.

Rustin had another beef with the antiwar movement. He objected mightily to its demonization of Lyndon Johnson and to its insistence that the war, and nothing else, should determine one's stance toward the Johnson administration. Make Johnson and American liberals the enemy, Rustin warned, and support for changing the racial status quo would unravel. Support for a social and economic agenda that uprooted inequality would evaporate. Rustin was keenly attuned to history. He knew the difference it made that, under Lyndon Johnson, for the first time since Reconstruction, the power of the federal government was wielded on behalf of Black Americans. He knew how fragile and tenuous such commitments could be. And he was not willing to aid and abet a conservative backlash that was waiting for any opportunity.

Of course, these were the very arguments that got Rustin into trouble. They clinched, for his former comrades, the belief that he had sold his soul for a mess of pottage, for invitations to White House meetings and presidential pens from legislative signings. But, though Rustin himself often framed his comments in the language of pragmatic politics, his views rested on a moral basis—his insistence that one treat opponents respectfully, that criticism *and* support could be combined, that pathways to communication must always remain open.

I, too, react viscerally against what Rustin had to say about the antiwar movement. The emotionalism of those years was intense. A common chant at antiwar demonstrations was "Hey, hey, LBJ, how many kids did you kill today?" I hear Rustin's nitpicking criticisms of the antiwar movement and I want to tell him to get over it: "Don't you *know* what's going on over there?" I hear his call for critical support of the Johnson Administration and I want to lecture him about the police power of the state: "Don't you know what's going on over here?" With the self-righteous certainty of a new convert to radical politics, I want to explain the world to a man who had endured Northern and Southern racism, who had seen first hand the effects of colonization in Africa and Asia, and whose encounters with homophobia make life since Stonewall a cake walk.

Except in my dreams, these conversations can never happen. But if I had to imaginatively construct what he might have said, I can almost hear the clipped diction, tinged with the arrogance that sometimes leaked from him in political debates:

"Don't you think it odd," he might say, "that the American war which produced the most vigorous sustained opposition in the nation's history, lasted longer than any other American war? Do you think that perhaps the way you opposed the war might have subverted your own goals? Do you take no responsibility for the election of Richard Nixon in 1968? Do you not see that while you were ranting and raving outside the citadels of power, while you were vilifying Lyndon Johnson, political demons you could barely imagine where plotting a slow but systematic rise to power? Do you not see that, a generation later, we are still living with the political results of your self-righteous emotionalism?"

Contrary to what you might be thinking, I'm not especially trying to demonstrate that Bayard Rustin was correct. I'm not trying to transform myself into his defender. I still don't know *what* I think about all this, and I will only find out what I think as I write this period in his life.

I do know that Rustin's career offers as much to chew on about our own times as it does about the '60s. Rustin challenges us to scrutinize orthodoxy in whatever form we encounter, or defend, it. He challenges us to recognize the emptiness of rhetorical militancy. He challenges us to take the call for coalition seriously, and apply it in ways that make many leftists, and progressives, uncomfortable. He asks us to discipline our untamed emotions, not so that we become like unfeeling robots, but so that our politics are shaped by critical thinking. He insists that there is a universalism that can flatten the differences of identity, and that this universalism will be found on a field of justice.

I also know that the opportunity to deliver this year's Kessler lecture has pushed the envelope for me—for which I thank you. Wrestling with this lecture has allowed me to discard emotional baggage that stood between me and an open-ended appraisal of Rustin's life. It has made it much more likely that the biography I finish will be about him, and not about me.

And the wrestling, so far, has been very much worth it. For in this life which began obscurely in a small Pennsylvania town, almost a century ago, is a wealth of wisdom and courage and moral integrity that deserves transmission as Bayard Rustin's legacy to us.

NOTES

1. References in this lecture to Columbia University reflect the fact that the 1999 Kessler Lecture was held on the Columbia University campus, at the Casa Italiana.

2000

JOAN NESTLE
EDMUND WHITE
BARBARA SMITH
MONIQUE WITTIG
ESTHER NEWTON
SAMUEL R. DELANY
EVE KOSOFSKY SEDGWICK
JOHN D'EMILIO

CHERRÍE MORAGA

JUDITH BUTLER

CHERRÍE MORAGA

Writer and activist **Cherríe Moraga** has been an important formulator of Chicana feminism. In 1983 she co-founded Kitchen Table: Women of Color Press, an organization dedicated to publishing and distributing works by women of color. She was co-editor of the feminist classic *This Bridge Called My Back: Writings by Radical Women of Color* (1984), which won the Before Columbus Foundation American Book Award in 1986. She has also published the memoir *Waiting in the Wings: Portrait of a Queer Motherhood* (1997), as well as collections of poetry and prose, including *The Last Generation* (1993) and *Loving in the War Years* (1983). Also a playwright, Moraga belongs to the Theatre Communications Group and has received the NEA Theater Playwrit-ing Fellowship Award. Her play *Heart of the Earth,* a feminist revisioning of the Mayan Popul Vuh, was produced at The Public Theater in New York in 1994, while her latest theatrical production, *Watsonville: Some Place Not Here,* won the Fund for New American Plays Award from the Kennedy Center for the Performing Arts. Recently, Moraga was also Artist-in-Residence at Stanford University.

A XICANADYKE CODEX OF CHANGING CONSCIOUSNESS

THE COLOR OF A NATION

In 1996, I wrote a memoir entitled, *Waiting in the Wings: Portrait of a Queer Motherhood*. The book, which was initiated by my now seven-year-old son's premature and threatened birth in 1993, was completed three years later, marked by the death of my son's paternal grandfather and the death of a beloved uncle. And in this manner, pass the generations, and our lives.

Wings was an extended narrative describing my growing relationship with my child through conception, his birth in Los Angeles, his many months in the hospital, through the first three years of his life, and his final emergence into a thriving boyhood. I learned to write fiction in that narrative, drawing from whatever skills about dramatic tension and character development I had garnered as a playwright. Through the act of writing that so-called autobiography, I learned that a story well told is a story embellished and re-visioned just like the stories that rose from my mother's mouth in our family kitchen some forty years earlier. The fiction of our lives—how we conceive our histories by heart—can sometimes provide a truth far greater than any telling of a tale frozen to the facts.

Through writing *Waiting in the Wings*, I learned to reconfigure and rearrange dates, names, chronologies in the effort to create a narrative generated by a relentless faith in dreams, memory, and desire. Since the completion of that memoir, I have witnessed my journal entries moving away from an "I" fixed on the exact record of my experience, to something, I hope, much deeper: I have encountered the "I" of character who is and who is not me, but one which allows me the freedom of incorrect politics and a bravery not realized in my own life. So, what I present to you today is as much an autobiographical narrative as it is a dream waiting to happen based on some irrefutable facts. Here are several.

Fact. I am a middle-aged dyke living in Oakland with my beloved and her sometimes-grown son and her growing pre-teen granddaughter and my blood-son, Rafael Angel. Fact. I got it all. A ridiculously high mortgage, but with a woman and a sunset I can witness every clear night la creadora provides right from my front porch, above it all. I sit *above it all*, above the bay's horizon and the Airport Hyatt and Alameda's military base turned back Indian territory and the Fruitvale barrio. I live with the barrio in my horizon, just south of my Berkeley whitedyke days and eight miles east of my early woman(of color)hood in San Francisco. I got history in this territory and a woman my age that's as old as the hills, which is why I took her on new cuz she remembered the hills of her own girlhood in Sacramento and southward all the way to Sandias, Tephuanes. And that matters to both of us. She taught me how to smoke a stick of tobacco like you're praying to some god; although I knew it before. Somehow. When she taught me, I remembered like most things she taught me that it was a matter of remembering. She taught me how to burn fire, even in the city. She taught me the importance of fire on a daily basis. Something you had to keep watch over, tend, nurture, coax along and control. Like a boy. Who'da thought we'd live this long, raising babies and our babies' babies into our middle age? Like I said, I got it all.

Fact. My literary and theater career has been "marred" as much by my cultural essentialism as by my sexualized undomesticized lesbianism, to say nothing of my habitual disregard for the requirements of genre and other literary conventions. I don't know that I am a good writer. I believe I have, at times, well-articulated moments of insight, but I am not always convinced, no matter how many letters I get from those lonely queer and colored ones telling me that my words save lives, that, in fact, words can.

Fact. We are a colonized people, we meXicanos, my woman reminds me when I find my stomach tied in knots each time I sit down to write. I experience myself writing beneath the suffocation of a blanket of isolation and censorship. The most virulent is self-imposed and lacks the high-drama of senator-sanctioned obscenity charges. The censorship I have experienced has come in the not-so-idle threats of gun-toting maddog envidiosa coloreddykes and in just plain ole commercial disregard, where the money you need to do the work you do ain't there for the kind of work you do. This has especially been the case with my work in theater. I don't know, really, who my friends are as a writer, those with whom I share common cause. I wonder why so many of us, Chicana/o writers, remain so enamored with white people, their privileges, their goodies: the seduction of success. Why do we remain confused about who we are? Not Black. Not Indian. Not white. Then what? I believe that our confusion causes our writing to fall miserably short of the truly revolutionary literature it could be. I tend to read American Indian writers these days because they aren't afraid to betray America and always Toni Morrison because she's stayed Black looking back.

Fact. I have always lusted for women and am grateful that there was a lesbian feminist movement in 1974, which at the age of twenty-one allowed me to recognize and act on this loving without shame, justified it without apology, and propelled me into oppositional consciousness with Patriarchy. Mostly, I am grateful to that movement for saving me from many years of heartbreaking repression, I'm sure.

I'm also grateful, plain and simple for her, my beloved, that there was a Chicano movement that invited her entrance, politicized and betrayed her, right around the same time that the white-entitlement of lesbianfeminism betrayed me. I am grateful for those first moments of consciousness, always born from a living experience of injustice turned to righteous rage, that first experience of genuine collectivism, that blessed epiphany of art-inspired action. And I am

equally grateful for those early betrayals that forced both of us to keep on looking elsewhere for a radical revisioning of our lives. Those betrayals have shaped
my political consciousness more profoundly than any easy solidarity. There is no
home, I learned, except what we build with a handful of others through a tena-
cious resistance to compromise.

In the small world that is my queer familia we live as if our values shaped the
world at large or more accurately as if our values chisel away at some monolithic monoculture we attempt to subvert with our art, our blood, our daily
prayer. This may be the truest fiction we inhabit, but it sustains us. For now.

Another maker of fiction, Spokane/Coeur d'Alene Indian Sherman Alexie
writes: "I made a very conscious decision to marry an Indian woman, who
made a very conscious decision to marry me. Our hope: to give birth to and
raise Indian children who love themselves. That is the most revolutionary act."
When I stumbled upon these lines in Alexie's collection of poems and essays,
One Stick Song, my heart opened at the pure courage and simplicity of the
statement. I felt him my relative in the naming of what I, as a Xicanalesbian,
have kept secret for so long. For as taboo as it is to admit within the context of
the firmly inscribed multiracial social democracy progressives paint of their
imagined America, I had a child to make nation, one regenerated from the
blood nations Mexicans in this country are forced to abandon. I had an Indian
child to counter the loss of my family's working-class mexicanindianism with
each succeeding generation. I had a Xicano child cuz Raza's turning white all
over the states.

Sometimes I think it is the "social advantage" of looking white enough to
travel unnoticed amongst them that has put me in the position to recognize on
a visceral level how spiritually unrewarding the white nation is. It may feed your
belly but not your soul, I tell my Chicano students. And beneath this writing, I
hear my son ask of his beloved gringo grandpa, my father, "What about Papa
Joe?" How do you teach a seven-year-old the difference between institutionalized
ignorance, racism, bigotry, class arrogance, and the individual white people,
breeds and mixed-bloods that make up his family? How do you teach a child the
word "genocide" and still give him reason to love beyond his front door?

The evolution of my own changing lesbianchicana consciousness led me to
make the same basic decision Alexie made: "to marry an Indian woman and to
give birth to, and raise Indian children who love themselves." Not necessarily in
that order, but, I believe, prompted by the same moral imperative. I can't write
those lines, however, without acknowledging that from the perspective of most
North American Indians, Chicanos are perceived as second-class Indians at best
or not Indian at all, i.e., "Hispanic." I also can't write those lines without conced-
ing that when most heterosexuals of color discuss "breeding" as a revolutionary
act, they aren't necessarily thinking of their lesbian sisters and gay brothers as
comrades in those reproductive acts of sexual resistance (especially given the
whitewashing queer identity has endured in the national consciousness.
Historically, we may have been invited to bed by those cultural nationalists, but
not to the tribal councils.

But for Indian children to love themselves, they must love their sex organs and their sexual desire. They must love their lesbian mothers and aunties and queer fathers and cousins. They must develop a living critical consciousness about their land-based history (outside of the whiteman's fiction), a history which remains undocumented by mainstream culture and is ignored by the queer, feminist, and "Hispanic" communities. They must remember they were here first and always, whether they call themselves Chicano, Diné, Apache, Yaqui, or Choctaw; for that memory can alter consciousness and consciousness can alter institutionalized self-loathing in the service of genocide. Our children must become rigorous abolitionists of the slavery of the mind. They must think the taboo thought and cultivate in their own lives a profound knowledge about who they are, outside the framework of the U.S. Nation-state. I don't know exactly how to teach a counterculture of courage to my children, but I am working on it. And in this, I am not alone.

For these reasons, I believe my conversation about strategies for revolution as a Xicanadykemama resides more solidly within the cultural-political framework of American Indigenism (North and South) than in any U.S. gay and lesbian or feminist movement, which remain, at their cultural core, Euro-American, in spite of a twenty-year history of people of color activism within those movements. I have for the most part removed myself from conversation with the gay and lesbian feminist movement because most of its activists do not share my fears and as such do not share my hopes.

Genocide is what I'm afraid of, as well as the complete cultural obliteration of those I call my pueblo and the planet that sustains us. Gay men and lesbians (regardless of race) have, in the last two decades, become intimately connected to the question of survival because of the AIDS pandemic. But, as AIDS activists have already learned, sometimes the hard way, AIDS and the threat of death impact people of color communities differently, gay *and* heterosexual. AIDS is just one more murderous face in the long history of the systemic annihilation of poor and colored folk across the globe.

So, I fear AIDS as I fear gang violence as I fear the prison industrial complex as I fear breast cancer. But I also fear the loss of Nuevo México to New York artists; the loss of Mexican Indian curanderismo to new age healers; the loss of Día de los Muertos to a San Francisco-style Halloween; the loss of Native tribal and familia social structures to the nuclear family (gay and straight); the cultural loss of kids of color to mixed-race adoptions (gay and straight); the loss of art to commerce.

I think of Adrienne Rich's words from a generation ago, "Every woman's death diminishes me." Twenty years later, I would amend Rich's statement and assert with equal lesbian feminist passion, "Every barrio boy's death diminishes me." I never knew I would experience it this way; this intimate sense de un pueblo in the body of a boy. Maybe motherhood has changed me. And then, I think not, except for a growing compassion for those I have loved the most intimately in my life: Mexican women (madres) unspoken and unspoken for. This love is what fundamentally propelled me to be a lesbian in the first place and remains so. And so, I suffer their sons, their fathers, our men. But I continue, a resistant combatant.

The police delivered Linda's son to our door just before dawn this morning. He returned home a broken boy, crying as his mother, my woman, patched him up from a yanked IV. Twenty-six-years-old, but in our bathroom, he is a boy of sixteen, wondering what had gone wrong, everything was going all right—the job, the car, the room, the "stuff"—I was doing so good, he cried. I watch the back of his neck as his head falls onto his chest wet with tequila tears, the sun-darkened brown of his skin against the white shirt collar, still crisp with starch. I see in him my own son's elegantly sculpted neck, the same silk of brown boy color. I want to look away from this meeting of generations, this juxtaposition of contradictions. My son of seven sleeping safely between the sheets, my woman of forty-seven, hours later, on the street with her grown son in search of the car he had abandoned the night before after a tequila-and-testosterone-driven fist fight after macho bravado and father failure and mother abandonment. Or so he sees it.

A week later the white Latin American therapist asks Linda, "What are you afraid of?" "That he'll be killed," she answers. I watch the therapist's face. He thinks she is being *exagerada*. Metaphoric. My woman, a veterana of a war the therapist does not witness. How is it we feel that our children's ability to flourish, to achieve some kind of real ánimo in their lives, is on our backs to carry. Their failure, our failure. How do we separate mother-guilt, collective and individual, from a righteous resistance to genocide? I am reminded of my comadre, Marsha. How she acknowledged in her mid-forties that she would never be free of the burden of her boy, that her son's "condition," as she called it, meant he would never be a fully functioning adult. I felt an unbearable sadness for her. Diagnosed schizophrenic, I sometimes wondered was her son's condition anything more than colored and queer in América: mixed-blood, mad, and male. A year later, he has murdered her. Marsha, like me, like my woman: a Xicanadykemama.

He was one of the lost tribe. No romance about it. One of the lost ones who are so many of our sons now. I gotta boy following him. Somehow think if I do good by Linda's boy, twenty-six going on sixteen, my little boy got a chance. But it's hard to live up to. Big boy aint my blood. I tell his mother, "I didn't break it." But I know in that resides the lie. We all "broke it," him, them. And I'm only as good as the chance I give him, even if we fail. "His blood is on my hands." I write these words like the beginning of a fiction about the end of a fact, but the question of his survival remains for both of us—for me and his mother. Somehow, this notion of us as a people, un pueblo, makes us mutually and collectively responsible for one another's survival. The privatization of the American household makes no sense to us. He is family because he is Raza, although he and his kind hold my own life and my lesbianism in contempt. A living contradiction: the mutuality of our responsibility to one another in an individualistic culture that divides and most surely continues to conquer us through those divisions. This son of ours, my antagonist and this country's volatile victim at once. This threatened and threatening machito, who is my gente, child, brother. I want to write "brethren," for it is biblical, this grand story of nations and dislocations, exile and homecomings.

HOMECOMING

On Día de los Muertos, my Linda gathers all the orphans together—Mexican Indians and a few dispossessed white folk—and we pray. It is a vigil of sorts. By 9 P.M. my son is already a bundle of bones and cobija on the hardwood floor Linda's granddaughter, Camerina, on the threshold of her bloods, stays up. Is it the pending menstruation, the hormonal eruption of her organism, which keeps her up? She has something to strive for.

I strive only for my son some days. Some days the pure joy I experience watching him jump off the play structure in the school playground at the sight of my car pulling up to the curb, his running toward it at full speed, backpack falling off one shoulder, an earnestness in his face is enough. What is enough for me is this pure recognition of the moment: these monkey bars, this asphalt playground with painted-on kickball fields and tetherball circles, *this momma arriving to pick me up as promised, knowing the afternoon snack will be waiting, the two hours of homework sitting at the table with sorta sister across from me, we both working word problems onto a sheet of Xeroxed preguntas. Momma working all the time with her hands, as we with our minds, cleaning the kitchen, banging around pots and pans, chop chop chop ajo, cebolla, celery into our evening dinner. My mother is not a housewife. She is queer and writes books, and wants something more for herself and her children—something more than careers and portfolios and mortgages.* And what she wants is enough for all of us for now.

I am wondering what is happening in my middle age. I have changed. I have less hope, it seems, but deeper dreams in my writing. I reference my son as I do because I know this is a fleeting moment of well-being, extended in his blessed childhood, where he is awake and full of hope which propels him forward into his life like the gestating hormones of his almost-sister. My lover's hormones and mine are not gestating so much anymore. They are, I imagine, taking leave of their previous missions, four babies in total between us. Is this why I am sad? This death of the illusion that we are not dying?

Days later, I am on a plane returning from Los Angeles and my mother's eighty-sixth birthday celebration. I measure the ages of the passengers around me. There are those striving upward, ignorant of death. They are making money, careers, plans. There are those whose careers are what they have been. Their bodies worry them so. They try not to think about it, its enormous weight (the daily discomfort of those extra thirty pounds), the aching left hip, frozen knee, the sudden palpitations of the heart.

My mother is eighty-six years old today and continues to change into a woman I've never met, but must quickly learn to know. She repeats descriptions of events from yesterday and last week over and over again because they still interest her as she remembers them brand new with each telling. She asks the same question two and three times within a ten-minute span of conversation. She brings out the same cup of coffee to serve someone, forgetting in the trip from kitchen to dining room who the someone was, although she's already asked and been told twice. The coffee she offered to serve me goes cold.

My mother is eighty-six years old today. My mother and Linda's son teach me daily not to expect anything. She is a deep bruise in my heart; he, the constant ache of uncertainty. As I return home to Oakland, the sun sets pink and purple outside my window. I read Chicano poet Alfred Arteaga's new collection of verse, *Frozen Accident*. He writes, "Gato and Xeritzín and all other / souls alive, live only in the inks, / in the red and the black, for only in / codices do bodies truly animate." Then, I think, can't we just make art? There is a prayer in the writing. How is it I stray so far away? How is it I do not daily drag my woman into this prayer of art that sustains in the face of grave disappointment, all the small dyings of heart?

SOME OF MY BEST FRIENDS ARE

Fact. Nearly thirty years out of the closet and I don't really know what I have left to say to the white gay and lesbian community, except that I continue to be one, a lesbian, that just last night, on the eve of my woman's forty-eighth birthday, I made love to her like I remember wanting it as an adolescent. Thirty years ago, desire was a sad dream, thinking how queer (in the pre-eighties sense of the word) it was to want as I did.

Lesbian. Dyke. Queer. I'll go to the grave queer, I announce, fully knowing that no one can shake me from that rock bottom place of conviction about my desire. My racial identity has always been more ambiguous. The ground it stands on is built upon a memory for which I can make no clear accounting. I never met one of my Yaqui ancestors; never a relative who named us anything but Mexican, so Mexican it is, but since my earliest childhood I knew Mexican meant Indian. And it was that naming of "Chicano" in the seventies that reminded me of that fact and that sent most of my relatives into political hiding. So, I knew "Indian" was dangerous, like lesbianism. Knew it could not be domesticated, tamed, colonized. Like "dyke." People (white, Black, and Brown alike) have tried to dislocate me from Chicanismo, half-breed that I am; but it is getting harder and harder to do so. I'm getting older. I've been standing on this ground for too long now. There are enemies from within and without. I've slept under the same roof and in the same bed with people for whom I remain unknown and unknowable. The bitter irony is that they never knew that they didn't know me. And *that*'s a fact.

Several years ago, my compadre, Chicano playwright Ricardo Bracho, asked me how I identified myself politically, as a "Chicana Lesbian" or a "Lesbian Chicana?" As wordsmiths, of course, these distinctions matter to us. I remember there was some discussion about how Spanish forces one to choose because "Lesbiana" and "Lésbica" occupy distinct locations as parts of speech, the first a noun, the second an adjective. English, on the other hand, allows for a bit more ambivalence, where the same "lesbian" is used for both the noun and the adjective and its signification relies exclusively on syntax. At the same time, nearly a decade ago, we both agreed that I was surely a Chicana Lesbian, in that order, where Chicana is the cultural *modifier* of the indisputable fact of my lesbianism. In a call for just such cultural specification, critiquing white middle-class women's cultural hegemony of lesbian sexuality, I wrote in 1982:

> What I need to explore will not be found in the lesbian feminist bedroom, but more likely in the mostly heterosexual bedrooms of South Texas, L.A., or even Sonora, México.[1]

What I didn't know was how a thorough exploration of that sexuality on the sheets of my bed and the sheets of my writing would eventually separate me from the lesbian and gay movement. In contrast to what Ricardo and I had concluded in that kitchen conversation in the early nineties, today I feel that my lesbianism modifies a growing Chicanismo, where the revolutionary consequence of my *cultural* identification generates my activism, my art *and* my sexuality.

I still got white friends (most at a distance now), queer girls who sleep with each other and some who sleep with men, and who remain my friends because they are not safe women. They are not secure at night. They do not believe middle-class security will secure them. They are not fooled by professions and insurance policies and retirement funds. They are not fooled into believing that post-modern theory is the same as radical action or that tenure is a tent against the elements of oppression. And so, they remain my allies, these white women. Still, I don't see them that much anymore.

There was a time, living in New York City in the early eighties, when I ran with a buncha white and Black literary girls and we had shared purpose. Cuz I was still thinking kind of black and white back then, never naming, except with great pains in my own private writings, what really wracked my soul at night: a desire for return more primordial than any simple cross-country relocation to Califas could fulfill. A longing for that Mexican Indian mother waiting for me at home in the body of my relatives here and gone, in the body of my age and wanting.

For me, New York in the early eighties was *Conditions* magazine, Kitchen Table: Women of Color Press, and New York Women Against Rape. It was a growing feminism of color that grew in its autonomous conversation just amongst us coloredgirls. And as that conversation evolved, so grew an activism which separated many of us from white women, drawing us closer and closer not only to one another, but also to our specific cultural experience as Chicanas, cubanas, Lakota, English- and Spanish-speaking Afro-Caribbean women; as Chinese American and immigrant South East Asian.

In that specificity, I learned that for the most part, when white women spoke of women of color and racism, they were usually thinking black/white relations and, too often, African Americans were equally politically engaged in the same bi-polared version of the history of U.S. race relations. Four years after the publication of *This Bridge Called My Back,* it seemed that, in spite of my *theoretical* faith in an international feminism of color proposed by *Bridge* (which I still believe in), in *practice* my feminism of color was taking on a decidedly meXicana formation.

In the meantime, at night me and the Puerto Rican girls and the Black girls that could dance salsa went out and made out in bathrooms and somehow in that there was a place to be me. And I thank Sandra and Alma and Vienna y las dos Mirthas for that. I thank Leota for an "Indianness" I couldn't even yet put a name to then, but knew my heart was working to live out in another decade. I thank even all "the women who hate me," to quote lesbian author Dorothy Allison's book of poems. Maybe cuz inspiring hatred gotta mean something was given and got up and gone when you left and that's somehow a tribute to what once was.

WHAT ONCE WAS: A STORY FORETOLD

Reading Amber Hollibaugh's *My Dangerous Desires*, the history of a poor-whitegypsytrashfemcommiedyke is rendered in the manner of a beautiful adventure book. It is my friend Amber's history and fantasy at once, the facts that make up *her* fiction. Closing the book, I think, *A damn worthy life. And she aint even dead yet.* And through the history told of this complex and compelling woman and activist, the history of a movement is documented. I must confess I was a bit jealous of Amber's story; that for all its class betrayals, the gay and lesbian movement—that one movement—is where Amber finally found home. I was jealous because no movement has ever sustained me like that. My history, a solo journey it seems, traversing many movements of diverse, seemingly contradictory identities.

A few weeks ago, my Linda returned home with the news of Dolores Huerta's critical condition. She is mostly recovered now, but earlier that day I had a premonition of sorts, for some reason, about Dolores. I remembered Cesar Chavez's funeral, how I was unable to attend. How the "circumstances" of my life had prevented it. Today those "circumstances" have changed. Thinking of Dolores, I told myself that when she passed, I wanted to be present con mi familia, that this time I had a familia to be present with. Selfish thoughts about the markers of meaning in our own lives. These leaders: both persons (our friends) and at the same time symbols. Audre Lorde was a symbol and a person and a friend. Artist-activist Marsha Gómez's intimate death by the hand of her son continues to symbolize something great and powerfully humbling in my life. Maybe I, too, am a symbol to others, to young ones, as I age. I don't write this to aggrandize myself, only knowing that we are all just moments in a small and devastating history of a planet and its people.

I watch my mother aging daily and I live inside her body, watch the markings of my own body like the prediction of the future she already lives. I can't wait for her to die to write of that history. I can't wait to be a centenarian to remember. I remember now a future I fear I will witness and I quiet my justified paranoia by writing counter-tales of courage I may never live up to. It is autobiography in the truest sense: a record of my imaginings, as much as that of my experience. So that when I write in the voice of some one-hundred-year-old Xicanadyke, armed and barricaded in her desert adobe, her lover of sixty years by her side, it is as much "me" as I can conjure in the best and worst of scenarios.

We are in a war against the U.S. government. We knew (hoped) it would finally come to pass, this meaningful way to end our lives here. Too horrible to think of dying without a fight, without reason for fighting. When I turned fifty, I began to mourn my ancestors, the recent ones known in my lifetime, who left with little resistance, except an entrenched bitterness. Flor and I shared this, this commitment to not die as one of them, to leave for our ungrateful children a legacy of self-defense, por los menos.[2]

The old women of this story, as much as the personal and political portraits painted in an essay, are my Xicanadyke codices of changing consciousness. As a child clandestinely dreaming of women in the early sixties, I could never have imagined how "legitimate" in some select circles queerness would become. I also never knew how the color of that queerness (and its political consequences) would once again render my desire not only unlawful, but thoroughly revolutionary in its political promise.

A codex is a history told and foretold. I know a little bit about where I've been in the almost-fifty-years that is my life. I don't know where we're going. I can only guess, which is why I write, to guess at a future for which we must prepare. To that end, may we strive always for illegitimacy and unlawfulness, in this criminal culture. May our thoughts and actions remain illicit. May we continue to make art that incites censorship and threatens to bring the army beating down our desert door.

NOTES
1. *Loving in the War Years: Lo Que Nunca Pasó por Sus Labios* (Second Edition). Boston, MA: South End Press, 2001, 117.
2. From "A Cactus Tuna Bleeding in the Heat," a work-in-progress.

JUDITH BUTLER

Judith Butler is Maxine Elliot Professor in the Departments of Rhetoric and Comparative Literature at the University of California, Berkeley. She received her Ph.D. in philosophy from Yale University in 1984. She is the author of *Antigone's Claim: Kinship Between Life and Death* (Columbia University Press, 2000), *Hegemony, Contingency, Universality*, with Ernesto Laclau and Slavoj Zizek, (Verso Press, 2000), *Subjects of Desire: Hegelian Reflections in Twentieth-Century France* (Columbia University Press, 1987), *Gender Trouble: Feminism and the Subversion of Identity* (Routledge, 1990), *Bodies That Matter: On the Discursive Limits of "Sex"* (Routledge, 1993), *The Psychic Life of Power: Theories of Subjection* (Stanford University Press, 1997), *Excitable Speech* (Routledge, 1997), as well as numerous articles and contributions on philosophy, feminist and queer theory. Her recent project is a critique of ethical violence and an effort to formulate a theory of responsibility for a subject who cannot always know herself. This manuscript works with Kafka, Freud, Foucault, Adorno, and Levinas. She is also working on a set of essays engaged with grievable and ungrievable lives, war, politics and the suspension of civil liberties.

GLOBAL VIOLENCE, SEXUAL POLITICS[1]

I am enormously honored to be here this evening, and very pleased, if also a bit daunted to be asked to speak to you on this occasion. It is wonderful for me to think that I have made a significant contribution of some sort to the work you do, and perhaps also to the lives you live, but the truth is that I would be nowhere without you. I am not sure I would have stayed in the academy if it were not for this emerging field. It has given me more than I have given it—a home, an incitement, a provocation—so let me take this opportunity to thank you.

I'd like to speak to you this evening on the matter of politics and, specifically, how the struggles of gender and sexual minorities might offer a perspective on current issues that are before us, questions of mourning and violence, which we have to deal with as part of an international community. I'd like to start, and to end, with the question of the human, of who counts as the human, and the related question of whose lives count as lives, and with a question that has pre-occupied many of us for years: *What makes for a grievable life*? I believe that whatever our differences as a community, and there are many, we all have some notion of what it is to have lost somebody. And if we've lost, then it seems to follow that we have had, that we have desired and loved, and struggled to find the conditions for our desire. We have all lost in recent decades from AIDS, but there are other losses that inflict us, other diseases, and there is the fact as well that we are, as a community, subjected to violence, even if some of us have not been. This means that we are constituted politically in part by virtue of the social vulnerability of our bodies; as a field of desire and physical vulnerability, of a publicity at once assertive and targeted.

I am not sure I know when mourning is successful, or when one has fully mourned another human being. I'm certain, though, that it does not mean that you have forgotten them, or that something else comes along to take their place. I don't think it works that way. I think instead that one mourns when one accepts the fact that the loss one undergoes will be one that changes you, changes you possibly forever, and that mourning has to do with agreeing to undergo a transformation the full result of which you cannot know in advance. So there is losing, and there is the transformative effect of loss, and this latter cannot be charted or planned. I don't think, for instance, you can invoke a protestant ethic when it comes to loss. You can't say, oh, I'll go through loss this way, and that will be the result, and I'll apply myself to the task, and I'll endeavor to achieve the resolution of grief that is before me. I think you get hit by waves, and that you start out the day, with an aim, a project, a plan, and you find yourself foiled. You find yourself fallen. You're exhausted, and you don't know why. Something is larger than your own deliberate plan, your own project, your own knowing. Something takes hold of you, and what sense does this make? What is it that claims us at such moments, such that we are not the masters of ourselves? To what are we tied? And by what are we seized?

Is it simply the case that we are undergoing something temporary? Or is it rather that, in undergoing what we do, something about who we are is revealed, something that delineates the ties we have to others, that shows us that the ties are what we are, what we are composed of, and that when we lose them, especially some of them, we do not know who we are, or what to do? Many people think that grief is privatizing, that it returns us to a solitary situation, but I think it has and can furnish a sense of political community of a complex order.

It is not just that I might be said to "have" these relations, and sit back and enumerate them to you, explaining what this friendship means, what that lover meant or means to me. On the contrary, it seems that what grief displays is the way in which we are in the thrall of our relations with others in ways that we cannot always recount or explain, in ways that often interrupt the self-conscious account of ourselves we might try to provide, in ways that challenge the very notion of ourselves as autonomous and in control. I might try to tell a story here, about what I am feeling, but it would have to be a story in which the very "I" who seeks to tell the story is stopped in the midst of the telling, the very "I" is called into question by its relation to the Other, a relation that does not precisely reduce me to speechlessness, but does nevertheless clutter my speech with signs of its undoing.

Let's face it. We're undone by each other. And if we're not, we're missing something.

This seems so clearly the case with grief, but this can be so only because it was already the case with desire. One does not always stay intact. It may be that one wants to, or does, but it may also be that despite one's best efforts, one is undone, in the face of the other, by the touch, by the scent, by the feel, by the prospect of the touch, by the memory of the feel. So when we speak about *my* sexuality or *my* gender, as we do, and as we must, we mean something complicated by it, since it is not precisely a possession, but, rather, a mode of being dispossessed, a way of being for another, or by virtue of another. It won't even do to say that I am promoting a relational view of the self over an autonomous one, or trying to redescribe autonomy in terms of relationality. We tend to narrate the history of the movement in such a way that ecstasy figures in the '60s and '70s, and mid-way through the '80s. But maybe ecstasy is more persistent than that, maybe it is with us all along. To be ec-static means, literally, to be outside oneself, and this can have several meanings: to be transported beyond oneself by a passion, but also to be *beside oneself* with rage or grief. I think that if I can still speak to a "we," or include myself within its terms, I am speaking to those of us who are living in certain ways *beside ourselves*, whether it is in sexual passion, or emotional grief, or political rage.

I'm arguing, if I am "arguing" at all, that we have an interesting political predicament, since most of the time when we hear about "rights," we understand them as pertaining to individuals, or when we argue for protection against discrimination, we argue as a group or a class. And in that language and in that context, we have to present ourselves as bounded beings, distinct, recognizable, delineated, subjects before the law, communities defined by sameness. Indeed, we had better be able to use that language to secure legal protections and entitlements. But perhaps we make a mistake if we take the definitions of who we are legally to be adequate descriptions of what we are about. Though this language might well establish our legitimacy within a legal framework ensconced in liberal versions of human ontology, it doesn't do justice to passion and grief and rage, all of which tear us from ourselves, bind us to others, transport us, undo us, and fatally, irreversibly implicate us in lives that are not our own.

It is not easy to understand how a political community is wrought from such ties. One speaks, and one speaks for another, to another, and yet there is no way to collapse the distinction between the other and myself. When we say "we" we do nothing more than designate this very problematic. We do not solve it. And perhaps it is, and ought to be, insoluble. I don't want to forget that there are bodies here, and that bodies are in a certain sense our own, and that we must claim rights of autonomy over them: this is as true for lesbian and gays rights claims in favor of sexual freedom as it is for transsexual and transgender claims to self-determination; as it is for intersex claims to be free of coerced medical and psychiatric interventions; as it is for all claims to be free from racist attacks, physical and verbal; as it is for feminism's claim to reproductive freedom. It is difficult, if not impossible, to make these claims without recourse to autonomy. I am not suggesting that we should cease to make these claims. We have to make them, we must. And I'm not saying that we have to make these claims reluctantly or strategically. They are part of any normative aspiration of a movement that seeks to maximize the protection and the freedoms of sexual and gender minorities, of women, defined with the broadest possible compass, of racial and ethnic minorities, especially as they cut across all the other categories. But is there another normative aspiration that we must also seek to articulate and to defend? Is there a way in which the place of the body in all of these struggles opens up a different conception of politics?

The body implies mortality, vulnerability, agency: the skin and flesh expose us to the gaze of others, but also to touch, and to violence; the body can be the agency and instrument of all these as well. Although we struggle for rights over our own bodies, the very bodies for which we struggle are never quite only our own. The body has its invariably public dimension: it is constituted as a social phenomenon in the public sphere, so that my body is and is not mine. It is given over from the start to the world of others, bearing their imprint, formed within the crucible of social life. Only later, with some uncertainty, do I lay claim to my body as my own. Indeed, if I seek to deny the fact that against my will, and from the start, my body relates me to others whom I did not choose to be in proximity, if I build a notion of "autonomy" on the basis of the denial of this sphere of a primary and unwilled physical proximity, then do I precisely deny the social and political conditions of my embodiment in the name of autonomy? If I am struggling for autonomy, I need to be struggling for something else as well: a conception of myself as invariably in community, impressed upon by others and impressing them as well, in ways that are not fully predictable.

Is there a way that we might struggle for autonomy in many spheres, but also consider the demands that are imposed upon us by living in a world of beings who are, by definition, physically dependent on one another, physically vulnerable to one another? This would be another way of imagining community, and imagining it in such a way that it becomes incumbent upon us to consider very carefully when and where we use violence, for violence is, always, an exploitation of that primary tie, that primary way in which we are, as bodies, outside ourselves, for one another.

If I might then return to the problem of grief, to the moments in which one undergoes something outside of one's control, finds that one is beside oneself, not at one with oneself, perhaps we can say grief contains within it the possibility of apprehending the fundamental sociality of embodied life, the ways in which we are, from the start, and by virtue of being a bodily being, already given over, beyond ourselves, implicated in lives that are not our own. Can this situation, which is so dramatic for us and establishes a very specific political perspective for anyone who works in the field of sexual and gender politics, supply a perspective by which to begin to apprehend the contemporary global situation?

Mourning, fear, anxiety, rage. And in the United States, we are everywhere now surrounded with violence, of having perpetrated it, having suffered it, living in fear of it, planning more of it. Violence is surely a touch of the worst order, in which the human vulnerability to other humans is exposed in its most terrifying way, in which we are given over, without control, to the will of another, in which life itself can be expunged by the willful action of another. To the extent that we commit violence, we are acting upon another, putting the other at risk, causing the other damage, expunging the other. In a way, we all live with this particular vulnerability, a vulnerability to the other which is part of bodily life, but this vulnerability becomes highly exacerbated under certain social and political conditions. It becomes the basis of claims for non-militaristic political solutions, as a vulnerability that we cannot will away, that we must attend to, even abide by, as we begin to think about what politics might be implied by staying with the thought of corporeal vulnerability itself.

I think we have seen, are seeing, various ways of dealing with grief. For instance, William Safire, citing Milton, writes in the *New York Times* that we must banish melancholy; and President Bush announces on September 21, 2001, that we have finished grieving and that *now* it is time for resolute action to take the place of grief.[2] When grieving is feared, it seeks to resolve itself quickly, to banish itself in the name of an action that is invested with the power to restore the loss or rectify the world. Is there something to be gained from grieving, from tarrying with grief, remaining exposed to its unbearability and not endeavoring to seek a resolution of grief through violence? Is there something to be gained in the political domain by maintaining grief as part of the framework by which we think our international ties? If we stay with the sense of loss, are we left feeling only passive and powerless, as some fear? Or are we, rather, returned to a sense of human vulnerability, to our collective responsibility for the physical lives of one another? The attempt to foreclose that vulnerability, to banish it, to make ourselves secure at the expense of every other human consideration, is surely also to eradicate one of the most important resources from which we must take our bearings, and find our way.

To grieve, and to make grief itself into a resource for politics is not to be resigned to a simple passivity or powerlessness. It is, rather, to allow oneself to extrapolate from our own experience of vulnerability to that experience that others undergo, others whom we may well be able to protect from violence.

There is a more general conception of the human with which I am trying to work here, one in which we are, from the start, given over to the other, even prior to individuation itself, and by virtue of our embodiment. This makes us vulnerable to violence, but also to another range of touch, a range that includes the eradication of our being at the one end, and the physical support for our lives, at the other.

And there is a further point: we cannot recover the source of this vulnerability, for it precedes the formation of "I," and this is a condition of being laid bare from the start, with which we cannot argue. Rather, we *can* argue with it, but we are doubtless foolish, if not dangerous, when we do. Of course, for some this primary scene is one of abandonment or violence or starvation, and in this case, we are referring to bodies given over to nothing, or to brutality, or to no sustenance. But to understand what is dire here, it is still necessary to understand that they are "given over." Part of understanding the conditions of oppression requires understanding how this primary need is or is not met by the social and economic world. We cannot understand the oppression of children without this conception of what it is to be human, or through what primary vulnerability human life emerges. There is no way to argue away this condition of primary vulnerability, of being given over to the touch of the other, even if, or precisely when, there is no other there, and no support for our lives. Lives are supported and maintained differentially, and there are radically different ways in which human physical vulnerability is distributed across the globe. Certain lives will be highly protected, and the abrogation of their claims to sanctity will be sufficient to mobilize the forces of war. Other lives will not find such fast and furious support and will not even qualify as "grievable."

A hierarchy of grief could no doubt be enumerated, and we've seen it already (December 2001), in the genre of the obituary, where lives are so quickly tidied up and summarized, humanized, usually married, or on the way to be, heterosexual, happy, monogamous. But this is just a sign of another differential relation to life, since we rarely, if ever, hear the names of the thousands of Palestinians who have died at the hands of Israeli military with U.S. support, or of any number of Afghani people, children and adults. What defense against the apprehension of loss is at work in the blithe way in which we accept deaths caused by military means with a shrug or with self-righteousness or with clear vindictiveness? Do those who support the war consider these as lives at all? Do these lives conform to the notion of the human? And if not, what are the cultural contours of the notion of the human at work here? And how do the contours that we accept as the cultural frame for the human limit the extent to which we can avow loss as loss? This is surely a question that lesbian, gay and bi- studies has asked, in relation to violence against sexual minorities, that transgendered people have asked as they have been singled out for harassment and sometimes murder, that intersexed people have asked, whose formative years have so often been marked by an unwanted violence against their bodies in the name of a normative notion of the human and what the body of the human must be. This is no doubt as well the basis of a profound affinity between movements revolving around gender and sexuality with efforts to counter the normative human morphologies and capacities that condemn or efface those who are physically challenged. And it must also be part of the affinity with anti-racist struggles, given the racial differential that undergirds the culturally viable notions of the human, ones that we see acted out in dramatic and terrifying ways in the global arena at the present time.

It should be added that violence is not an abstraction. If one learns non-violence, one finds that it is an ongoing struggle, a practice, an arduous ethical demand. Non-violence doesn't mean doing away with rage: it is the ethical practice of cultivating one's rage into articulation. And if I had to say what drove me to queer theory it was probably this ethical problematic, one that pertains to rage and to desire. I haven't been able to do very well without either. They are my resources, and they carry with them a set of risks.

So what is the relation between violence and dehumanization, between violence and the unreality that can attach to those who become the victims of violence, and where does the notion of the ungrievable life come in? Some would argue that at the level of discourse, certain lives are not considered lives at all, they cannot be humanized; they fit no dominant frame for the human, and their dehumanization occurs first, at this level. This level then gives rise to a physical violence that in some sense delivers the message of dehumanization that is already at work in the culture. Two hundred thousand Iraqi children were killed in the Gulf War and its aftermath:[3] do we have an image, a frame for any of those lives, singly or collectively? Is there a story we might find about those deaths in the media? Are there names attached to those children? There is no obituary for the war casualties that the U.S. inflicts, and there cannot be. For there to be an obituary, there would have had to have been a life, a life worth noting, a life worth valuing and preserving, a life that would qualify for recognition. Though we might argue that it would be impractical to include obituaries for all those people, or for all people, I think we have to ask, again and again, how the obituary functions as the instrument by which grievability is publicly distributed, the means by which a life becomes, or fails to become, a publicly grievable life, an icon for national self-recognition, the means by which a life becomes noteworthy. As a result, we have to think of the obituary as an act of nation building. And the matter is not so simple, since if the life is not grievable, it is not quite a life; it does not qualify as a life and is not worth a note; it is already the unburied, the unburiable. It's not that the death is poorly marked, but that it is unmarkable. It vanishes, not into explicit discourse, but into the ellipses by which discourse proceeds.

The queer lives that vanished on September 11th are not publicly welcomed into the idea of national identity currently being built in the obituary pages. But this should come as no surprise, when we think as well about how many deaths from AIDS were publicly ungrievable losses, and how, for instance, the extensive deaths now taking place in Africa are also, in the media, for the most part unmarkable and ungrievable.

So it is not just that a discourse exists in which there is no frame and no story and no name for such a life, and that violence might be said to realize or apply this discourse. Rather, violence against those who are already not quite lives, who are living in a state of suspension between life and death, leaves a mark that is no mark. If there is a discourse, it is a silent and melancholic writing in which there have been no lives, and no losses, there has been no common physical condition, no vulnerability that serves as the basis for an apprehension of our commonality, and there has been no sundering of that commonality. None of this takes place on the order of the event. None of this takes place. Don't get me wrong: it may be reported, there may be a story, there may even be a picture of the face of this or that leader of a terrorist gang who is dramatically personified for us. But even these personifications are not *humanizations*; they become, like the face of bin Laden, visual icons of the only apparently human, what the media wants to portray as the deceptively human. In the images he supplies, and the media absorbs and distributes, he smiles, but implicit in the presentation is that this is no smile; that his eyes seem kind, but he is most certainly not kind: such an image is the lure of surface, the personification of a lie, the appearance of a face that distorts the very expressivity of the face. And it wouldn't matter if it were just bin Laden, but he is standing for, he is representing, he is being generalized into the Islamic menace, the true meaning of Islam, the terror that lies behind every Islamic charity, the lie that Islam is, for the government, and for the media, which so quickly and consistently forgets the difference between the various practices of Islam and its extremist version or, rather, takes the former to be the lie behind which the latter hides.

I began these remarks this evening with a suggestion that perhaps the interrelated movements and modes of inquiry that collect here might need; to consider autonomy as one dimension of its normative aspiration, one value to realize when we ask ourselves, in what direction ought we to proceed, and what kinds of values ought we to be realizing? I also suggested that the way in which the body figures in gender and sexuality studies, and in the struggles for a less oppressive world for the otherwise gendered and for sexual minorities of all kinds, is precisely to underscore the value of being beside oneself, of being a porous boundary, given over to others, finding oneself in a trajectory of desire that takes one out of oneself, resituates one irreversibly in the field of others. The particular sociality that belongs to bodily life, to sexual life, and to becoming gendered (which is always, to a certain extent, becoming gendered for others) establishes a field of ethical enmeshment with others. We are, as bodies, always for something more than, and other than, ourselves. To articulate this as an entitlement is not always easy, but perhaps not impossible. It would be to suggest, for instance, that "association" is not luxury, but one of the very conditions and prerogatives of freedom. Indeed, the kinds of associations we maintain importantly have many forms, and it will not do to extol the marriage norm as the new ideal for this movement. It should certainly be there as an option, but to instate as the exclusive site of sexuality or legitimacy is precisely to constrain the sociality of the body. And though it is clear that it is crucial to expand our notions of kinship beyond the heterosexual frame, especially in light of seriously damaging judicial decisions against second parent adoptions in recent years, it would be a mistake to reduce kinship to family, or to assume that all community ties are extrapolations of kinship relations.

Kinship ties that bind persons to one another may well be no more or less than the intensification of community ties, may or may not be based on enduring or exclusive sexual relations, may well consist of ex-lovers, non-lovers, friends, community members. In this sense, then, the relations of kinship arrive at boundaries that call into question the differentiation of kinship from community, or that, perhaps, call for a different conception of friendship. These modes of association constitute a breakdown of traditional kinship that not only displaces the central place of biological and sexual relations from its definition, but also gives sexuality a separate domain from that of kinship, allowing as well for the durable tie to be thought outside of the conjugal frame, and opening sexuality to a number of social articulations that do not always imply binding relations or conjugal ties. That not all of our relations last or are meant to, however, does not mean that we are immune to grief. On the contrary, sexuality outside the field of monogamy well may open us to a different sense of community, intensifying the question of where one finds enduring ties, and so may become the condition for an attunement to losses that exceed the private realm.

So in response to the question of what political perspectives might be derived from the resources of this complex notion of community, we might supply a perspective on violence, on the public distribution of legitimate grief, and on the public or, rather, national allocation of grievable lives. We can also, I think, consider what politics comes from grief, and what politics comes from its hasty foreclosure. If revenge is the quick way to escape from the feeling of loss, it allows for this only by instigating a cycle of revenge that redoubles the loss in the end. Perhaps we should be providing queer readings of Aeschylus for the nation-state. But perhaps we also wonder whether perspectives emerging from sexuality and gender studies have political implications right now. Are we secondary, or beside the point?

It is crucial to make our claims for autonomy, our claims for rights of association, and our claims on reality, all the more active and vigilant, precisely because the nation-state is being produced again and again along lines of consensus that centralize the heterosexual family, property and national boundaries, and that degrade not only civil liberties and the practice of dissent, but freedom itself, as democratic values. Reality is being made and remade during these times in dramatic and consequential ways. And for those who know what it is to be treated as unreal, it is all the more important that the unreal speak, in reality's name, if only to disrupt and to compel its reshaping in another direction.

The question of who and what is considered real and true is apparently a question of knowledge. But it is also, as Foucault makes plain, a question of power. Having or bearing "truth" and "reality" is an enormously powerful prerogative within the social world, one way which power dissimulates as ontology. According to Foucault, one of the first tasks of a radical critique is to discern the relation "between mechanisms of coercion and elements of knowledge."[4] Here we are confronted with the limits of what is knowable, limits that exercise a certain force, but are not grounded in any necessity, limits that can only be tread or interrogated by risking a certain security within an available ontology: "[N]othing can exist as an element of knowledge if, on the one hand, it . . . does not conform to a set of rules and constraints characteristic, for example, of a given type of scientific discourse in a given period, and if, on the other hand, it does not possess the effects of coercion or simply the incentives peculiar to what is scientifically validated or simply rational or simply generally accepted, etc."[5] Knowledge and power are not finally separable, but work together to establish a set of subtle and explicit criteria for thinking the world: "It is therefore not a matter of describing what knowledge is and what power is and how one would repress the other or how the other would abuse the one, but rather, a nexus of knowledge-power has to be described so that we can grasp what constitutes the acceptability of a system."[6]

What this means is that one looks *both* for the conditions by which the object field is constituted, and for the limits of those conditions, the moments that point to their contingency and their transformability. In Foucault's terms, "schematically speaking, we have perpetual mobility, essential fragility or rather the complex interplay between what replicates the same process and what transforms it."[7] To intervene in the name of transformation means precisely to disrupt what has become settled knowledge and knowable reality, and to use, as it were, one's unreality to make an otherwise impossible or illegible claim. I think that when those who are deemed "unreal" nevertheless lay claim to reality, or enter into its domain, something other than a simple assimilation into prevailing norms can and does take place. The norms themselves can become rattled, display their instability, become open to a resignification.

I think we have seen this in recent years as the new gender politics has offered numerous challenges from transgendered and transsexual peoples, and as the intersex movement has gained some place in public life. My earlier example of drag was no doubt too simple and too quick to come close to doing justice to this terrain.[8] But one of the criticisms of it, namely, that butch, femme, and transgendered lives are not essential to refashioning politics, not only failed to acknowledge the violence that the otherwise gendered suffer in the public world, but failed as well to recognize that embodiment is crucial to politics. Indeed, if we consider that embodiment cannot really proceed without a relation to a norm, or a set of norms, that that relation can be transformative, and that fantasy is part of that very relation, then it is not possible to demean transgendered lives as so many individuals living out their private fantasies and having no real impact on political life.

I would insist not only that the struggle to survive is not really separable from the cultural life of fantasy, but also that the foreclosure of fantasy is one strategy for providing for the social death of persons. Fantasy is not the opposite of reality: it is what reality forecloses, and it operates to delimit and to challenge the limits of what will and will not be called reality. Fantasy is what allows us to imagine ourselves and others otherwise; it establishes the possible in excess of the real; it points elsewhere, and when it is embodied, it brings the elsewhere home.

How does drag or, indeed, much more than drag, how do butch, femme, transgender, transsexual enter into the political field? They do this, I would suggest, by making us not only question what is real, and what has to be, but by showing us how the norms that govern contemporary notions of reality can be questioned, and new modes of reality instituted. They show that we can do this, in our very embodiment, and as a consequence of being a body in the mode of becoming, which in becoming otherwise exceeds the norm, reworks the norm, makes us see how realities to which we thought we were confined are not written in stone. Although some people have asked me what is finally the use of simply increasing possibilities for gender, I would suggest that possibility is not a luxury: it is as crucial as bread. I think we should not underestimate what the thought of the possible does for those for whom the very issue of survival is most urgent. If the answer to the question, is life possible, is yes, that is surely something. It cannot be taken for granted. That is an affirmation which, for many, is an accomplishment, one that is fundamentally conditioned by reality being structured or restructured in such a way that that very affirmation becomes possible.

This is one way in which the matter is and continues to be political, but there is something more. What the perhaps naive example of drag sought to do in *Gender Trouble* was to make us question the means by which reality is made, and to consider the way in which being called real, being called unreal, can be not only a means of social control, but also dehumanizing violence. I would put it this way: to be called unreal, and to have that call, as it were, institutionalized as a form of differential treatment, is to become the other against whom (or against which) the human is made. It is the inhuman, the beyond the human, the less than human, the border that secures the human in its ostensible reality. To be called a copy, to be called unreal, is thus one way in which one can be oppressed, but consider that it is more fundamental than that. To be oppressed means that you already exist as a subject of some kind, you are there as the visible and oppressed other for the master subject, as a possible or potential subject. But to be unreal is something else again. To be oppressed you must first become intelligible. To find that you are fundamentally unintelligible—indeed, that the laws of culture and of language find you to be an impossibility—is to find that you have not yet achieved access to the human; it is to find yourself speaking only and always *as if you were* human, but with the sense that you are not, it is to find that your language is hollow, that no recognition is forthcoming because the norms by which recognition takes place are not in your favor.

The point about drag is not simply to produce a pleasurable and subversive spectacle, but to allegorize the spectacular and consequential ways in which reality is both reproduced and contested. And this has consequences for how gender presentations are criminalized, pathologized, how subjects who cross genders risk internment and imprisonment, why violence against transgendered subjects is not recognized as violence, why it is sometimes inflicted by the very states that should be offering such subjects protection from violence.

I take this to be essential to politics. As I mentioned, I am sometimes asked the following question: so what if new forms of gender are possible? How does this affect the ways that we live, the concrete needs of the human community? And how are we to distinguish between forms of gender possibility that are valuable and those that are not? First, I would say that it is not a question merely of producing a new future for genders that do not yet exist. The genders I have in mind have existed for a long time, but they have not been admitted into the terms that govern reality. So it is a question of developing, within law, within psychiatry, within social and literary theory, a new legitimating lexicon for the gender complexity that we have always lived. Because the norms governing reality have not admitted these forms to be real, we will, of necessity, call them new. But I hope we will, at least, laugh knowingly when and if we do. If we think this is a theory of mere indulgence, then consider that the question of survival provides the necessary background for *Gender Trouble*, specifically, the question of how to create a world in which those who understand their gender and their desire to be non-normative can live and thrive not only without the threat of violence from the outside, but without the pervasive sense of their own unreality which can and has led to suicide, both suicidal life and quite literal suicide. Lastly, I would ask what place the thinking of the possible has within political theorizing. One can object and say, ah, but you are trying only to make gender complexity possible, but that does not tell us which forms are good or bad—it does not supply the measure, the gauge, the norm. And that is right. It does not supply the measure, the gauge, the norm. But there is a normative aspiration here, and it has to do with the ability to live and breathe and move, and would no doubt belong somewhere in what is called a philosophy of freedom. The thought of a possible life is only an indulgence for those who already know themselves to be possible. For those who are still looking to become possible, possibility is a necessity.

The desire to kill someone, or killing someone, for not conforming to the gender norm by which he or she is "supposed" to live suggests that life itself requires this norm, and that to be outside it, to live outside it, is to court death. The person who threatens this life with violence emerges from the anxious and rigid belief that a sense of world and a sense of self will be radically undermined if such an uncategorizable being is permitted to live within the social world. The negation, through violence, of that body is a vain and brutal effort to restore order, to renew the social world on the basis of intelligible gender, and to refuse the challenge to rethink that world as something other than natural or necessary. This is not far removed from the threat of death, or the actual murder, of transsexuals in various countries, and of gay men who read as "feminine" or gay women who read as "masculine." I can give you many examples, and they are graphic, and they are widespread, sometimes countered by local police, sometimes aided and abetted by local police.[9] They are sometimes denounced by governments and international agencies, sometimes not included as legible or "real" crimes against humanity by those very institutions.

I understand this violence to emerge from a profound desire to keep the order of binary gender natural or necessary, to make of it a structure, either natural or cultural, or both, that no "human" can oppose, and still remain human. If someone opposes these norms, and not just by having a point of view on them, but if someone opposes these norms, and this opposition is incorporated into the body, the corporeal style, of this person, and that stylized opposition is legible, then it seems that violence emerges precisely as the demand to counter that opposition. But this is not a simple difference in point of views. To counter that opposition by violence is to say, effectively, that this body, this challenge, to an accepted version of the world is and shall be unthinkable. It is an effort to expunge what renders the gendered order of intelligibility contingent, frail, open to fundamental transformation. But if we oppose this violence, then we oppose it in the name of what? What is the alternative to this violence, and for what transformation of the social world do I call?

The ethical task that emerges is to find a way in which we might encounter the difference that calls our grids of intelligibility into question without trying to foreclose the challenge that the difference delivers. This is to learn to live in the anxiety of that challenge, to feel the surety of one's epistemological and ontological anchor go, but to be willing, in the name of the human, to allow the human to become something other than what it is traditionally assumed to be. It means that we must learn to live, and to embrace, the destruction and rearticulation of the human in the name of a more capacious and, finally, less violent world, not to know in advance what precise form our humanness does and will take, but to be open to its permutations, in the name of non-violence. Emanuel Levinas has taught us, wisely, that the question we pose to the Other is simple and unanswerable: "who are you?"[10] The violent response is the one which does not ask, and does not seek to know. It wants to shore up what it knows, to expunge what threatens it with not-knowing, what forces it to reconsider the presuppositions of its world, their contingency, their malleability. The non-violent response lives with its unknowingness about the Other, in the face of the Other, since sustaining the bond that the question opens is finally more valuable than knowing in advance what holds us in common, as if we already have all the resources we need to know what defines the human, what its future life might be.

But the fact that we cannot predict or control what permutations of the human might arise does not mean that we must value all possible permutations of the human; it doesn't mean that we cannot struggle for the realization of certain values, democratic and non-violent, international and anti-racist. The point is only that to struggle for those values is precisely to avow that one's own position is not sufficient to elaborate the spectrum of the human, that one must enter into a collective work in which one's own status as a subject must, for democratic reasons, become disoriented, exposed to what it does not know.

The point is not to apply social norms to lived social instances, to order and define them, nor is it to find justificatory mechanisms for the grounding of social norms that are extra-social (even as they operate under the name of the "social"). There are times when both of these activities do and must take place: we level judgments against criminals for illegal acts, and so subject them to a normalizing procedure; we consider our grounds for action in collective contexts, and try to find modes of deliberation and reflection about which we can agree. But neither of these is all we do with norms. Through recourse to norms, the sphere of the humanly intelligible is circumscribed, and this circumscription is consequential for any ethics and any conception of social transformation. We might say, "we must know the fundamentals of the human in order to act in such a way that we preserve and promote human life as we know it." But what if the very categories of the human have excluded those who should be operating within its terms, who do not accept the modes of reasoning and justifying "validity claims" that have been proffered by Western forms of rationalism? Have we ever yet known the "human"? And what might it take to approach that knowing? Should we be wary of knowing it too soon or of any final or definitive knowing? If we take the field of the human for granted, then we fail to think critically—and ethically—about the consequential ways that the human is being produced, reproduced, de-produced. This latter inquiry does not exhaust the field of ethics, but I cannot imagine a responsible ethics or theory of social transformation operating without it.

Let me suggest here as a way of offering a closing discussion that the necessity of keeping our notion of the "human" open to a future articulation is essential to the project of international human rights discourse and politics. We see this time and again when the very notion of the "human" is presupposed; it is defined in advance, and in terms that are distinctively Western, very often American, and therefore parochial. The paradox emerges that the "human" at issue in human rights is already known, already defined, and yet it is supposed to be the ground for a set of rights and obligations that are international. How we move from the local to the international is a major question for international politics, but it takes a specific form for international lesbian, gay, bi-, trans- and intersex struggles as well as for feminism. And I would suggest to you that an anti-imperialist or, minimally, non-imperialist conception of international human rights must call into question what is meant by the human, and learn from the various ways and means by which it is defined across cultural venues. This means that local conceptions of what is "human" or, indeed, of what the basic conditions and needs of human life are, must be subjected to reinterpretation, since there are historical and cultural circumstances in which the "human" is defined differently, and its basic needs and, hence, basic entitlements are also defined differently.

I do not mean to be offering a reductively relativist argument. I think that a reductive relativism would say that we cannot speak of the human or of international human rights, since there are only and always local and provisional understandings of these terms, and that the generalizations themselves do violence to the specificity of the meanings in question. This is not my view. I'm not ready to rest there. Indeed, I think we are compelled to speak of the human, and of the international, and to find out in particular how "human rights" do and do not work, say, in favor of women, of what "women" are, and what they are not. But to speak in this way, and to call for social transformations in the name of women, we must also be part of a critical democratic project, one which understands that the category of the human has been used differentially and with exclusionary aims, that not all humans have been included within its terms, that the category of women has been used differentially and with exclusionary aims, and that not all women have been included within its terms, and that women have not been fully incorporated into the human, and that both categories are still in process, underway, unfulfilled. This means that we must follow a double path in politics: we must use this language, and use it to assert an entitlement to conditions of life in ways that are sensitive to the questions of sexuality and gender. We must also subject our very categories to critical scrutiny, find out the limits of their inclusivity, the presuppositions they include, the ways in which they must be expanded to encompass the diversity of what it is to be human and gendered. When the U.N. conference at Beijing met a few years ago, and we heard there a discourse on "women's human rights" or when we have heard from the Inter-national Gay and Lesbian Human Rights Commission, many of us detected a paradox. Women's human rights? Lesbian and gay human rights? But think about what this coupling actually does. It performs the "human" as contingent, suggests that it has been so in the past, and continues to be in the present, defining a variable and restricted population, which may or may not include lesbians and gays, may not include women. It says that such groups have their own set of human rights, that what "human" comes to mean when we think about the human-ness of women is perhaps different than what "human" has meant when it has functioned as presumptively male. It also says that these terms are defined variably, in relation to one another. And we could certainly make a similar argument about race. Which populations have qualified as the "human" and which have not? What is the history of this category? Where are we in its history at this time?

I would suggest that in this last process, we can only rearticulate or resignify the basic categories of ontology, of being human, of being gendered, of being recognizably sexual, to the extent that we submit ourselves to a process of cultural translation. The point here is not to assimilate foreign or unfamiliar notions of gender or humanness into our own, as if it is simply a matter of incorporation. It is also a process of yielding our most fundamental categories, that is, seeing how and why they yield to a rupture and a resignification when they encounter what is unknown or not yet known. It is crucial to recognize that the notion of the human will only be built over time in and by the process of cultural translation, where it is not a translation between two languages which stay enclosed, distinct, unified. But rather, *translation will compel each language to change in order to apprehend the other*, and this apprehension, at the limit of what is familiar, parochial, and already known, will be the occasion for both an ethical and social transformation. It will constitute a loss, a disorientation, but also a gain.

When we ask what makes a life livable, we are asking about certain normative conditions that must be fulfilled for life to become life. There are at least two senses of life: one that refers to the minimum biological form of living, and another, that intervenes at the start, which establishes minimum conditions for a livable life in order to qualify for the category of human.[11] This does not imply that we can disregard the merely living in favor of the "livable life," but rather that we must ask, as we asked about gender violence, what humans require in order to maintain and reproduce the conditions of their own livability. And what do our politics need to be such that we are, in whatever way is possible, both conceptualizing the possibility of the livable life and arranging for its institutional support?

There will always be disagreement about what this means, and those who claim that a single political direction is necessitated by virtue of this commitment will be mistaken. But this is only because to live is to live a life politically, in relation to power, in relation to others, in the act of assuming responsibility for a collective future. To assume responsibility for a future, however, is not to know its direction fully in advance, since the future, especially the future with and for others, requires a certain openness and unknowingness. A certain agonism and contestation will and must also be in play. They must be in play for politics to become democratic. Democracy does not speak in unison; its tunes are dissonant, and necessarily so. It is not a predictable process; it must be undergone, like a passion must be undergone. It may also be that life itself becomes foreclosed when the right way is decided in advance, when we impose what is right for everyone and without finding a way to enter into community, and to discover there the "right" in the midst of cultural translation. It may be that what is "right" and what is "good" consist in staying open to the tensions that beset the most fundamental categories we require, in knowing unknowingness at the core of what we know, and what we need, and in recognizing the sign of life—and its prospects—in the contestations which are ours to undergo with one another.

NOTES
1. A revised version of this essay was published as "Violence, Mourning, Politics" in *Studies in Gender and Sexuality*, 4, no. 1 (2003): 9–7.

2. William Safire, "All Is Not Changed," *New York Times*, September 27, 2001, A: 21.
3. Richard Garfield, "Morbidity and Mortality Among Iraqi Children from 1990 Through 1998: Assessing the Impact of the Gulf War and Economic Sanctions," in *Occasional Papers* (Notre Dame, IN: The Joan B. Kroc Institute for International Peace Studies, March 1999).
4. Ibid., 50
5. Ibid., 52.
6. Ibid., 52–3.
7. Ibid., 54.
8. See Judith Butler, *Gender Trouble: Feminism and the Subversion of Identity* (New York: Routledge, 1990).
9. Consult The International Gay and Lesbian Rights Commission (www.iglhrc.org) for a comprehensive archive of violence done internationally against sexual minorities.
10. See Adriana Cavarrero, *Relating Narratives: Storytelling and Selfhood*, trans. P. Kottman (New York: Routledge, 2000).
11. See Giorgio Agamben, *Homo Sacer: Sovereign Power and Bare Life*, trans. Daniel Heller-Roazen, (Stanford: Stanford University Press, 1998).

PERMISSIONS ACKNOWLEDGMENTS

"I Lift My Face to the Hill": The Life of Mabel Hampton as Told by a White Woman" is reprinted here from Joan Nestle, *A Fragile Union*, copyright © 1998, by permission of Cleis Press.

"The Personal Is Political: Queer Fiction and Criticism" is reprinted from Edmund White, *The Burning Library*, copyright © 1994, by permission of Alfred A. Knopf, a division of Random House, Inc., and International Creative Management.

"African American Lesbian and Gay History: An Exploration" is reprinted from Barbara Smith, *The Truth That Never Hurts*, copyright © 1998, by permission of Rutgers University Press.

Excerpts from Monique Wittig, *Virgile, non,* copyright © 1985, and *Across the Acheron*, translation copyright © 1987, are reprinted by permission of Les Éditions des Minuit and Peter Owen Publishers.

"My Butch Career: A Memoir" is reprinted from Esther Newton, *Margaret Mead Made Me Gay*, copyright © 2000, by permission of Duke University Press.

". . . 3, 2, 1, Contact" by Samuel R. Delany is reprinted from Joan Copjec and Michael Sorkin, eds, *Giving Ground: The Politics of Propinquity*, copyright © 1999, by permission of Verso Press.

"A Dialogue on Love" is reprinted from Eve Kosofsky Sedgwick, *A Dialogue on Love*, copyright © 1999, by permission of Beacon Press.

"A Biographer and His Subject: Wrestling with Bayard Rustin" is reprinted from John D'Emilio, *The World Turned: Essays on Gay History, Politics, and Culture*, copyright © 2002, by permission of Duke University Press.

"A Xicanadyke Codex of Changing Consciousness" by Cherríe Moraga, copyright © 2000, is published here by permission of the author.

"Global Violence, Sexual Politics" by Judith Butler, copyright © 2001, is published here by permission of the author.